THE ETHICAL RELIGION OF
ZOROASTER

THE ETHICAL RELIGION OF ZOROASTER

An account of what Zoroaster taught, as perhaps the very oldest and surely the most accurate code of ethics for man, accompanied by the essentials of his religion

BY

MILES MENANDER DAWSON

AMS PRESS
NEW YORK

Reprinted from the edition of 1931, New York
First AMS EDITION published 1969
Manufactured in the United States of America

Library of Congress Catalogue Card Number: 73-90100

AMS PRESS, INC.
NEW YORK, N.Y. 10003

TO THE MEMORY OF

REVEREND ANDREW JACKSON JUTKINS, D.D.,
*who, an eminent clergyman of the Methodist
Episcopal faith, forty years ago, in his
elderly years, became my unfailing friend,
suggesting to me who was then alive with
the ethical teachings of Socrates and Confucius, the study of the ethics of Zoroaster*

INTRODUCTION

The Gathas as embodying the precepts of the prophet, introduce a great reform, a notable advance over anything hitherto known in the field of human ethics. Dhalla's (The High Priest's) *Zoroastrian Theology.*

To Zoroaster is due the same rank, the same respect, the same reverential regard that is due to such seekers after light as Buddha, Confucius, Socrates. Jackson's *Zoroaster, the Prophet of Ancient Iran.*

If the Gathas contain the earliest printed effort of their kind to reform the human heart, being also alive today in all our faiths, on which, too, futurity may hang, they are, indeed, unique in morals. Mills' *Our Own Religion in Ancient Persia.*

IT might indeed be said that Zoroaster was the discoverer, or at least the uncoverer, of *individual morals;* the very evolution of the most primitive but fundamental and therefore eternal notions of right and wrong, is first of all discernible in earnest activity in the original Gathas, Zoroaster's own contribution to the enlightenment of mankind.

The purely spiritual conception of divinity by Zoroaster (who is in the Persian language called Zarathustra) is witness, how rapturously beautiful to him was true good and right; for the first person in his sevenfold unity of God was Mazda, Light; the second person was Aramaïti, the Good Mind; and the third was Asha, Right.

All these names, likewise, except Mazda which became part of the name of God, stood in the Yasnas, or canticles, of the Gathas quite as often for these qualities, as for the divine person, Ahura Mazda, distinguished by them, who with six others compose the one Godhead.

This presentation of what Zoroaster and his disciples have taught, is given in their own words, translated into English, with reference to the passage in the book from which the quotation is taken.

The ethics of Zoroaster subject all conduct to the acid test, whether or not its consequence, reasonably to be expected, is the weal or woe of men.

The largest remnant of the followers of Zoroaster, called the Parsis, chiefly residing in India, in and about Bombay, maintain the ancient reputation of the Zoroastrian code of morals and are most highly and generally esteemed for their integrity and loftiness of character.

High Priest Dhalla, of the Parsis, in his *Zoroastrian Theology*, says "Zoroastrian virtues have made the modern Parsis great. The community has secured a pioneer place in the social, intellectual and industrial life of the teeming millions of India. They have amassed vast fortunes and have given away equally vast sums for philanthropic purposes without distinction of caste, color or creed. An individual member among the Parsis today is a better cared for unit than one in any society" (p. 370).

The Hebrew scriptures pay tribute, the more worth while because unconscious and even involuntary, to the sterling merit of Zoroaster's rules of conduct, when they speak of the law of the Medes and Persians as one "which altereth not."

These rules and the religious precepts in which they

were laid contain so many things that are found in Christian or Jewish creed and practice. They came into existence centuries ahead of Judaism and Christianity, and in fact are the relics of the race from which sprang the religions of Greece, of Rome, of Germany, of Scandinavia, and in short, of European countries, and of America, Australia, and other places which Europe has colonized.

Zoroaster lived at least several centuries earlier than any other of the four whom Professor Jackson names as entitled to "the same rank, the same respect, the same reverential regard," Zoroaster, Buddha, Confucius, Socrates.

The latest period assigned the religion by the competent among critics is between 600 and 700 B.C., although all the Greek scholars have set his date more than six thousand years before Christ. The Parsis' late traditions, however, since their studies in our time, fix the date between the latter half of the seventh century and middle of the sixth century. (For a complete list of the authorities and a full discussion see Appendix II of Professor Jackson's *Zoroaster*.)

Professor Jackson, in stating his definite personal conclusion, says of this (p. 176):

"The above results, if they be accepted in the light at least of our present information on the subject, seem to be not without importance for the history of early religious thought and of the development of ethical and moral teaching. If one carefully works through the material, it must be acknowledged that the most consistent and the most authoritative of all the actual statements upon the subject place the appearance of the prophet at a period between the closing century of Median rule and the rising wave of Persian power, that

is, between the latter half of the seventh century and
the middle of the sixth century B.C. (better between the
middle of the seventh century and the former half of
the sixth century B.C.). It is the sowing of the fallow
land that is to bring forth the rich fruits of the harvest.
The teaching of Zoroaster must have taken deep root in
the soil of Iran at the time when the Jews were carried
up into captivity at Babylon (586-536 B.C.), where they
became acquainted with 'the law of the Medes and
Persians which altereth not'; the time was not far
remote when the sage Confucius should expound to
China the national tenets of its people, and the gentle
Buddha on Ganges' bank should preach to longing
souls the doctrine of redemption through renunciation.
How interesting the picture, how full of instruction the
contrast!"

It is thought that, in view of the difference between
this late date and the date, thousands of years earlier,
that is given by Greek authorities, this date is appropriate in any event for the coming into use among the
Persians, pretty generally, of this religion.

Some of the higher critics have placed the name,
Pharisee, with Parsi; the claims of that Hebrew sect
to superior sanctity, its aloofness and cleanliness, its
belief in the continuance of life after death and in
future rewards and punishments, have been traced to
the religion with which the Jews had come in contact
during the Babylonian captivity.[1]

[1] Since "Thus Spake Zarathustra" was used by Nietzsche as the
title for one of his books, and his ascription to a "Zarathustra rediv-
idus" of the sayings which have greatly disturbed men's thinking
about ethics, this memorandum was made.

It does not appear that Nietzsche was, in fact, at all acquainted
with the work of the ancient Persian, Zoroaster (in Persian, Zarathustra) or his teaching. The Zend Avesta and the later Parsi scrip-

The method pursued in preparing this book for pub-
lication is the same as that by which my earlier works,
The Ethics of Confucius, and *The Ethics of Socrates,*
were produced, viz., the presentation of authoritative
texts regarding conduct or religion, including all which
are deemed of real significance, arranged with reference
to the subjects dealt with and accompanied by intro-
ductory and explanatory comment, the purpose of
which is to hold the interest and supply the connection
which the process of taking these passages out of their
context may have destroyed.

To obtain these passages, every scrap of the ancient
books available in English translation has been ex-
plored, and to confirm the construction which these
passages have been given, every recognized authority
upon Zoroaster and Parseeism has been consulted.

The translation is followed in each case except the
Gathas, in which Professor Moulton's *Early Zoroas-*

tures were then being made known to the world in difficult translations, the meaning of the text often involved in much doubt and
only a ripple of interest—barely enough to cause "Zarathustra" to be
heralded abroad as the prophet's name, instead of Zoroaster which
had come down to us through the Greeks—had been aroused, outside of very narrow circles.

The result, however, little that may have been intended, is most
incongruous. The Nietzschean philosophy certainly lauds to the sky
nearly everything which Zoroaster of old hated and reviled and also
depreciates all that his followers have been taught to hold sacred and
pure. This is illustrated in the Prologue (VIII) in the following
concerning Zarathustra's bearing a corpse about with him. "When
Zarathustra had said this to his heart, he put the corpse on his
shoulders and set out upon his way"; for, according to the Parsis
scriptures, if he carried forth the body alone, it would have been
a crime involving deadly punishment. The Zend Avesta says, "Let no
man himself carry a dead body . . . he is unclean thenceforth for
ever and ever" (Vendidad Fargard III, c. III, 14). Thus, this Zarathustra is, in his thoughts and deeds, most unlike the ancient Zoroaster.

trianism is followed and is at times slightly amended, without change of meaning.

Aside from its value and interest in the regards already mentioned, it is confidently expected that these sayings will be found a genuine and important contribution to the study of comparative ethics which inevitably must precede the evolution of higher and nobler standards for mankind. A higher basis of individual ethics will surely not be found; and better results than in the life of the ancient Persians or the more modern Parsis will not be discovered.

The Gathas may have been lost to the extent of four-fifths of their stanzas, at least, which appears to show their age; and the clarity of their conception, as well as the appropriateness of the thoughts and acts suggested, cause us to mourn that any portion should be missing.

The preparation of this book has taken nearly fifteen years; during which obligations were incurred to Rev. William Norman Guthrie for again recommending the study to me; to Dr. Paul Carus (since dead), of Chicago, for letters of encouragement while the work was in progress; to Dr. Abraham Yohannan, whose recent death I deplore, to whom, by reason of his assistance in the Department of Zend Literature in Columbia University, the first draft of this book was submitted; and to all those who make up the Department, including a student from Bombay, who took a valuable part in determining the merits of the translations.

M. M. D.

New York
May 1, 1931

BIRTH AND CAREER OF ZOROASTER

A GOOD deal is known concerning Zoroaster from the sacred writings themselves. Thus, that his surname was Spitata; that his father's name was Porushaspa, and his mother's name, Dukhdav; that he was married three times and was survived by all his wives; that by his first wife he was the father of one son and three daughters, by his second wife of two sons, and by his third wife, of no progeny, though it is true that spiritual offspring, later brought forth by miraculous means and from which Saöshyant, the savior, as he was called, was to spring, is accredited as the result of this marriage.

There is also the account that he entered upon his sacred ministry at the age of thirty; that his first and for a long time, his only convert was his cousin; that between thirty and forty, he had seven revelations, each devoted to one of the attributes of the Godhead which his followers adore as the seven Holy Ghosts or Amesha Spentas; that he converted King Vishtaspa, who became the ardent champion of his religion; that a holy war, which he waged against the infidels, was successful; that the results of such a second war were in doubt when Isfendiar, the son of Vishtaspa, who had been confined but was set free to defend the kingdom and the religion, changed the fortunes of battle, though unfortunately not before Zoroaster had been slain at the altar at Balkh, on the Persian steppes, in his seventy-seventh year, by Turi-Bratar-Vakhsh.

There is, unfortunately, much greater uncertainty in these days about the era when he lived than about any of the leading events of his life.

The ancient references to him in the Greek classics, of which there is an astonishingly great number, uniformly or almost uniformly ascribe his life to about 6000 years B.C. To this precise effect testifies Pliny, the Second, in his Natural History, who speaks of Zoroaster in nine separate passages, and cites Eudoxus and Aristotle, both of whom lived in the *fourth* century, B.C., and Hermippus, who lived in the *third* century, B.C.; to this effect, also, Plutarch, who made no less than eight references in six books; and Plato in a scolium on *The Republic*; in three other writings, ascribed to Plato, which are now believed to be the work of contemporaries. Plato wrote in the first half of the *fourth* century, B.C.; Pliny and Plutarch in the *first* century A.D., but giving the older writers as authorities. A writer of the *first* century, B.C., Nikolaos of Damascus, quotes Zanthus, living in the *fifth* century, B.C., as authority that Zoroaster lived 6000 years before Xerxes, i.e. about 6500 years B.C.

These are the oldest, known, classical references; but Diogenes Laertius, writing early in the *third* century, A.D., cites also many writers of the *third* and *fourth* centuries, B.C., as authorities for statements concerning Zoroaster. There are many references to him both in Greek and in Assyrian texts which were well known, not merely to the Medes and Persians, but to the Greeks, as well.

Thus Herodotus, living in the *fifth* century, B.C., gives a remarkably accurate account, in general, of Zoroastrian tenets and practices, though he makes no mention of Zoroaster by name, speaking merely of the

Magi, who certainly became Zoroastrian long after he had left the earth.

The famous inscription at Behistun shows, by the repeated references of King Darius to the one god, Ahura Mazda, that Zoroaster's religion was dominant among the Medes in the latter part of the *sixth* century, B.C.; and to Ahura Mazda (i.e. God) the great king gave thanks for his victories.

This name of God, i.e. Ahura Mazda, Professor Hummel has also found upon an Assyrian inscription, assigned by him to an age *earlier* than 1000 B.C., and perhaps well toward the beginning of the *second* millennium B.C.

The names of all the Amesha Spentas, with three angels or minor deities, later accepted by Zoroastrians, are found in the Cappadocian calendar, the introduction of which cannot have been later than the middle of the *fourth* century, B.C.

Notwithstanding all of which things, modern Parsi savants, followed by, or following, some of the leading higher critics of our time, have inclined to place the period of Zoroaster at not more than *three* centuries before Alexander.

The oldest authority for this is Ammianus Marcellinus in the *fifth* century, A.D., who thought to identify Vishtaspa with Hytaspes, father of Darius. His opinion, thus fanciful, is decidedly condemned, however.

A goodly number of Occidental scholars follow the chronology of the Pahlavi text of Sassanian times, though many contend for, at least, a few centuries earlier.

The language, literary construction and idea contents of the Gathas, which nearly all the critics ascribe chiefly to Zoroaster himself, indicates a primitive era in human history; few, if any, sacred writings, extant to this day, are so naïve, simple, unsophisticated.[1]

That out of this should so quickly have developed the religion of adepts, the Magi, in full ritual form, famed even in distant Greece and really well understood there, and, in addition, established as the royal creed in Persia's days of splendor, may have been true; but, if so, it is indeed singular that no note should have been taken of how remarkable a thing this was but that, instead, the ancient testimony is virtually unanimous that its origin was much earlier in human history.

It is said that Pythagoras visited Zoroaster, which fixes his date much later, and that Plato designed to go to the East for study with the Magi when a new war with Persia broke out and prevented the journey. The disciples of Prodicus, a contemporary of Socrates, are reported to have had a copy of Zoroaster's scriptures, the Gathas.

He was so highly esteemed by Greek and Roman writers that, as stated, a vast number of references to him and to his conceptions have been found in ancient books; these have been collected with marvelous fitness in *Zoroaster, the Prophet of Ancient Iran,* by Professor Jackson, and in *Early Zoroastrianism,* by Professor Moulton. The information concerning him has largely reached the West within the last hundred years in translations from the Parsi scriptures and other writings. For instance, the translation of the Gathas into English by Moulton, which is easily the best, appeared in print in 1913.

[1] Signs of a great antiquity are found to attach to the language of certain rhythmical compositions, called Gathas or hymns; and the religious ideas contained in these are found to be at once harmonious and also of a simpler and a more primitive character than those contained in the rest of the volume." Rawlinson, *The Religions of the Ancient World.*

BIBLIOGRAPHY

THE chief source from which the sayings, which, together with the author's comments, compose this book, have been drawn is, of course, the books of which the sacred canon of the Persians has for upwards of two thousand five hundred years consisted, which are known by the collective name, the Zend Avesta. So far as it has come down to us, it consists of, or may be said to embrace, the following books and parts of books, all of which have been consulted, in translation:

The Gathas
The Vendidad
Fragments of the Nasks
    Westergard's Fragments
    Zend Fragments
    Tahmura's Fragments
    Fragments of the Erpatistan Nask
    Fragments of the Nirangistan Nask
    Sundry Fragments
    Aögemaïde Nask
The Sirozahs, I and II
The Yasts; as follows:
    Ormazd
    Haptan
    Ardebehist
    Khordad
    Aban
    Khorshed
    Mah
    Tir
    Gos
    Mihir

Srosh Yast Hadhokht
Rashn
Farvardin
Bahram
Ram
Din
Ashi
Ashtad
Zamyad
Vanant
XXI, a Fragment
XXII, a Fragment
Afrin Païghambar Zartust
Vistasp
Khorshed Nyasis
Mihir Nyasis
Mah Nyasis
Aban Nyasis
Atas Nyasis

Reference is also made to each of the following:

The Bundahis
Selections of Zad Sparam
Bahman Yast
Shayast-La-Shayast
Andaz-i Atarpat-i Maraspand
Arda Viraf
Dinkard
Gangi-i Shayigan
Menuk-i-Khrat
Sad Dar

Quotations from the last six Parsi books are taken from an excellent book, *Zoroastrian Ethics,* by Magaular A. Buch, printed in India.

The Bundahis and other books are of later issue, though very ancient—the Bundahis quite 2000 years old—and contain many passages, sometimes literally quoted, sometimes paraphrased, from lost portions of the Zend Avesta, and also comment upon them and the Parsi interpretation of them.

The early simplicity of the Gathas, that remain, is remarkable; the nature in general of the later text is shown in the following: "The lofty tone of the earlier compositions gradually declines, and the greater part of the Yasna, Yashts and Vendid becomes heavy and monotonous." Dhalla's *Zoroastrian Theology*.

Quotations are from, and citations to, West's translation, which forms Volume XI, Parts I and II, of the *Sacred Books of the East,* and, with slight changes, to Moulton's *Gathas,* much the best of all translations.

Jackson's *Zoroaster, the Prophet of Ancient Iran* (Macmillan), Moulton's *Early Zoroastrianism* (Williams and Norgate), Mills' *Our Own Religion in Ancient Persia* (Open Court Publishing Company).

PARALLELS WITH JEWISH AND CHRISTIAN SAYINGS

NOTHING is more extraordinary, perhaps, than the great number of parallels or near-parallels between texts to be found in the Zoroastrian scriptures and doctrines in the Old Testament and sometimes only in the New Testament, or the sacred traditions of the churches.

Surely the teachers of both these religions will wish the text of both Zoroaster and his disciples before them, arranged to show his splendid ethics and the trend of his religion.

Among these are the following:

ZOROASTRIAN	JEWISH AND CHRISTIAN
God, Ahura Mazda	God, Jehovah Elohim
King of Kings	King of Kings
A spirit	A spirit
Not anthropomorphic	Not anthropomorphic
Made himself partly visible to Zoroaster	His hinder parts seen by Moses
A sevenfold Godhead, composed of the Amesha Spentas	A triune Godhead, composed of Father, Son and Holy Spirit
The incarnate word, the priest	The Incarnate Word, Jesus
God, the creator of all things	God, the creator of all things
Period of creation, six days	The world created in six days
A diurnal order of creation	Separate creations, each day
The greatest creation, a righteous man	Man the last and greatest creation
Man and woman driven from Paradise for sin	Man and woman banished from Eden for disobedience
Ahriman, the devil	Satan, the devil
The father of lies	The father of lies
Heaven or Paradise	Heaven
Hell and Purgatory	Hell, Hades, Gehenna, and Purgatory

Resurrection from the dead
The Last Judgment
Immortality of the soul
God's omniscience and foreknowledge
God "is not to be deceived."
"Turning misfortunes and calamities into lessons and blessings."
Zoroaster: "Whoso concedeth my divine office, shall share in the best . . . but torments will I set upon him who is for us a grievous oppressor." Also, "unto him shall be given the reward of the future life."
"Whatsoever He in His wisdom thinketh, ought to be."
"The same at every now."

"Spirit Bountiful, Giver of all things."
"Where findeth my soul a helper . . . save in Right and in Thee, oh God"
"That nature alone is good which shall not do unto another whatever is not good for its own self."
"Also think of them as thine own and this is thy religion."
"Such an one . . . shall then arrive, as the best of intercessors, who here below intercedeth for the poor man and the poor woman in their distress."
"The holy law standeth ever at thy door in the persons of thy brethren."

"Standeth both for those of the faith and for those not of the faith."

Resurrection of the body
The Last Judgment
Immortality of the soul
God is all-knowing

"God is not mocked."
"All things work out for good unto them that love God."
Jesus: "Whoso believeth in me shall not perish but have everlasting life, but whosoever believeth not, shall be damned."

"Thy will, not mine, be done."

"The same from everylasting unto everlasting."
"Giver of all good things."

"The Lord is my shepherd, I shall not want."

"Do unto others as you would have them do unto you."

"Thy neighbor as thyself."

"Pure religion and undefiled is to visit the widow and orphan in their distress."

"Even as thou hast done it unto the least of these, my brethren, thou hast done it also unto me."
"Behold, God hath made of one blood all the peoples of the earth." "He causeth the rain to fall upon the just and the unjust."

"Upon the very first time that this deed (i.e. perjury) is done . . . down there the pain for it shall be as severe as any pain in this world."

"God will not hold him guiltless who taketh his name in vain."

"It is necessary for us to promote whatever is His wish that our wish may be realized."

"Seek thou first the Kingdom of Heaven—and all things will be added unto thee."

"So unto us shall it be as Thou willeth!"

"Thy will be done!"

Next-of-kin Marriage.

The "Song of Solomon"

"Well-principled and obedient to her husband."

"Wives, obey your husbands!"

"Such beings (courtesans) ought to be slain even more than gliding serpents, than howling wolves."

"Suffer not a whore to live!"

"He that wasteth seed causeth death of progeny."

This is also condemned.

"For no sodomist was acceptable unto Him."

Sodomy, a capital offense

No usury among the faithful

Among the Jews, the same

"Purity is for man, next to life, the greatest good."

"The pure in heart shall see God."

"He that in this world of flesh, . . . deemeth overweening well of his own merit, all the time that he doeth it, his soul becometh weighed down with sin."

"Pride goeth before a fall!"

"This, too, that, as respects the world, anxiety is not to be suffered!"

"Take no thought for the morrow!"

"May I obtain . . . abiding serenity of soul."

"The peace that passeth understanding."

"If he hath committed ought other sin, it is remitted also by his repentance."

"He that repenteth and is baptized shall be saved, he that repenteth not, shall be damned."

"A full atonement for his sin is made by means of the religion of God."

"The Lamb of God that taketh away the sin of the world."

"If he have no means, it shall not be accounted unto the godly man for unrighteousness."

The widow's mite

xxiv PARALLEL SAYINGS

"Then this man is the best-healing of all healers who heals with the Holy Word."

The healings by Jesus and his apostles

The call of those about to die, "We come, we rejoice, we submit."

"Oh grave, where is thy victory? Oh death, where is thy sting?"

"To make the good creatures again fresh and pure, and to keep them constant and progressing in pure and virtuous conduct, is to render them immortal."

"To be spiritually minded is life everlasting; to be carnally minded is death."

"If thou wilt make me immortal as the tree opposed to harm."

"The Tree of Life" in the Garden of Eden

"Whoever, in that time, appealeth for the body, is not able to save the soul."

"Fear not him who hath power only to destroy the body but fear rather Him who hath power to destroy both body and soul."

"He hath gained nothing that hath not gained the soul."

"What profiteth it a man though he gain the whole world and lose his own soul?"

"Also out of his sin cometh the punishment connected with it."

"Be sure thy sin will find thee out."

"Thou shouldest not consider anyone whatever without hope of Heaven."

"Judge not, that ye be not judged."

Religious services to relieve souls in Hell, or Purgatory

Masses for the dead

"The dead shall rise, life shall return to the bodies and they shall breathe again."

The resurrection of the dead

"Each one of them when created by me, was therein more difficult than causing the resurrection."

Arguments about power of God to raise the dead

"The whole world shall become free from old age and death, from corruption and decay, forever and ever."

Revelations concerning Last Judgment

Purification of the Earth by melting in fire

The same

Ahriman destroyed at the end of time

The devil destroyed at the last day

NOTATION

"GOD" is used for "Ahura Mazda" which *name is also given,* opposed to the word "God," when it appears first in each quotation.

The pronouns "thou" "thee" or "thine" are used because to use "Thou," "Thee," or "Thine," when God, i.e. Ahura Mazda, is concerned, seems to speak irreverently of the six others albeit he is recognized as the chief of the gods and what we would call God as distinguished from what we would call archangels.

Zoroaster, instead of new spelling, "Zarathustra," is used because he is already known to the English and, indeed, to all Europeans and Americans, by that name, used by Greek authors dating from about 500 B.C.

CONTENTS

xxvii

THE ETHICAL RELIGION OF
ZOROASTER

CHAPTER I

THE MISSION OF ZOROASTER

"WHAT award thou givest by thy spirit and the Fire and hast taught by Right [1] to the two parties and what decision unto the wise and what law governeth the enlightened, this do thou tell us, oh God (Ahura Mazda), that we may know even with the tongue of thine own mouth, so that I may cause all who live to choose aright" (Yasna XXXI, 3).

In these words the Gathas set forth what Zoroaster himself esteemed to be his mission, that is, to cause all living beings to choose rightly between good and evil.

Again the Gathas [2] pronounce that Zoroaster is chosen, saying:

"Come thou, with Good Mind; [3] give through Right, oh God (Ahura Mazda), as thy gift to Zoroaster by thy sure words, long-enduring, mighty help and so to us, oh God, whereby we may overcome our enemies." (Yasna XXVIII, 6).

And the same spiritual aid does Zoroaster ask for in the earlier words of the same Gatha:

"Give thou me who would serve you, oh God (Ahura

[1] Fire is the image of God to the people; and Right is the name of the second of his followers; the holy spirits, of which the Good Mind was the first. See the next chapter.

[2] 6500 years B.C., it is told; the *Bull* religion, the critics say, 2600 years ago.

[3] See Footnote 1.

1

Mazda), and Good Mind, through the Right the blessings of both worlds, that of body and of mind which set the faithful in felicity" (Yasna XXVIII, 2).

One of the Nasks (Tahmura's Fragments, c. XLIV, 99), describes the condition of the world to which Zoroaster addressed himself:

"At present in this world below, oh Spitama Zoroaster, there is not one just man, not two, nor three, not several."

It was to a world, thus desolate and forgotten, that the prophet was sent.

And to it Zoroaster came, urged by the triune that caused his program to have the support of God; for they said unto him:

"What help hast thou, oh Right, for Zoroaster who calls upon thee? What hast thou, Good Mind, for me who with praises seek your favor, oh Lord (Ahura Mazda), longing for that which is the best in your possession" (Yasna XLXIX, 12).

And he, with trembling, begs that what he is bid to say shall in verity be the truth:

"This I ask thee, tell me truly, oh Lord (Ahura Mazda), whether what I shall proclaim is verily the truth" (Yasna XLIV, 6).

And, when he has with courage complied, he proclaims his authority and looks on those who would dispute with contempt:

"I was ordained at the first by thee; all others I look upon with hatred of spirit" (Yasna XLIV, 11).

The terror of the Daëvas (who were demons) at the birth of Zoroaster is thus portrayed in the Zend Avesta:

"They rush away shouting, the wicked, evil-doing Daëvas; they run away shouting, the wicked, evil-doing Daëvas; 'Let us gather together at the head of Aresura!

For he is just born, the holy Zoroaster, in the house of Porushaspa. How can we procure his death He is the weapon that fells the fiends; he is a counter-fiend to the fiends; he is a Druj to the Druj!' Vanished are the Daëva-worshipers, the Nasu * made by the Daëvas, the false-speaking lie" (Vendidad, Fargard XIX c. VI, 45, 46)!

The infant Zoroaster, it is narrated, escaped destruction because the fire, the holy manifestation of God in the household, was maintained and therefore the demons could not enter.

That which Zoroaster asked of God in order that he ' might serve mankind by causing them to know the right and to choose it, is amply phrased in the same book (Fargard XIX, c. I, 10) thus:

"The holy Zoroaster said aloud, 'This I ask of thee: Teach me the truth, oh Lord (Ahura Mazda)!'"

In the Gathas (Yasna XLIII, 11) Zoroaster asserts:

"As the holy one I recognized thee, oh God (Ahura Mazda), when the Good Mind came to me, when first by thy words I was instructed. Shall it bring me grief among men, my devotion, in doing that which thou didst declare unto me to be the best?"

Again in the Gathas (Yasna XXXIII, 7) the prophet asks help and support:

"Come hither to me, oh ye Best Ones, hither, oh God (Ahura Mazda), in thine own person and to the sight, oh Right and Good Mind, that I may be heard beyond the limits of the people. Let the august duties be manifest to all of us and clearly be seen" (Yasna XXXIII, 7).

Here is yet another prayer of Zoroaster and the answer to it of the Amesha Spentas, promising him

* The contagion of corruption.

bliss in Paradise* as a reward for his labors; it is from the Vishtasp Yast (c. IV, 32, 33):

"'Help me! Forgive me!'—We, the Amesha Spentas, will come and show thee, oh Zoroaster, the way to that world, to abiding glory in the spiritual world, to abiding happiness of the soul in Paradise.

"To bliss and Paradise, to the Heaven of God (Ahura Mazda), beautifully made and fully-adorned, when a man's soul goeth out of his body through the will of fate, when I, God (Ahura Mazda), when I, the Lord, gently show him the way as he asketh for it!"

The Bundahis (c. IV, 1, 4) relates this concerning what took place in Heaven before Zoroaster was born, the primeval ox having made a plea for the protection of the domestic animals against the cruel raids of the bandits:

"Gosurvan, as the soul of the primeval ox came out from the body of the ox, stood up before the ox and cried unto God (Ahura Mazda), as much as a thousand men when they sustain a cry at one time, thus, 'With whom is the guardianship of the creatures left by thee, when ruin hath broken upon the earth, and vegetation is withered, and water is troubled? Where is the man of whom it was said by thee, "I will produce him, so that he may preach carefulness?"' . . . .

"Then the guardian spirit* of Zoroaster was exhibited to her, and God spake, saying, 'I will produce for the world him who will preach carefulness.'"

The word here translated "carefulness" means the same as the hovering care of her young by the mother

* The place for the disembodied spirits of just men.

* This was a separate, eternal spirit which ever accompanies him; such were believed in by the followers of Zoroaster, as shown by later books.

bird; that is, as regards man's duty, it is the preservation of all useful things and beings.

Thus one of the Gathas (Yasna XXIX, 6) identifies his mission with the care of herds,

"Thereupon God (Ahura Mazda) himself spake, who knows the laws, with wisdom, 'There is found no lord or judge, according to the Right; for the Creator hath formed thee for cattle-breeding and as a husbandman.' "

However, before God created Zoroaster to preach to men this religion of beneficence, Yima of old was said to have been offered this mission, according to the Vendidad, which gives the following account of it:

"Zoroaster inquired of God (Ahura Mazda) saying, 'Oh Lord God, most beneficent spirit, Maker of the material world, thou Holy One, who was the first mortal, before myself, Zoroaster, with whom thou, oh God, didst converse, to whom thou didst teach the religion of God, the religion of Zoroaster?'

"And God (Ahura Mazda) made answer and said, 'The fair Yima, the good shepherd, oh holy Zoroaster; he was the first mortal, before thee, Zoroaster, with whom I, God, did converse, to whom I taught the religion of God, the religion of Zoroaster. Unto him, oh Zoroaster, I, God, spake, saying, "Well, fair Yima, son of Vivanghat, be thou the preacher and the bearer of my religion!"

" 'Then I, God, spake thus unto him, oh Zoroaster, "Since thou dost not consent to be the preacher and the bearer of my religion, then make thou my world increase, make my world grow; consent thou to nourish, to rule, and to watch over my world"; and the fair Yima replied unto me, oh Zoroaster, saying, "Yes, I will make thy world increase, I will make thy world grow. Yes, I will nourish, and rule, and watch over thy world. There shall be, while I am king, neither cold wind nor hot wind, neither disease nor death."

" 'Then I, God, brought two implements unto him, a golden seal and a poniard inlaid with gold. Behold, here Yima bears the royal sway' " (Vendidad, Fargard II, c. I, 1-7)!

The promise of Zoroaster concerning the work which he would do in the world, that is, teach men how to behave in conformity with universal law, is recorded by the Gathas, in these words:

"I, who have set my heart to watch over the soul in union with the Good Mind, having known the rewards given by God (Ahura Mazda) for our deeds, will teach men to strive after the Right, the while I have power and strength" (Yasna, XXVIII, 4).

Thus it is affirmed that his mission was primarily and essentially ethical, to cause men to elect, with intelligence and good motive, to do the right thing.

This is also seen in this pronouncement of the prophet of Iran, in the Gathas (Yasna XXX, 11):

"If, oh ye mortals, ye shall mark those commandments that God (Ahura Mazda) hath ordained, of happiness and pain, of punishment for liars and blessings for the virtuous, then hereafter ye shall have bliss."

And also this:

"Thus will I speak forth what the Most Bountiful spake unto me as the word that is best for mortals to obey, 'Whoso at my will offereth obedience proceedeth unto the twain, Well-Being and Immortality, through deeds of the Good Mind,' saith the Lord (Ahura Mazda)" (Yasna XLV, 5).

Zoroaster appears to have been the first of those who are in the world's scriptures called "the incarnate word,"[7] a name given in these scriptures generally to the priests of this religion, merely meaning those who could repeat in proper form and with proper observances, the Gathas and the other sacred writings.

Thus the Aban Yast (c. XXI, 91) records:

"Ardvi Sura Anahita[8] answered, 'Oh pure, holy Spitama, this is the sacrifice wherewith thou shalt worship me, this is the sacrifice wherewith thou shalt worship and forward me, from the time when the sun is rising to the time when the sun is setting. Of this libation of mine thou shalt drink, thou who art a priest, who hast asked and learnt the revealed law, who art wise, clever, and the word incarnate.'"

The following is also recorded in another place in the same Yast (c. XXI, 88, 89) of the same conversation with Zoroaster:

"Then Ardvi Sura Anahita came forth, oh Zoroaster, down from those stars to the earth made by God (Ahura Mazda); and Ardvi Sura Anahita spake thus, 'Oh pure, holy Zoroaster, God hath established thee as the master of the material world; God hath established me to keep the whole of the holy creation. Through my brightness and glory flocks and herds and two-legged men continue upon the earth. I, forsooth, preserve all good things, made by God, the offspring of the holy principle, as a shepherd keepeth his flock.'"

The Ashi Yast (c. II, 17-22), gives this narration of divine appreciation of Zoroaster:

[7] An expression very much later given by the author of the Gospel of St. John and by Philo-Judæus a much deeper and more mystical significance.

[8] A semigoddess or angel, presiding over a spring, of fabulous life-giving qualities.

"Praised of the gods, unoffended by the righteous, the great Ashi Vanguhi[9] stood up on her chariot, thus speaking: 'Who art thou who dost invoke me, whose voice is to my ear the sweetest of all that invoked me most?'

"And he spake aloud, 'I am Spitama Zoroaster, he who, first of mortals, recited the praise of glorious Right and offered up sacrifice unto God (Ahura Mazda) and the Amesha Spentas; at whose birth and growth the waters and the plants rejoiced; at whose birth and growth the waters and the plants grew; at whose birth and growth all the creatures of the good creation cried out, "Hail!"

" 'At whose birth and growth Ahriman[10] rushed away from this wide, round earth, whose ends lie afar, and he, the evil-doing Ahriman, who is all death, said, "All the gods together have not been able to smite me down in spite of myself, and Zoroaster alone can reach me in spite of myself. He smiteth me with the Ahuna Vairya,[11] as strong a weapon as a stone big as a house; he burneth me with Asha-Vahista,[12] as if it were melting brass. He maketh it better for me that I should leave this earth, he, Spitama Zoroaster, the only one who can daunt me.' "

"And the great Ashi Vanguhi exclaimed, 'Come nearer unto me, thou pure, holy Spitama; lean thou against my chariot!'

"Spitama Zoroaster came nearer unto her, he leant against her chariot.

"And she caressed him with her left arm and the

[9] Another semigoddess or angel, said in later books to be a daughter of God.
[10] The devil, i.e. Ahriman.
[11] A saying ever on the lips of the devout follower of Zoroaster.
[12] Another familiar saying.

right, with the right arm and the left, saying unto him, 'Thou art beautiful, oh Zoroaster; thou art well-shapen, oh Spitama; strong are thy legs and long are thy arms. Glory is given to thy body and abiding serenity to thy soul, as sure as I proclaim it unto thee.' "

In the Gathas (Yasna XXVIII, 11) is this invocation of the prophet of Iran:

"Teach thou me, oh Lord (Ahura Mazda), who am to guard the Right and the Good Mind for all time, from thy spirit, by thy mouth, how it will be at the beginning of life."

The Ormazd Yast (26) puts these words concerning Zoroaster's discerning knowledge of these things, upon the lips of the Almighty, himself:

"Thou knowest this, and how it is, oh holy Zoroaster, from my understanding and from my knowledge, namely, how the world first began, and how it will end."

And in the Gathas (Yasna XXIX, 8) this testimonial is related to have been given to his ministry, also by the Good Mind:

"This one is here found for me, who alone hath hearkened to our doctrines of command, Zoroaster Spitama. He desireth to cause our counsels to be heard, oh God (Ahura Mazda), and those of the Right; wherefore I will bestow upon him the blest charm of speech."

The Vendidad, in question and answer, develops this tribute to the compelling excellence of the law of God, as announced to men by Zoroaster, again ascribing the words to God, himself:

" 'Oh Maker of the material world, thou Holy One, this law, this demon-destroying law of Zoroaster, by what greatness, goodness, and fairness is it great, good and fair above all other utterances?'

"God (Ahura Mazda) made answer and said, 'As much above all other floods as is the sea, Vouru-Kasha, so much above all other utterances in greatness, goodness, and fairness is this law, this demon-destroying law of Zoroaster.

" 'As much as a great stream flows more swiftly than a slender rivulet, so much above all other utterances in greatness, goodness, and fairness is this law, this demon-destroying law of Zoroaster.

" 'As high as the great tree stands above the small plants it overshadows, so high above all other utterances in greatness, goodness, and fairness is this law, this demon-destroying law of Zoroaster.

" 'As high as the heavens are above the earth that they compass about, so high above all other utterances is this law, this demon-destroying law of God' " (Vendidad, Fargard V, c. V, 22-25).

The Gathas (Yasna XXXIII, 14) thus celebrate the devotion and self-sacrifice with which the prophet fulfilled his mission:

"Zoroaster giveth the very life of his own person as a sacrifice, the choiceness of good thought, action and speech unto God (Ahura Mazda) unto Right, Piety and Dominion."

The same book in another place (Yasna XLVI, 18) causes Zoroaster to promise rewards for submission to his authority and dire consequences to those who persecuted his followers, in these words:

"Whoso holdeth with me, shall share in the best in my possession through the Good Mind; but torments will I set upon him who is for us a grievous oppressor, oh God (Ahura Mazda), and the Right, desiring to satisfy your will. This is the discerning resolution of my mind and heart."

That which Zoroaster would forward upon the earth, the spread of the religion of beneficence and spiritual worship, is called in the Persian scriptures the Maga or Great Cause; the reward for helping it on was Paradise or Heaven, the "Abode of Song," into which God enters first; as it is put in the Gathas (Yasna LI, 15):

"Since Zoroaster appointed a reward to them of his covenant, which, first of all, God (Ahura Mazda) will pass into the Abode of Song; for all of this I have, looked through your blessings, the Good Mind and the Right."

This Maga is, fundamentally, the inculcation of beneficence, the development among men of the Good Mind; it is so termed in the following despairing question in the Gathas (Yasna LI, 11):

"What person, nobly upright, hath cared for the Great Cause of the Good Mind?"

His first followers were his kinsmen, by birth or marriage, to whom he said:

"Ye Haëhtospes Spitamas, of you I declare that ye discern the wise and unwise. Through these deeds ye inherit the Right in accordance with the primeval laws of God (Ahura Mazda)" (Yasna XLVI, 15).

There is something in this prayer for a long life and a good one for Zoroaster in order that he might convert and instruct persons who had betrayed him:

"The best possession known is that of Zoroaster Spitama, and it is that God (Ahura Mazda) will bestow the glories of a blessed life forever through the Right, and likewise to them that practice and learn the words and actions of his Good Cause (Yasna LIII, 1).

The Gathas also (Yasna XLVI, 13) record that God himself will give his blessings unto mankind:

"Whoso among mortals finds grace with Zoroaster Spitama, by his willingness, himself worthy to have good repute, unto him God (Ahura Mazda), will grant life, and the Good Mind shall increase the substance; him we regard the familiar friend with the Right."

And, with trepidation, he cries, in contemplation of that which he was to do and that which he has done, that there may be a close relation between his understanding and his act:

"Oh God (Ahura Mazda) and sovereign, grant that your prophet may perform the word of hearing" (Yasna XXVIII, 7).

And the God (Ahura Mazda) who sent him said concerning his mission most fervently:

"Associating him with Piety, I have come hither. Ask us now what things we are here for thee to ask. For thine asking is as that of a mighty one, since he that is able should make thee as a mighty one possessed of thy desire" (Yasna XLIII, 11).

CHAPTER II

GOD

"AHURA MAZDA (God), by thy spirit, which is ever the same!"

Thus the Gathas (Yasna XXXI, 7) in the earliest centuries known to men salute the Almighty Spirit as God and as Lord, the one and only, unchanging through all eternity.

To Zoroaster and his followers, the ancient Persians, the so-called "fire-worshipers," and the Parsis of later times and our own, God is a spirit.

No image, therefore, could represent him; and idolatry has always been proscribed.

It explains the favor with which the ancient Babylonians and the Persian king, Cyrus, who had taken and ruled the city, as a follower of Zoroaster, are said to have looked upon the Israelitish religion, with its one God, a spirit, not to be represented by images, when they in later days learned of it.

Whether or not the Jews obtained their notion of condemning idolatry from the great people whose king restored the Temple for the pure adoration of Jehovah, may be left for the speculation of archæologists and higher critics.

The Zoroastrian religion, however, is wonderfully pure; its very fundamental things are transcendently ethical and the moral motive is ever present. In consequence, it is of great interest and has been of the highest value, from the standpoint of considering what is right; for it gives almost, or perhaps quite, the earliest example, the records of which are yet extant, of an earnest, uncomplicated search for the right.

This is so true that Mr. Dhalla, High Priest of the Parsis, says:

"The ethical principles of Zoroaster transcend all these. They are the eternal elements that constitute his religion" (*Zoroastrian Theology*, pp. 359 and 360).

Indeed, the entire scheme of virtuous conduct and of its rewards is embraced in the mere names of the deities who compose the Zoroastrian Godhead; they represent the divine things which men see and know.

The Holy Spirits, constituting this Godhead and called in the Zend or ancient Persian language, the "Amesha Spentas," adored by followers of Zoroaster, were seven and were known by the following names:

Ahura Mazda [1]	God, the Eternal Light
Vohu Manah	The Good Mind
Asha	Right
Khshathra	Dominion
Aramaïti	Piety
Haürvetat	Well-Being
Ameretat	Immortality

The tremendous ethical significance of such a selection as the divine attributes and as the active influences for good, among men and throughout the universe, will not fail to be apparent to all to whom these names become known. As the qualities which make the character of Almighty God they are indeed supreme.

They constitute, in order, the very inception of man's ethical life, his reason; its development through beneficent purpose; its discipline by observing and comply-

[1] An expression translated Lord of Hosts or Lord God.

ing with the laws that control the universe; the rich
resources which such a course of thought and action
sets free; the abundance of triumphant life which the
exercise of these powers generates; the reward of well-
being, physical and spiritual, which follows inevitably,
as fruit comes after flowering; and the immortality
which makes of the after existence an endless continuance of this great joy in beneficial usefulness.

The whole story of the ethical life of man, here and
hereafter, is there summarized.²

Though Ahura Mazda, called Ormazd by the Greeks
and therefore usually so known to Occidentals, is God,
the Almighty, the Supreme, and though the other
Amesha Spentas are particular aspects of God, as is
made clear in many places, yet each is spoken of as a
personality.

There is little mention in later writings of the
"Amesha Spentas," by which name they were spoken
of as on a level with God. The Gathas are indeed
sung and they are thus kept in mind.

To the Amesha Spentas, the Zamyad Yast (c. III,
14-20) pays this glowing, enthusiastic tribute:

"We sacrifice unto the awful, kingly glory, created
by God (Ahura Mazda) . . . which belongs to the

² "The Zoroastrian religion was a religion of life in the noblest
sense of the word; it brought two things of which the old Aryan
religions in the midst of which it arose had no idea or only a dim
perception; those two things were *immortality* and *hope;* so that
the Zoroastrian faith not only gives its follower a moral rule through
life; not only directs his heart, his tongue, his hand, teaching him
good thought, good word, good deed; but it tells him that the good
will prevail at last if he does his duty; that a son of the prophet,
Saöshyant, will come and open the eternal reign of Ormazd (Ahura
Mazda), and exterminate the evil from the world. The poorest, the
meanest Zoroastrian in the world knows that he is born a soldier of
Saöshyant and that Ormazd will conquer through him." Hastings,
Encyclopedia of Religion and Ethics.

Amesha Spentas, the bright ones, whose very glance performs their wish, august, quick to act, mighty, glorious, undecaying and holy; who, being seven, are one in thought; being seven, are one in speech; being seven, are one in deed; whose thought is the same, whose speech is the same, whose deed is the same; whose father and ruler is the same, that is God, Creator of all things; who look into one another's soul intent upon good thoughts, intent upon good words, intent upon good deeds, intent upon Paradise and whose path through the heavens shines with glory as they descend to the libations; who are the makers and rulers, the fashioners and overseers, the keepers and preservers of the creation of God."

The Dinkard well says of it:

"From humility arises the recognition of God (Ahura Mazda), and from the recognition of God, spiritual belief" (XII, 65).

In the Shayast-La-Shayast (c. XV, 3) God is said to have replied to a question concerning the Amesha Spentas, put by Zoroaster, in these words, giving what purports to be, but falls far short of being, a statement of the divine activities through each of these agencies, characterizing the entire Godhead as spiritual:

"Zoroaster spake thus, 'Thou art intangible and Vohu Manah, Asha, Khshathra, Aramaïti, Haürvetat and Ameretat are also intangible; and, when I depart from thy presence and see thee not nor even them, then, since there is something of each person whom I see and to whom I pay homage, am I to worship thee and the Amesha Spentas?'

"Unto him God (Ahura Mazda) made answer and said, 'Yea; for I say unto thee, oh Zoroaster, the

Spitaman, that each of us hath produced for the world his own unique creation, by means of which there may be set in motion in the body of that world, the activity which each exerciseth in the spiritual existence. That in the world which belongeth unto me who am God, is the righteous man; unto Vohu Manah, the cattle; unto Asha, fire; unto Khshathra, metals; unto Aramaïti, the soil and virtuous women; unto Haürvetat, water; and unto Ameretat, plants. Whoever hath learned the care of these seven, behaveth as is pleasing in our sight and his soul will never pass under the dominion of the devil and his demons; when he hath bestowed this care upon these, even so hath he done unto the Amesha Spentas.' "

This again, it will be observed, is fundamentally moral, involving man's behavior toward every material thing which constitutes his environment.

In the Shayast-La-Shayast, also (c. XXII, 1-7) is found this composite prayer to the Amesha Spentas, which seeks to give an account, in many respects crude and far-fetched, yet filled with moral purpose, of the respective blessings conferred by the Amesha Spentas upon mankind:

"May Ahura Mazda (God) grant thee the august rank and throne of a master!

"May Vohu Manah (the Good Mind) grant thee wisdom and may the benefit to thee of knowing the Good Mind be good thoughts; and mayst thou follow virtuous conduct, to the salvation of thy soul!

"May Asha (Right), the glorious grant the understanding and insight!

"May Khshathra (Dominion) grant thee resources, poured forth from every generous source!

"May Aramaïti (Piety) grant thee credit and honor

among men through thine offspring and bestow upon thee, as wife, a woman from a strong race!

"May Haürvetat (Well-Being) grant thee plenty and prosperity!

"May Ameretat (Immortality) grant thee herds of four-footed creatures!"

The coupling of herds with Ameretat (Immortality), signifying reproduction, and the joining of good purpose and righteous conduct with Vohu Manah (the Good Mind) are a departure from the connections named in the other passage; but, to perhaps even a greater degree, these sayings illustrate the moral ends which the authors of the sacred texts had in view.

In the Khorshed Nyasis (c. I, 4) is found this prayer, not asking aught of the sacred seven, but pledging unto them, as the Godhead and so as the great, worthwhile ethical forces of the universe, service and devotion even unto death:

"I give sacrifices and pray unto you, oh Amesha Spentas, in the fullness of thought, of word and of deed, and of my heart; unto you I give freely even my life!"

The religion of Zoroaster is so extraordinarily spiritual and in all its conceptions so squares with the ethics which he taught, that it is necessary at the very outset to examine with great care what he and his followers thought about God and the attributes or personalities which compose their conception of the Godhead, as has already been said.

Though the name by which God is known in their scriptures is Ahura Mazda, which may be translated Eternal Light, or, by a figure of speech, Abiding Wisdom, it must not be supposed that God, in this personality or aspect, was viewed as an abstraction; the Gathas (Yasna XLV, 10) says of him and of his associates, "Him (Ahura Mazda) thou should seek to exalt with prayers of Piety, him that is called ever God, for he hath promised through his own Right and Good Mind that Well-Being and Immortality shall be in his Dominion, strength and perpetuity in his house," showing him to be a real, living being, forever to be served, and adored, of men.

First and foremost, he is the Creator, not only of the material universe but of all spiritual existences as well. The Vendidad (Fargard XVIII, c. 1, 13) speaks of him as "the Creator and the Most Beneficent of all things," conferring his blessings upon all other beings in the universe.

Man is, as the scriptures assert, the crowning act of his creation; this the Aögemaïde Nask (30) declares in his name, thus:

"Oh, Spitama Zoroaster, I created the stars, the moon, the sun and red-burning fire, the dogs, the birds and the five kinds of animals; but, better and greater than all, created I the righteous man. . . ."

Though, as will be seen, the counter-creations of evil are ascribed to Angra Mainyu, the evil spirit, whom later writers have called Ahriman, the name adopted for use in this volume, yet it was conceded that, since God (Ahura Mazda) is, by hypothesis, almighty, he must accept responsibility for all that is; so the Aban Yast (c. XXVIII, 81) testifies:

"For whom God (Ahura Mazda) hath created four horses, the wind, rain, mist and sleet; and thus ever upon the earth, it is blowing, raining, hailing and sleeting."

It could hardly be said, however, that the gifts of the heavens, the wind, the rain, the snow or sleet, are really evils and not blessings, howsoever they may at times interfere with man's comfort; and that was really the view the followers of Zoroaster took of the matter.

The Vendidad gives the following surprisingly scientific account of how God (Ahura Mazda) moves the waters from the reservoir of the sea back to that great reservoir again, illustrating the orderly activities of God, working through the unvarying laws of nature:

" 'Oh thou Maker of the material world, thou Holy One (Ahura Mazda), is it true that thou seizest the waters from the sea, Vouru-Kasha, with the wind and the clouds? That thou takest them down to the corpses? That thou takest them down to the Dakhmas?* That thou takest them down to the unclean remains? That thou takest them down to the bones? And that then thou makest them flow back unseen? That thou makest them flow back to the sea, Puïtika?'

"God (Ahura Mazda) made answer and said, 'It is even so as thou hast said, oh righteous Zoroaster! I seize the waters from the sea, Vouru-Kasha, with the wind and the clouds; I take them to the corpses; I take them down to the unclean remains; I make them flow back unseen; I make them flow back to the sea, Puïtika' " (Vendidad, Fargard V, c. IV, 15-18).

That God is purely spirit and intangible, though not always invisible, is affirmed by the Shayast-La-Shayast (c. XV) in the following anecdote:

"It is revealed in a passage of the Avesta* that

*Elevated places constructed for the exposure of corpses.
* This passage of the Zend Avesta has been lost.

Zoroaster in the presence of God (Ahura Mazda)
sought continually to obtain light from him; he spake
to God, saying, 'Thy head, hands, feet, hair, face and
tongue are, in my eyes, just like unto those which are
mine, and thou hast the raiment of men; give me a
hand that I may grasp thy hand!' God made answer
and said, 'I am an intangible spirit; it is not possible
to grasp my hand.' "

The similarity of this to the passage from the same
book, already quoted, in which the Amesha Spentas are
all described as intangible spirits, will of course be
noted.

God as the All-Seeing and All-Knowing, is thus celebrated in the Gathas:

"God (Ahura Mazda) knoweth best the purposes
that have been wrought already by demons and mortals and that will be wrought hereafter" (Yasna
XXIX, 4).

And in another place:

"Not to be deceived is the all-seeing God (Ahura
Mazda)" (Yasna, XLV, 4).

The Zend Avesta echoes this, by causing Zoroaster
to address him, "Thou All-Wise God (Ahura Mazda),
who sleepeth never" (Vendidad, Fargard IX, c. IV,
20)!

Also the Aögemaïde Nask (76) in describing God
as, "Him whom no one can deceive or mislead."

The Ormazd Yast (5, 7) records this declaration of
God concerning his names among men and angels:

"Then Zoroaster said, 'Reveal thou unto me that
name of thine, that is greatest, best, fairest, most effective, most fiend-smiting, best-healing, that destroyeth
best the malice of demons and men . . . '

"God (Ahura Mazda) replied unto him, saying, 'My

name is, first, He of whom questions are asked,⁵ oh holy Zoroaster!

" 'My second name is the Giver of Herds.

" 'My third name is the Strong One.

" 'My fourth name is Perfect Holiness.

" 'My fifth name is All Good Things created by Mazda, the offspring of the holy principle.

" 'My sixth name is Understanding.

" 'My seventh name is He that possesseth understanding.

" 'My eighth name is Knowledge.

" 'My ninth name is He that possesseth knowledge.

" 'My tenth name is Blessing.

" 'My eleventh name is He that causeth blessing.

" 'My twelfth name is Ahura (the Eternal).

" 'My thirteenth name is the Most Beneficent.

" 'My fourteenth name is He in whom there is no harm.

" 'My fifteenth name is the Unconquerable.

" 'My sixteenth name is He that maketh the true account.

" 'My seventeenth name is the All-Seeing.

" 'My eighteenth name is Healing.

" 'My nineteenth name is Creator.

" 'My twentieth name is Mazda (Light).' "

⁵ The law was generally revealed by Zoroaster in the form of questions, addressed to, and answered by, God (Ahura Mazda).

CHAPTER III

THE HOLY SPIRITS

"AND thus Zoroaster himself, oh Lord (Ahura Mazda), chooses that spirit of thine that is holiest, oh Lord. May Right have a body strong with vital vigor! May Piety abide in the Dominion where the sun shines! May the Good Mind grant a destiny to men according to their works (Yasna XLIII, 16).

Such is God, as conceived by the ancient Zoroaster, an exalted spiritual being, ruling the universe by his spiritual power.

Emanating from him and existing together with him, were, as said, six other divine intelligences, constituting, with their Creator, the Amesha Spentas, or Holy Spirits, the elements of God.

These emanations from God who, together with him, make up God, are worshiped as distinct, but wholly spiritual, personalities, by the early, as well as the late, followers of Zoroaster.

The first and second of them, Vohu Manah, the Good Mind, and Asha, the Right, stand out clearly as individuals; Khshathra, Dominion, and Aramaïti, Piety, not so clearly; and Haürvetat, Well-Being, and Ameretat, Immortality, as scarcely more than abstractions and merely attributes, indeed, of the divine.

They are, however, important, and indeed indispensable, factors in the Zoroastrian scheme.

Vohu Manah, the Good Mind, is the first creation,

or, more particularly, the offspring of God (Ahura Mazda) according to the traditions of the Persians.

Through the instrumentality of Vohu Manah, his Good Mind, the ancient scriptures say, he did all his good and mighty works. By this Good Mind, also, his first and most potent emanation, he is made known unto his creatures as the moving, beneficent power of the universe.

"Then I shall recognize thee as powerful and holy, oh God (Ahura Mazda), when . . . the might of Good Mind shall come to me."

Thus the Gathas (Yasna XLIII, 4) celebrate the manner in which frail man, by searching, may find out God, that is, by recognizing the beneficent purpose of the Creator.

Again in the same Yasna (7) this is made yet clearer, as is the duty of man to rank himself on the side of God, thus:

"Yea, as the holy one I recognized thee, oh God (Ahura Mazda), when the Good Mind came to me and asked me, 'Who art thou?' and 'To whom dost thou belong?' "

That what is meant, is that the Good Mind, meaning thereby sound reason, impelled by the motive to benefit mankind, and, indeed, all living creatures, is the revealer of God unto man, this sentence, taken from a later verse of the same Yasna (11) shows:

"As the holy one I recognized thee, Lord (Ahura Mazda), when the Good Mind came to me, when first with thy words I was instructed."

That this Good Mind is of God and is the means and medium by which he blesses mortals, another of the Gathas (XXXI, 21) asserts, thus:

"God (Ahura Mazda) by virtue of his absolute Godhead, will give in perpetuity a communion with Well-Being, Immortality, Right, Dominion, and Good Mind, to him who in spirit and deed is his friend."

In another of the Gathas (Yasna L, 11) is found this invocation, showing in what way God may directly aid his servants,

"Yea, thy servant, instant in praise, may I call myself, oh God (Ahura Mazda), and such may I truly be, so far as by means of the Right it in me lies and as my powers avail. Let him who called the universe into being, give aid with the Good Mind to its fulfillment of all that most perfectly answers to his will."

The duty of "the recording angel" is by Zoroastrians assigned to the Good Mind; of this the Dadistan-i-Dinik (c. XIV, 1, 2) says that:

"The account of one's deeds, both of good works and evil, the archangel,[1] the Good Mind, must record three times every day; for to take note of the thoughts, words and deeds of men while in the flesh, is one of his duties."

That whatsoever man does, by being and acting in accord with the Good Mind of God, belongs to God as his very own, as inevitably the result of his beneficence, as are all the manifestations of the Right throughout all creation, this beautiful passage declares:

"Whatso I may do or have already done, and whatso, oh Good Mind, may be precious in thy sight, the rays of the sun, the bright uprising of the dawns, these are for your praise alone, oh thou Right and God (Ahura Mazda)" (Yasna L, 10).

Asha, the Right, is, according to Zoroaster, the second creation of God, his offspring in the second genera-

[1] Note that Good Mind is called here, not a god, but the archangel.

tion springing from the Good Mind; that is, out of God's beneficence have sprung the unchanging laws that control the universe, laws wisely designed to bless and benefit mankind.

In one of the Gathas, it appears: "Oh God (Ahura Mazda), might one like thee, teach it to his friend, such as I am, and through friendly Right, give us support that the Good Mind may come to us" (Yasna XLIV, 1).

This appears to signify that full recognition of the uniformity of God's laws would convince the sinner of the evil of his ways—that is, of his failure to conform with their manifest intent.

Accordingly, the Gathas (Yasna XLIII, 12) thus invoke God:

"And since that thou hast spoken, 'Thou mayest go unto the Right for knowledge,' then didst thou not issue a command that I did not obey."

Mills, in *Our Own Religion in Ancient Persia,* says that the significance of Asha, or the Right, grew "out of the observation of the undeviating regularity of natural phenomena."

It was this, of course, which caused the rules of conduct in ancient Persia to be so strict and undeviating; and it was that strictness, based upon the idea of the laws of nature, without shadow of turning, to which the Hebrew scriptures have reference, when speaking of laws being as invariable as those of the Medes and Persians.

The benefits that accrue unto the man who first conceives aright the Right and the manner in which that leads him on to the consequent, ineffable blessings of the Godhead, the Ardibehist Yast (c. I, 3) celebrates, saying:

"I proclaim Asha-Vahista.[2] When I proclaim Asha-Vahista, then easy is the road unto the other Amesha Spentas, whom God (Ahura Mazda) keepeth with good thoughts, whom God keepeth with good words, whom God keepeth with good deeds."

A prayer for insight is offered up by Zoroaster in the Vendidad (Fargard XIX, 10) as follows:

"This I ask of thee, teach thou me the truth, oh Lord God (Ahura Mazda)!"

This prayer is not so much for revelation as for power to see what truly exists and governs.

This, when imparted to Zoroaster, he promised to transmit to others, saying in the Gathas:

"I . . . will, while I have power and strength, teach men to seek after the Right" (Yasna XXVIII, 4).

The character of the lessons which careful observation of the order of nature may teach and how it may do so, this inquiry, taken from the Yasna (XXXIV, 7), exemplifies:

"None know I, other than thee, oh Right; so do ye protect us!"

It was the prayer of the devout Zoroaster that the Right be in very truth might to bless and save, as in this:

"May Right be provided with a body, strong with vital vigor" (Yasna XLIII, 16)!

It was, therefore, in his view, no mere, impotent abstraction, but the living, working manifestation of God in the outer universe.

The Nasks give the obverse of this, meaning the same thing, that one must first see the Right and then do it, in the following:

"He hath achieved nought, oh Zoroaster, nor shall

[2] Vahista, an appellation of Asha, meaning "perfect."

he achieve aught, who doth not fulfill the laws of perfect holiness, well pondered in his heart . . . " (Tahmura's Fragments of the Nasks, c. XLVIII, 105, 106).

This is further explained in this saying, taken from Yasna (XXXI, 22), which emphasizes the fundamental requirement of sincere thinking and that he who does right, aids God's governance of his universe,

"Unto him that thinketh sincerely, as also unto him that knoweth in his mind, these things are clear. By word and deed followeth he the Right, with the good Dominion; and unto thee, oh God (Ahura Mazda), shall he be a most helpful companion."

Khshathra, Dominion, is rather the resources of the universe, freely operating for beneficent ends and open to utilization by man so long as he also seeks those ends, than the power of the Almighty which can make or mar man at will.

It is the power which flows in unlimited measure, as beneficence, enlightened by reason, learns the meaning and uses of the laws of the universe.

The Zoroastrian scriptures do not celebrate so fulsomely the almighty power of God, as do the scriptures of many other peoples.[3]

The Yasna (XLIV), however, eloquently sets forth the omnipotence of God and his creative power, thus in part:

"Oh God (Ahura Mazda), might one like thee teach it to his friend, such as I am, and through the friendly Right give us support that the Good Mind may come to us.

"This I ask thee, tell me truly, oh God, whether at the beginning of the best existence the recompenses

---

[3] There is abundant literature about the persistency of believing in powers of good and of evil, *equally.*

shall bring blessedness to him that meets with them. Surely he, oh Right, the holy one, who watches in his spirit the transgression of all, is himself the benefactor of all the living, oh God.

"This I ask thee, tell me truly, oh God, who was the father of the Right in generation—who determined the paths of suns and stars—who is it by whom the moon waxes and wanes? This, oh Lord, and yet more I am fain to know.

"This I ask thee, tell me truly, oh God, who, from below, sustained the earth and the firmament from falling—who sustained the waters and plants—who yoked swiftness with the winds and the clouds—who, oh God (Ahura Mazda), called forth the Good Mind" (Yasna XLIV, 1-4)?

Aramaïti, Piety, abundant, overflowing, full of energy and vigor, comes next in order in the persons that compose the Godhead.

The Gathas say of its office in the divine plan: "And to him came, then, Dominion, Good Mind, and Right. Piety thereupon gave continued life to their bodies and indestructibility" (Yasna XXX, 7).

In another of the Gathas (Yasna XLIII, 16) is this prayer:

"May the Good Mind grant a destiny to men according to their works."

Thus the ancient writings characterize the dynamic force of vitality as that which makes alive and real all things in the material universe which otherwise would be inert.

In another place (Yasna XXXI, 8) God is identified as peculiarly the inspirer of life and energy, thus:

"I conceived thee, oh God (Ahura Mazda), in my thought, that thou, the first, were also the last; that thou also art the father of the Good Mind for thus I saw all with mine eye; that truly thou didst create Right; and art the Lord to judge the deeds of life."

Piety is also represented in the Gathas as the lawgiver through which God's laws are made known to man, thus:

"Their judgments shall Piety proclaim, even those of thy wisdom which none can deceive" (Yasna XLIII, 6).

This, also, is no mere euphemism to the followers of Zoroaster. Instead, it goes back to the very beginning of the conception by the plainsmen among whom this religion came into existence, of the Good Mind, that is, the fostering care of cattle, and especially of the cow and her calf, as well as of men, women and children, against marauders, as is set forth in this passage from the Gathas:

"For such precious reward, oh God (Ahura Mazda), bestowest thou through the workings of the Good Mind, to the bodily life of those in the community to care for the pregnant cow (the promise of) thy blest doctrine, oh Lord, that of the wisdom which exalts communities through Right" (Yasna XXXIV, 14).

And out of this life, as Zoroaster conceived it, came immortality, for he said in the Gathas (Yasna XXVIII, 3):

"I who would praise you as never before, Right, Good Mind, and God (Ahura Mazda), and those for whom Piety causeth the Dominion that passeth not away, to increase; come ye to my help at my call."

Haürvetat, Well-Being, comes next, the normal state of him who has done well. Of this, one of the Yasts gives this account:

"God (Ahura Mazda) spake unto Spitama Zoroaster,

saying, 'I created for the faithful the assistance, the enjoyments, the comforts and the delights of Well-Being' " (Khordad Yast, 1).

Rarely, if ever, is this effluence of God mentioned in the Persian scriptures except as a thing shared by God with man, when he is deserving of such a blessing, and accompanied, also, by Immortality, the sixth and final emanation of God. Thus again the Gathas say:

"Oh, thou who hast created the kine, the waters, the plants, Well-Being and Immortality, by the holiest spirit, oh God (Ahura Mazda), strength and continuance through the Good Mind as the judge shall sentence" (Yasna LI, 7).

And in this prayer is set forth the same conception:

"By his holy spirit and by Good Mind, by good deed and word, may God (Ahura Mazda) in accordance with Right, by his Dominion, together with Piety, bestow upon us the twain, Well-Being and Immortality" (Yasna XLVII, 1).

These are often, even usually, merely called "the twain" in the Zoroastrian writings, which expression always means the same as in this passage, also from the Gathas,

"Grant, oh Well-Being and Immortality, your own blessings forever" (Yasna XXXIII, 8).

The Gathas (Yasna XLV, 10) thus praise God for these gifts:

"Him thou shouldst seek to exalt with prayers of Piety, him that is called forever God (Ahura Mazda), because he hath promised through his own Right and by Good Mind that Well-Being and Immortality shall be in his Dominion and strength and perpetuity in his house."

In the Yasna (XXXIV, 1) it is made clear that both

these blessings should follow right conduct and a saintly life, in this passage:

"The deed, the word and the worship by which I will ask of thee, Immortality and Right, oh God (Ahura Mazda), and the realm of Well-Being—the multitude of these, oh God, we wish that you would grant."

And in yet another Yasna (XXXI, 6) the tribute is paid to God:

"To him shall the best come who as one who knows speaks to me Right's very word of Well-Being and Immortality, even that Dominion of God (Ahura Mazda) which the Good Mind will render prosperous for him."

Ameretat, Immortality, follows as indeed a boon to him who would throughout endless years use his rich powers to serve beneficently all God's creatures.

It was not so certain at the outset as to be asserted always with confidence; the Gathas signify this in this passage which alone might leave the question one unsolved:

"As the holy one I recognized thee, oh Lord (Ahura Mazda), when the Good Mind came to me to learn the state of my desire. Grant it me, that which none may compel you to allow, the wish for long continuance of blessed existence that they say is in thy Dominion" (Yasna XLIII, 13).

Though Well-Being is rarely mentioned except in company with Immortality, there are not wanting passages referring to the latter by itself.

And in the Gathas is found this prayer for the twain:

"This I ask thee, tell me truly, oh Lord (Ahura Mazda), whether through you I shall attain my goal, oh Lord, even attachment unto you, and that my voice may be effectual, that Well-Being and Immortality may be ready to unite according to that promise with him who joins himself with Right" (Yasna XLIV, 17).

And this, in another Gatha, he speaks of as being the characteristic blessing of them who stand with God as the foes of his foes:

"And both thy gifts shall be for sustenance, even Well-Being and Immortality. Piety linked to the Right shall advance the Dominion of Good Mind, its permanence and might. By these, oh God (Ahura Mazda), dost thou bless the foes of thy foes" (Yasna XXXIV, 11).

The following prayer that the devil be not able to destroy Immortality is offered in the Aögemaïde Nask (4-7):

"May the accursed Ahriman be smitten, destroyed, and broken, he who hath no knowledge, who hath evil knowledge, who is full of death!

"Who destroyeth the body of the immortal soul!

"May the immortal soul have its share in Paradise!

"And may the pleasure and comfort that will dissipate the pain of the immortal soul, come to us!"

CHAPTER IV

WORSHIP OF THE SUN, FIRE, ATAR, MITHRA AND OTHERS

"THIS I ask thee! tell me truly, oh Lord (Ahura Mazda): As to prayer, how should it be to one of you? Oh God (Ahura Mazda), might one like thee teach it to his friend, such as I am, and through friendly Right, give us support, that the Good Mind may come to us" (Yasna XLIV, 1).

No office of the Right was more highly esteemed by followers of Zoroaster than control over worship and all religious performances. Worship of the Great Spirit was commanded, worship of idols or evil spirits prohibited; but for the more difficult, direct worship of God who is a spirit, two new forms of worship were *later* introduced, viz. the worship of the Sun, and, after that and as a symbol of it, the worship of the Fire. These were to be dealt with as symbols.

There is nothing so uncommon about worship of the Sun by primitive peoples that it should be necessary to give this feature prominence in a book on Zoroastrianism, were it not that this has been, and continues to be, together with the worship of Fire, perhaps the most distinctive thing in Parsi devotion, aside possibly from religious purification which is discussed in another chapter.

This practice had its beginning, apparently, in the very spirituality which caused Zoroaster and his plains-

34

men to adopt the name, "Daëvas,"[1] for the evil spirits, because that was the name applied, by the peoples of the East, to their anthropomorphic deities and idols.

Therefore, the Sun, afar in the heavens, giving light and heat unto the earth and causing life to spring forth abundantly, was selected as the symbol and manifestation of God, rather than anything which might even suggest a human form.

This turned the worship, likewise, to the abstract qualities of the Sun, its glory, its light, its warmth, its life-giving, its beneficence, its exposure of the delusions and phantoms of darkness.

The Khorshed Yast (1-4) thus commands Sun worship:

"We sacrifice unto the undying, shining, swift-horsed Sun.

"When the light of the Sun waxeth warmer, when the brightness of the Sun waxeth warmer, then up stand the heavenly Yazatas,[2] by hundreds and thousands; they gather together its Glory, they make its Glory pass down, they pour its Glory upon the earth made by God (Ahura Mazda), for the increase of the world of holiness, for the increase of the creatures of holiness, for the increase of the undying, shining, swift-horsed Sun.

"And when the Sun riseth up, then the earth, made by God, becometh clean; the running waters become clean, the waters of the wells become clean, the waters of the sea become clean, the standing waters become clean; all the holy creatures, the creatures of the Good Spirit, become clean.

"Should not the Sun rise up, then the Daëvas would

[1] These are demons; see the next chapter.
[2] Stable spiritual beings.

destroy all the things that are in the seven Karshvares, nor would the heavenly Yazatas find any way of withstanding or repelling them in the material world.

"He who offereth up a sacrifice unto the undying, shining, swift-horsed Sun—to withstand darkness, to withstand the Daëvas born of darkness, to withstand the robbers and bandits, to withstand the Yatus and Païrikas,[3] to withstand death that creepeth in, unseen —offereth it up to the Amesha Spentas, offereth it up to his own soul. He rejoiceth all the heavenly and worldly Yazatas, who offereth up a sacrifice unto the undying, shining, swift-horsed Sun."

The Shayast-La-Shayast (c. VII, 6, 7) thus enforces the obligation, resting upon every follower of Zoroaster, to be constant in his adoration of the Sun and also in cleanliness, which it thus connects with godliness:

"And, while men reverence not the Sun, the good works which they do that day are not their own. . . . While they wash not their dirty hands,[4] any good work which they do is not their own. For, while one doth not utterly destroy corruption, there is no coming of the angels to his body; when there is no coming of the angels to his body, he hath no steadfastness in the religion; and, when he hath no steadfastness in the religion, no good work whatever reacheth unto him."

In the first verse of the same chapter, the Shayast-La-Shayast declares:

"The morning Sun it is necessary to reverence till midday and that of midday it is necessary to reverence till the afternoon and that of the afternoon it is neces-

---

[3] Evil spirits of various kinds.

[4] Cleanliness is also highly supported by the Parsis: "Purity of body is a most salient feature in the life of a Zoroastrian. It is rated higher than anything else." Dhalla, *Zoroastrian Theology*, p. 93.

sary to reverence till night. Whenever one is quite prepared for this act and shall then do reverence, it is proper."

In like manner, instead of some idol in human form or monstrous guise, Fire, which also gives light and heat, was taken as the representative upon the earth, itself, of the Sun and, therefore, also of God.

Fire is also identified with God as his visible manifestation upon the earth, as in this passage from Atas Nyasis (c. V, 18):

"We gladden by our virtue thy mighty Fire, oh God (Ahura Mazda), thy most quick and powerful Fire, that showeth his assistance to him who hath ever comforted him, but delighteth in taking vengeance with his hands on the man that hath harmed him."

And thus in the Gathas:

"The glow of thy Fire, who works with the Right" (Yasna XLIII, 4).[5]

In another of the Gathas (Yasna XXXI, 19) this idea of inspiration and of inspired utterances in connection with the sacred Fire, is set forth, thus:

"To him should one listen who has the Right in his thoughts, a healer of life and one that knows,—one who, oh God (Ahura Mazda), can establish the truth of the words of his tongue at will when, by thy red Fire, oh God, assignment is made between the two parties."

And again in the Gathas stands the promise of Zoroaster:

"As the holy one I recognized thee, God (Ahura Mazda), when the Good Mind came to me. To his question, 'For which wilt thou decide?' (I made reply), At the gift of adoration to thy Fire, I will bethink

---

[5] Fire is thus spoken of in the Gathas, but not frequently.

me of the Right, so long as I have power'" (Yasna XLIII, 9).

The Dinkard speaks of this devotion.

"To Fire special reverence is due; because we owe to it the existence and sustenance of man" (IX, 644).

Fire is esteemed not the less holy by followers of Zoroaster because it performs lowly offices for men, such as heating and cooking, nor while put to such use. The fire on the hearthstone is the object of their adoration as is the fire upon the altar; indeed, it is regarded as then being one of the most sacred of all altars.

Thus the selections of Zad-Sparam (c. XI, 1-6) say of the various sorts of fire, classed according to their functions:

"As he (Ahriman) came seventhly to Fire, which was combined against him, the Fire separated into five kinds, which are called the Propitious, the Good Diffuser, the Aurvazist, the Vazist, and the Supremely-Benefiting. And it produced the Propitious Fire itself in Heaven; its manifestation is in the Fire which is burning on the earth, and its propitiousness is this, that all the kinds are of its nature. The Good Diffuser is that which is in men and animals, and its business consists in the digestion of the good, the sleeping of the body, and the brightening of the eyes. The Aurvazist is that which is in plants, in whose seed it is formed, and its business consists in piercing the earth, warming the chilled water and producing the qualities and fragrance of plants and blossoms therefrom, and elaborating the ripened produce into many fruits. The Vazist is that which has its motion in a cloud, and its business consists in destroying atmospheric gloom and darkness, and making the thickness of the atmosphere fine and

propitious in quality, sifting the hail, moderately
warming the water which the cloud holds, and making
sultry weather showery. The Supremely-Benefiting,
like the sky, is that glory whose lodgment is in the
Behram Fire,⁶ as the master of the house is over the
house, and whose propitious power arises from the
glowing brightness of the Fire, the blazing forth in the
purity of the place, the praise of God (Ahura Mazda),
and the practice of good works."

As the sun was taken to be the direct representation
of God, the most potent force of nature and the most
beneficent, so fire came to be, in the traditions of the
Persians, the representation of Atar, the Son of God,
in which his spirit is manifest, as perhaps next in power
and certainly in beneficence.⁷

This is the burden of Atas Nyasis which (c. V, 13)
speaks thus of the message of the fire while performing
the humble service of cooking:

"Atar, the Son of God (Ahura Mazda), lifteth up
his voice to all those for whom he cooketh their evening
meal and their morning meal. From all those he
wisheth a good offering, a beneficent offering, an offering of assistance, oh Spitama!"

This extends also to holding aloof evil spirits, intent
upon injuring members of the household or sowing a
sentiment of discord among them.

It also protects the expectant mother against efforts
of the powers of darkness to kill the babe within her
womb or to compel her to bring it forth unto evil.

Thus the Shayast-La-Shayast (c. X, 4) gives this
account of a legend of the birth of Zoroaster, ascribed

---

⁶ The fire on the altars at the temples, never quenched.
⁷ This Son of God calls for no such peculiar reverence as does
Christ.

to a passage in the Spend Nask, which has been lost:

"The rule is this, that when a woman becometh pregnant, as long as it is possible, the Fire is to be maintained most carefully in the dwelling, because it is declared in the Spend Nask that towards Dukhdav, the mother of Zoroaster, when she was pregnant with Zoroaster, for three nights every night a leader with a hundred and fifty demons rushed for the destruction of Zoroaster, but, owing to the existence of the Fire in the dwelling, they knew no means of accomplishing it."

Fire could be contaminated and profaned in certain ways, the Zoroastrian scriptures record, especially by being used to burn the bodies of the dead, whether of human beings or of animals. Burning the dead possibly seemed the more dreadful to the plainsmen, because fire, as they knew it upon the steppes, was the sun by day, the moon and stars by night, the burning gas wells of the neighborhood of Baku and the greatly treasured fire upon the hearth, preserved by the most careful use of the scanty combustibles available, twigs and branches and dried dung of cattle.

Save as fire might sweep over the dry and scant vegetation in a prairie conflagration, the burning of flesh was unknown, except as the marauders swept down from the hills and set the plantations afire, consuming the bodies of men and cattle in a holocaust.

The vultures and beasts and the dry air soon disposed of bodies and, especially if they were exposed on high and barren spots, without contamination being spread abroad in the air, water or soil.

The dead flesh of man was called "Nasu," meaning corruption. Of giving it to be consumed by fire, the

Vendidad reports this inquiry by Zoroaster and God's reply:

" 'Oh Maker of the material world, thou Holy One, if worshippers of God (Ahura Mazda) walking or running, or riding, or driving, come upon a Nasu-burning Fire, whereon Nasu is being burnt or cooked, what shall they do?'

"God made answer and said, 'They shall kill the man that cooketh the Nasu; surely they shall kill him' " (Vendidad, Fargard VIII, 73, 74).

Merely that a death took place in a house where there was a fire, accompanied by the sacred utensils that were in every pious Zoroastrian household, was enough to contaminate the place; this, and what should be done under these conditions, the same book thus expounds.

" 'Oh Creator of the material world, thou Holy One, when into our houses here below we have brought the Fire, the Baresma, the cups, the Haöma, and the mortar, oh Holy Lord, if it come to pass that either a dog or a man die there, what shall the worshippers of God do?'

"God (Ahura Mazda) made answer and said, 'Out of the house, oh Spitama Zoroaster, shall they take the Fire, the Baresma, the cups, the Haöma, and the mortar; they shall take the dead one out to the proper place, whereto, according to the law, corpses must be brought, to be devoured there.'

" 'Oh Creator of the material world, thou Holy One, when shall they bring back the Fire into the house wherein the man hath died?'

"God made answer and said, 'They shall wait for nine nights in winter, for a month in summer, and then they shall bring back the Fire to the house wherein the man hath died' " (Vendidad, Fargard V, c. VII, 39-42).

It was, of course, the custom of the plainsmen, as of all men of old, to "keep fire," since to let it go out was to incur the great inconvenience of kindling it anew by means of sunglass, of friction of wood upon wood, or of metal or flint upon flint, or else of borrowing fire from neighbors.

By the Zoroastrian scriptures, however, this was made a sacred duty; though, of course, upon occasion, the fire might be extinguished, as when the home or camp was deserted, or be permitted to go out, as when fuel could not be had. Of this the Shayast-La-Shayast says:

"This, too, that Fire is not to be extinguished, for this is a sin; and there is he that extinguisheth it, and yet is good" (Shayast-La-Shayast, c. XX, 15).

In the Atas Nyasis (c. V, 9) is found this invocation to the fire, calling upon it not to go out, to the end of time:

"Mayest thou burn in this house! Mayest thou ever burn in this house! Mayest thou blaze in this house! Mayest thou increase in this house, even for a long time, until the powerful restoration of the world, until the time of the good, powerful restoration of the world!"

And elsewhere in the same book (c. V, 12) this further prayer that Atar, the Son of God, present in the fire upon the hearthstone, will bless and save:

"Give me, oh Atar, Son of God (Ahura Mazda), however unworthy I am, now and forever, a seat in the bright, all-happy, blissful abode of the holy ones. May I obtain the good reward, a good name and abiding serenity for my soul!"

In worshiping Atar, the Son of God, in his manifestation in the form of fire, it was regarded essential that the means of kindling or of feeding the flames be not dishonest, that is, be not procured by theft or by extortion. Of this it is said:

"Whoever wisheth to propitiate Atar in the world is he who wisheth to promote his things; and it is necessary for him, so that Atar may be with him at every place and time, that he should propitiate the Fire of God (Ahura Mazda) in whatever has happened and whatever occurreth, and should act for its happiness; he should not put upon it wood, incense and holywater which are stolen and extorted, and he should not cook at it a ration which is violently extorted from men. Oft it is a counterpart of Atar, himself, in the world, the Fire of God (Ahura Mazda)" (Shayast-La-Shayast, c. XV, 12).

The following are some of the blessings for which the devout Parsi prays unto the sacred flames, invoking the Son of God:

"Give me, oh Atar, Son of God (Ahura Mazda), lively welfare, lively maintenance, lively living; fullness of welfare, fullness of maintenance, fullness of life;

"Knowledge, sagacity, quickness of tongue, (holiness of) soul; a good memory; and then the understanding that goes on growing and the one that is not acquired through learning;

"And then the manly courage;

"Firm-footed, unsleeping save for a third part of the day and of the night, quick to rise up from bed, ever awake;

"And a protecting, virtuous offspring, able to rule countries and assemblies of men, well-growing-up, good, freeing us from torment, endowed with a good intellect, that may increase my house, my borough, my town, my country, my empire" (Atas Nyasis, c. V, 10, 11)!

There are other demigods, such as Mithra—sometimes called Mihir—to whom the carrying out of specific commands is at times exercised.

CHAPTER V

AHRIMAN AND THE EVIL SPIRITS

"I WILL speak of the two spirits of the beginning of the world, of whom the holier thus spake of the enemy: 'Our thoughts, our teaching, our wills, our beliefs, our words, our deeds, our consciences, our very souls do not agree.' "

Thus the Gathas (Yasna XLV, 2) emphasize the contrast between beneficence and maleficence, in the respective persons of God (Ahura Mazda) and of Ahriman, the devil.

The Zend Avesta gives this circumstantial account of the part of the devil in the creation, viz. as the one responsible for all noxious and harmful things, for to him the Persians ascribed the origin of all such:

"Thereupon came Ahriman, who is all death, and he counter-created the serpent in the river and winter, a work of the demons. . . .

"There are ten winter months there, two summer months; and those are cold for the waters, cold for the earth, cold for the trees. Winter falls there, the worst of all plagues. . . .

"Thereupon came Ahriman who is all death, and he counter-created the locust, which brings death unto cattle and plants. . . .

"Thereupon came Ahriman who is all death, and he counter-created plunder and sin. . . .

"Thereupon came Ahriman who is all death, and he counter-created the ants and the anthills. . . .

"Thereupon came Ahriman who is all death, and he counter-created the sin of unbelief. . . .

"Thereupon came Ahriman who is all death, and he counter-created tears and wailing. . . .

"Thereupon came Ahriman, who is all death, and he counter-created the sin of pride. . . .

"Thereupon came Ahriman, who is all death, and he counter-created a sin for which there is no atonement, the unnatural sin. . . .

"Thereupon came Ahriman, who is all death, and he counter-created a sin for which there is no atonement, the burying of the dead. . . .

"Thereupon came Ahriman, who is all death, and he counter-created a sin for which there is no atonement, the cooking of corpses. . . .

"Thereupon came Ahriman, who is all death, and he counter-created winter, a work of the demons" (Vendidad, Fargard I).

The Bundahis (c. VIII, 1) gives Ahriman credit, also, for earthquakes and mountains, tracing the latter, as do modern scientists, to the former, i.e. to eruptions through the earth's crust, and saying of this:

"As the Evil Spirit rushed in, the earth shook and the masses of the mountains were made upon the earth."

The same book (c. I, 9) asserts, however, that "the Evil Spirit, on account of backward intelligence, was not aware of the existence of God (Ahura Mazda)."

The idea that evil is delusion and itself unreal is Zoroastrian, however, and is often found in these scriptures; the Epistles of Manuskihar (c. II, 2) set forth in the following the manner in which Ahriman, the father of lies, deceives the elect:

"Responsible for the malice and annoyance of unjust kinds which are encountering us, is the fiend of great strength, who is unobserving, seductive, astute in evil, eager for causing annihilation and full of deceit, so that it is possible for him to render doubtful, when himself so deceived, even him who is most a listener to essential righteousness, most desirous of steadfast truth, most performing proper religious customs, most acquainted with good ideas, most amazingly careful of his soul, most approved in the most wounding, hell-brought conflict, and most at home in truth of all kinds, and to show him a semblance of reality in unreality, and of unreality in reality."

One of the Yasts puts it thus in a warning to the wise:

"Let no thought of Ahriman ever infect thee, that thou shouldst indulge in evil lusts, be scornful, be an idolator and shut (to the poor) the door of thy house" (Vistasp Yast, c. V, 37).

The followers of Zoroaster have neither images nor ikons of God (Ahura Mazda) or of any other of the Amesha Spentas, all of whom, as has been said, they conceive of as intangible spirits; idolatry is, therefore, unknown among them and is strictly prohibited.

The Gathas (Yasna XXXII, 11) say of enmity of the unbelieving marauders toward the Good Mind:

"It is they, the liars, who destroy life, who are mightily determined to deprive mistress and master of the enjoyment of their heritage in that they restrain the saints, oh God (Ahura Mazda), from the Good Mind."

And that to overcome this, with God's help, is the

part and duty of man, they assert in another place (Yasna XLVIII, 2):

"Tell me, for thou art he that knows, oh God (Ahura Mazda), shall the righteous smite the liar ere the retributions come which thou hast conceived? That were indeed a message to bless the world."

As Ahriman made counter-creations to those of God, so the Zoroastrian scriptures present a complete counter-seven to the Sacred Seven, as follows:

Amesha Spentas	*Daëvas*
Ahura Mazda—God The Eternal Light	Ahriman—Devil, Prince of Darkness
Asha—Right	Druj—False Appearance
Vohu Manah—The Good Mind	Akem—Evil
Khshathra—Dominion	Dush-Khshathra—Pusilla-nimity
Aramaïti—Piety	Taromaïti—False Pretense
Haürvetat—Well-Being	Avetat—Misery
Ameretat—Immortality	Merethyn—Annihilation

It is interesting that the Sanskrit word which perhaps is the root from which Zeus, Deus, and other Occidental words, signifying the divine, are derived, should in Persian become Daëva or demon; but this must be due to the identification by Zoroaster of this expression with the idols of India and of other peoples, and with beings of whom maleficent things are recorded.

It is noteworthy, also, that it is not the mere images which are thus condemned, but the very things themselves, falsely personifying, as something godly, the views of conduct which are less than human.

Thus, as will be seen elsewhere in this book, the evil mind is fully identified in the Zoroastrian scriptures with the spirit of them who would destroy instead of create, would despoil others instead of labor, would work maleficence instead of beneficence toward God's creatures.

The Bundahis (c. XXVIII, 43) asserts that other evil spirits are produced indefinitely in the following way:

"Various new demons spring from the various new sins and are produced on account of them."

Elsewhere in the same book (c. XIV, 6) duties are assigned to these, as follows:

"The punishment of a sinful soul floweth from that demon with whom the sin, which it hath committed, is associated; the punishment evoked by the sin itself cometh upon the sinful and wicked man, first in this life, then in hell and last at the installation of the future existence."

The Gathas thus ascribe all the Daëvas, or demons, as to their origin, to the Evil Mind, that is to Ahriman:

"But ye, ye Daëvas all, and he that highly honors you, are of the Evil Mind, yea of the lie and arrogance; likewise your deeds, whereby are ye known to the seventh region of the earth" (Yasna XXXII, 3).

In another Yasna (XLIV, 13) the same thing is said, negatively but even more strikingly, in this passage:

"This I ask thee, tell me truly, oh God (Ahura Mazda), How shall we drive away the lie from us unto those who, being full of disobedience, will not strive after fellowship with Right, nor trouble themselves with the counsels of the Good Mind?"

And in yet another passage of the Gathas Zoroaster describes himself as a man who "desires to win through the Right, men that are neglected" (Yasna XLIX, 1), meaning thereby them who have taken the devil's view of what is desirable.

The wrong which those who are deluded by the demons would do mankind is depicted in these words elsewhere in the Gathas:

"Thereby ye defrauded mankind of Well-Being and Immortality by the deed which he and the evil spirit, with evil mind and evil word, taught you, ye Daëvas and the liars, for the purpose of destroying mankind" (Yasna XXXII, 5).

Followers of Zoroaster connected these demons and their progeny with all the destructive and noxious things which men encounter and particularly with the evil lusts which lead them astray and inspire them to evil.

Thus the Bundahis (c. XXVIII, 37) devotes a little space to the following description of their activities:

"With every one of them are many demons and friends coöperating, to specify whom a second time would be tedious; demons, too, who are furies, are in great multitude, it is said. They are demons of ruin, pain, and growing old; producers of vexation and bile; revivers of grief, the progeny of gloom; and bringers of stench, decay and vileness; who are many, very numerous, and very notorious; and a portion of all of them is mingled in the bodies of men, and their characteristics are glaring in mankind."

Here is a passage from the Vendidad, giving a formula for exorcism of the Druj,[1] by which is meant not merely the devil's chief adjutant, but also the whole brood of the evil seven and their progeny:

"Keep us from our hater, oh God (Ahura Mazda), and Aramaïti Spenta! Perish, oh fiendish Druj!

[1] An evil spirit.

Perish, oh brood of the fiend! Perish, oh creation of the fiend! Perish, oh world of the fiend! Perish away, oh Druj! Rush away, oh Druj! Perish away, oh Druj! Perish away to the regions of the north, nevermore to give unto death the living world of righteousness" (Fargard VIII, c. III, 21)!

The "regions of the north," from which the terrible "northers" came, rendering the plain desolate and chilling the plainsmen to the marrow, destructive to the sprouting grain, the budding tree, the young calf, the weak and old in every household, was deemed by Zoroaster's followers the infernal region.

The Bundahis (c. XXVIII, 39) repeats this saying concerning Ahriman elsewhere in the Zoroastrian scriptures, contrasted with a saying concerning God:

"Of the evil spirit are the law of violence, the religion of sorcery, the weapons of fiendishness and the perversion of God's (Ahura Mazda's) creations; and his desire is this, 'Inquire not concerning me, and do not understand me; for if ye ask about me and understand me, ye will not thereafter follow me.' "

CHAPTER VI

CREATION OF THE WORLD AND
PRIMITIVE AGES

"THE first of God's (Ahura Mazda's) creations in the world was the firmament and Good Mind, by a benign process, produced light for the world, which was joined unto the good religion of the followers of God; this was because the renovation that is to come unto all creatures, was known unto him. Then followed Right, Dominion, Piety, Well-Being and Immortality."

Thus speaks the Bundahis (c. I, 25, 26) concerning the order of spiritual creation; and follows it with this account of the order of creation upon the earth (28):

"Of the creations of God (Ahura Mazda) in the world, the first was the sky; the second, water; the third, soil; the fourth, plants; the fifth, animals; the sixth, mankind." [1]

There were therefore six periods in both the celestial, and the mundane, creation.

The Vendidad (Fargard I, 3) records of the order of creation, that:

"The first of the good lands and countries which I, God (Ahura Mazda), created, was the Aïryana Vaëgo [2] beside the Vanguhi Daïtya. . . ."

---

[1] The closeness to the creation as set forth in Genesis is remarkable.

[2] Aïryana Vaëgo is regarded the ancient seat of the Iranians where Zoroaster lived and founded his religion. It is supposed to have been near Balkh, a ruined city, lying near the northern border of what is now the Afghan Turkestan near the Oxus river. The Vanguhi Daïtya has been variously identified as the Oxus, the Arras or the Tigris river.

Into this earthly paradise, God introduced mankind in the persons of Mashya and Mashyoi, brother and sister, concerning whom the Bundahis gives the most circumstantial account:

"God (Ahura Mazda) spake to Mashya and Mashyoi, saying, 'You are man, you are the ancestry of the world, and you are created perfect in devotion by me. Perform devotedly the duty of the law, think good thoughts, speak good words, do good deeds, and worship no demons.'

"Both of them first thought this, that each of them should please the other, as each was a mate for the other and the first deed done by them was this, when they went out, they cleansed themselves thoroughly; and the first words spoken by them were these, that God (Ahura Mazda) created the water and the earth, the plants and the animals, the stars, moon and sun, and all prosperity, the source and nature of which are from the manifestation of righteousness.

"And, afterwards, antagonism rushed into their minds, and their minds were thoroughly corrupted, and they exclaimed that the Evil Spirit created the water and the earth, the plants and the animals and the other things named above. That false speech was spoken through the will of the demons, and the Evil Spirit possessed himself of his first enjoyment from them. Through that false speech they became wicked and their souls are in hell until the future existence.

"And they had gone thirty days without food, covered with clothing of herbage; and after thirty days they went forth unto the wilderness, came to a white-haired goat and milked the milk from the udder with their mouths. . . .

"Afterwards, in another thirty days and nights, they

came to a sheep, fat and white-jawed, and they slaughtered it; and fire was extracted by them out of the wood of the lote-plum and box-tree, through the guidance of the heavenly angels, since both woods were most productive of fire for them; and the fire was fanned by (the breath of) their mouths. The first fuel kindled by them was dry grass, kendar, lotos, date palm leaves, and myrtle; and they made a roast of the sheep.

"And, first, a clothing of skins covered them; afterwards, it is said, woven garments were prepared from a cloth woven in the wilderness. And they dug out a pit in the earth, and iron was obtained by them and beaten out with a stone, and without a forge they beat out a cutting edge from it; and they cut wood with it, and prepared a wooden shelter from the sun. . . .

"Mashya went forth and milked a cow's milk, and poured it out toward the northern quarter.[3] Through that the demons became more powerful; and, owing to them, they both became so dry-backed that in fifty winters they had no desire for intercourse, and, had they had intercourse, they would have had no children.

"And on the completion of fifty years the source of desire arose, first in Mashya and then in Mashyoi, for Mashya spake to Mashyoi thus, 'When I see thy nakedness my desires arise.' Then Mashyoi spake thus, 'Brother Mashya, when I see thy great desire I am also agitated.'

Afterwards, it became their mutual desire that the satisfaction of their desires should be accomplished, as

[3] To these plainsmen, the source of all ills was the North, whence the Evil One issues with his demons, bringing the winter and blighting the life upon the earth.

they reflected thus, 'Our duty even for those fifty years was this.' . . .

"And from them arose seven pairs, male and female, and each was a brother-husband and sister-wife; and from every one of them, in fifty years, children were born, and they themselves died in a hundred years" (c. XV, 6, 7-10, 15-16, 19-21, 24).

According to another chapter of the Bundahis (XXXIV, 3):

"After thirty years Mashya and Mashyoi grew up; for fifty years they were not husband and wife; and they ninety-three together as husband and wife before Hashyang was born," making our first parents to be no less than one hundred and seventy-three years old when they were blest with offspring.

The somewhat later Zoroastrian scriptures chronicle something akin to the great flood, recorded in the Bible, except that the flood was to come from melting snows instead of rain and that the human race and other beings were preserved by means of an enclosure instead of in an ark floating upon the waters. The account is given in the Zend Avesta, thus:

"And God spake unto Yima, saying:

" 'Oh fair Yima, son of Vivanghat, upon the material world the evil winters are about to fall, that shall bring the fierce, deadly frost; upon this material world the evil winters are about to fall, that shall make snow-flakes fall thick, even an aredvi deep on the highest tops of mountains.

" 'And the beasts that live in the wilderness, and those that live on the tops of the mountains, and those that live in the bosom of the dale shall take shelter in underground abodes.

" 'Before that winter, the country would bear plenty

of grass for cattle, before the waters had flooded it. Now after the melting of the snow, oh Yima, a place wherein the footprint of a sheep may be seen, will be a wonder in the world.

" 'Therefore make thee a Vara, long as a riding-ground on every side of the square, and thither bring the seeds of sheep and oxen, of men, of dogs, of birds, and of red, blazing fires.

" 'Therefore make thee a Vara, long as a riding-ground on every side of the square, to be an abode for men; a Vara, long as a riding-ground on every side of the square, for oxen and sheep.

" 'There thou shalt make waters flow in a bed a hathra long; where thou shalt settle birds, on the green that never fadeth, with food that never faileth. There thou shalt establish dwelling-places, consisting of a house with a balcony, a courtyard, and a gallery.

" 'Thither thou shalt bring the seeds of men and women, of the greatest, best, and finest on this earth; thither thou shalt bring the seeds of every kind of cattle, of the greatest, best, and finest on this earth.

" 'Thither thou shalt bring the seeds of every kind of tree, of the highest of size and sweetest of fragrance on this earth; thither thou shalt bring the seeds of every kind of fruit, the best of savor and sweetest of fragrance. All those seeds shalt thou bring, two of every kind, to be kept inexhaustible there, so long as those men shall stay in the Vara.

" 'There shall be no humpbacked, none bulged forward there; no impotent, no lunatic, no one malicious, no liar; no one spiteful, none jealous; no one with decayed teeth, no leprous to be pent up, nor any of the brands wherewith Ahriman stampeth the bodies of mortals.

" 'In the biggest space in the place thou shalt make nine streets, six in the middle space, three in the smallest space. To the streets of the biggest space thou shalt bring a thousand seeds of men and women; to the streets of the middle space, six hundred; to the streets of the smallest space, three hundred. That Vara shalt thou seal up with thy golden seal and thou shalt make a door and a window, self-shining within.'

"Then Yima said within himself, 'How shall I manage to build that Vara which God (Ahura Mazda) hath commanded me to build?'

"And God spake unto Yima, saying, 'Oh fair Yima, son of Vivanghat, crush thou the earth with a stamp of thy heel and then knead it with thy hands as doth the potter when kneading the potter's clay.'

"And Yima did as God desired of him; he crushed the earth with a stamp of his heel, he kneaded it with his hands as doth the potter when kneading the potter's clay.

"And Yima made a Vara, long as a riding-ground on every side of the square. There he brought the seeds of sheep and oxen, of men, of dogs, of birds, and of red, blazing fires. He made a Vara long as a riding-ground on every side of the square, to be an abode for men; a Vara long as a riding-ground on every side of the square, for oxen and sheep.

"There he made the waters to flow in a bed a hathra long; there he settled birds on the green that never fadeth, with food that never faileth. There established he dwelling-places, consisting each of a house, with a balcony, a courtyard and a gallery.

"There he brought the seeds of men and women, of the greatest, best and finest on this earth; there he brought the seeds of every kind of cattle, of the greatest, best and finest of this earth.

"There he brought the seeds of every kind of tree, of the tallest and sweetest of fragrance of this earth; there he brought the seeds of every kind of fruit, the best of savor and sweetest of fragrance. All those seeds he brought, two of every kind, to be kept inexhaustible there, so long as those men shall stay in the Vara.

"And there were no humpbacked, none bulged forward there; no impotent, no madman; no malevolent, no liar; no spiteful, no jealous; none with decayed teeth, none leprous to be pent up, nor any of the brands wherewith Ahriman stampeth the bodies of mortals.

"In the largest space of the place he made nine streets, six in the middle space, and three in the smallest. To the streets of the largest space he brought a thousand seeds of men and women; to the streets of the middle space six hundred; to the streets of the smallest space, three hundred. That Vara he sealed up with a golden ring and he made a door and a window self-shining within" (Vendidad, Fargard II, 22-38).

It seems, however, that the happy creatures who were thus saved in Yima's Vara never escaped but have survived there, in their progeny at least, if not in their proper persons, unto this day; for it is also recorded, "And the men in the Vara which Yima made, live the happiest life" (Idem. 41). And there is no account of their emerging.

CHAPTER VII

A RELIGIOUS PLACE FOR SINGING GATHAS

" 'Oh thou Maker of the material world, thou Holy One, which is the first place where the Earth feels most happy?' God (Ahura Mazda) made answer and said, 'It is the place, oh Spitama Zoroaster, whereon one of the faithful steps forward, with the wood, the baresma (i.e. the sacred twigs), the milk and the mortar in his hand, lifting up his voice in delightful harmony with religion and calling upon Mithra,[1] lord of the rolling countryside, and Rama Hyastra [2]."

Thus the Vendidad (Fargard III, c. 1) calls that, first and foremost, holy ground upon which religious ceremonies and observances are performed.

Such services, among the ancient Parsis, were chiefly prayer and songs of praise and thanksgiving; and the Srosh Yast Hadhokt (c. I, v. 2) says of prayer:

"Good prayer, excelling prayer to the worlds, oh Zoroaster. This it is that taketh away the friendship with the male and female fiends. This it is that turneth from giddiness men's eyes, minds, ears, hands, feet, mouths and tongues; for good prayer, free from deceit and desire to injure, constituteth the courage of a man and turneth away the Druj."

In the Nasks, this declaration of the quickening power of these devotions is found (Tahmura's Fragments c. XIX, 28):

[1] The god of the sun.
[2] An acolyte of Mithra, who gives food its flavor.

"Now that which we consider the best of all things, oh God (Ahura Mazda), is prayer and sacrifice offered unto thee."

The Nasks give many directions concerning chanting the Gathas, which became one of the most important things in the religious and moral life of a follower of Zoroaster.

Thus in the Nirangistan Fragments (Fargard I, Part II, I, 25) the warning runs:

"If he think the Gathas to himself or listen to another singing them or get another of those of the faith to sing them, he is not accepted, for he hath not himself sung them."

In the same connection (I, 22) it is noted:

"The assistant is accepted who singeth the Gathas and followeth to himself the Yasna and the Fehushomathra. The man is guilty who followeth not these texts, even as the Gathas; but he who singeth the Gathas and followeth the Yasna to himself, is accepted for all the Gathas."

According to another passage of the Nasks (Erpatistan, Fargard I, Part II, 14, 15) few excuses avail for failing to sing the Gathas:

"If he whose ears hear not, or who hath no voice, repeat not a word,

"He is not guilty for not repeating.

"If he can repeat, were it only one word, for not repeating it he is guilty.

"If he repeat not because he suffers from a wound;

"Or for any physical pain . . .

"Or by reason of drought, or cold, or thirst . . .

"Or by reason of the hard fare of travel,

"If he repeat not, he is not guilty.

"If he repeat not by reason of weariness, sadness, or slumber, he is guilty."

In yet another place (Tahmura's Fragments, c. XII, 11) it is said, as if to prevent other excuses being offered:

"Even uncovered and nude, he will chant."

But another Nask mentions one occasion (while performing the office of nature) when to sing would be profanation (Nirangistan Fragments, Fargard I, Part II, IV, 37).

The following question and answer, given in the same connection (IV, 31) is reminiscent of a saying of Jesus to his disciples upon parting:

" 'Which is the smallest assembly of which the singing is accepted?' 'Three.' "

In the same Nask (Fargard II, I, 44) the following condemnation is apportioned unto those of the faith who are negligent in performing the duty of chanting these songs of praise:

"If a man go half a year without singing the Gathas and also prevent another of the faith from singing the Gathas, for the half year that he did not sing the Gathas, he shall be in a state of sin and for the half, whether before or after, that he hath prevented their being sung, he shall be a Peshotanu."

And in the same connection (XI, 42) it is also written:

"He that goeth a year through without singing the Gathas becometh a Peshotanu."

Referring to the entire service, including sacrifice, the Mihir Yast (c. XXXII, 137) records this saying of God unto Zoroaster:

"Happy is that man, in my sight, oh holy Zoroaster, for whom a holy priest, as pious as any in the world, who is the incarnate word, offereth up a sacrifice unto Mithra, with bundles of baresma and with the appropriate words."

Among the Parsis from the earliest times, a woman could, if necessary, perform the priestly office; the Shayast-La-Shayast (c. X, 35) limits this, however, as follows:

"A woman is fit for priestly duty among women."

The Nasks (Erpatistan Fragments, Fargard I, Part I, 1) name the one paramount qualification of a priest, asking and answering:

" 'Who is he in the house who shall officiate as priest?' 'He that longeth most after holiness.' "

The praise of holiness is itself so important a part of all Parsi religious observances that the following account, recorded in the Yast (Fragment XXI, 1-5, inc.) is given here:

"Zoroaster inquired of God (Ahura Mazda) saying, 'Oh Lord God, Most Beneficent Spirit, Maker of the material world, thou Holy One, what is the only word in which is contained the glorification of all good things, of all the things that are the offspring of the good principle?'

"God made answer and said, 'It is the praise of holiness, oh Spitama Zoroaster! He who reciteth the praise of holiness, in the fullness of faith and with a devoted heart, praiseth me, the Lord God; he praiseth the waters, he praiseth the earth, he praiseth the cattle, he praiseth the plants, he praiseth all good things created by God, all the things that are the offspring of the good principle. For the reciting of that word of truth, oh Zoroaster, the pronouncing of that formula increaseth strength and victory in one's soul and piety. For that only recital of the praise of holiness is worth a hundred Khshnaōthras of the beings of holiness, when delivered while going to sleep, a thousand when delivered after eating, ten thousand when delivered during cohabitation, or any number delivered in departing this life.' "

It is to be observed that, unlike another situation, deemed vulgar by modern peoples, cohabitation is not one during which this religious formula is actually proscribed. This was because to Zoroaster and his followers cohabitation, save when sinful for reasons set forth in these pages, was not vulgar or in any sense a matter for shame, but was, instead, as ever among those who see clearly, itself a holy thing, to be withdrawn from public gaze, not because shameful but because sacred.

The one way, viz. by abandoning his wickedness, in which man can best and most effectively recite the praise of holiness is given in the same connection (Yast Fragment, XXI, 16, 17) by the following question and answer:

" 'What is the one recital of the praise of holiness that is worth all that is between the earth and the heavens, and this earth and that luminous space, and all the good things made by God (Ahura Mazda) that are the offspring of the good principle in greatness, goodness and fairness?'

"God made answer and said, 'It is that one, oh Holy Zoroaster, that a man delivereth, to renounce evil thoughts, evil words and evil deeds.' "

In the Zoroastrian scriptures there are many sayings, showing the futility, or worse, of wicked persons attempting to secure the favors of God by participating in the ceremonies or the sacrifice; among these, this from the Nasks:

"And he that offereth me the libations of a thief, of a robber or of a ravisher . . . or the libations of a liar, that man afflicteth me with the same burning that afflicteth a man who is possessed of Ahriman" (Tah-mura's Fragments, c. XXII, 36, 37).

In the Aban Yast (c. XXI, 92, 93) a much wider range of such prohibitions is found, thus:

"Of this libation let not an enemy partake nor a man with fever nor a liar, a coward, a jealous man, a woman, one of the faith who chanteth not the Gathas nor a leper who should be confined. I like not libations that are offered unto me by the blind, the deaf, the wicked, destroyers, niggards . . . nor any that are of a character not to stand up for the Holy Word. Let not any man partake of my libations that is hump-backed or sway-backed nor a wretch with decayed teeth."

This Yast gives evidence of having been wrought out by some priest in a vain attempt to glorify God by decrying the frailties and misfortunes of man. The exclusions were probably pretty well confined to those named in the earlier Nask, perhaps with these, also, who were inhibited by the Tir Yast (c. XVI, 59, 60) to take part in offerings to Tistrya:

"Let not a murderer take part in these offerings nor a prostitute nor an Ashaövo³ who chanteth not the Gathas, who spreadeth death throughout the world and withstandeth the law of God (Ahura Mazda), the statutes of Zoroaster."

There were certain hours, according to the Nasks, during the course of which the Gathas are to be chanted, as follows:

"At what hour doth the celebration of the Ushahina Gathas begin?

"It continueth from midnight to sunrise; thus, in winter time.

³ Infidel.

"In summer time, if one sing the Ahunavaïti Gatha before sunrise,

"As well as the Yasna Haptanghaïti and the Ustavaïti Ha,

"He may, without guilt, not sing the rest of the Gathas till the middle of the forenoon.

"At what hour doth the celebration of the Havani Gathas begin?

"It continueth from sunrise to the middle of the forenoon;

"Thus in summer time;

"In winter time till the middle of the afternoon.

"From what hour may the sacrifice to the Good Waters be offered?

"It continueth from sunrise to sunset;

"Thus both in summer time and in winter time" (Nirangistan Fragments, Fargard II, II, 46, 47).

This order, involving many hardships for lovers of ease, seems in accord with the following passage in the Vendidad (Fargard IV, c. IIIa, 45):

"So shall he sit up, in devotion and prayers, that he may be increased in intelligence; he shall rest during the middle part of the day, during the middle part of the night; and thus shall he continue until he can say all the words which former Aöthrapaïtis[4] have said."

The following from the Shayast-La-Shayast (c. IX, 9, 10) gives an interesting but very fanciful account of how various combinations of correct or incorrect ceremonies, with a good or a bad man conducting the same, are received:

"In a passage of the fifth Fargard of the Pazon Nask[5] it is declared that one mentions these characteristics

[4] Teaching priests.
[5] One of the Nasks which are lost.

of four kinds of worship of the celestial beings: one is that whose Avesta is correct, but the man is bad; the second is that whose Avesta is faulty, but the man is good; the third is that whose Avesta is correct, and the man is good; and the fourth is that whose Avesta is faulty and the man is bad. That whose Avesta is correct, but the man bad, the archangels will approach and will listen to, but do not accept; that whose Avesta is faulty, but the man good, the archangels and angels will approach, but do not listen to, and will accept; that whose Avesta is correct, and the man good, the archangels and angels will approach, will come to, will listen to, and will accept; that whose Avesta is faulty, and the man bad, they do not approach, do not listen to, and do not accept."

The Dinkard says of this:

"If at any place holy men find it very injurious and hurtful (to speak the truth), still it (the truth) must be spoken. And, if at any place, holy men should find untruth very convenient and beneficial, still it must never at any time be spoken" (I, 27).

The Sad Dar speaks of this as follows:

"When man becomes fifteen years of age it is necessary that he should take one of the angels as his own protection, one of the wise as his own sage, and one of the high priests . . . as his own high priest" (289).

The Vendidad (Fargard VIII, c. III, 20) joins fire, as the symbol of God, and the Good Mind as the protectors of the good, inquiring:

"Whom hast thou given unto me, as a protector, while the hatred of wicked men encompasseth me? Whom, forsooth, but Fire and the Good Mind, through whose good work I keep in the world of righteousness. Reveal, therefore, unto me, as thy rule, thy religion!"

And the Gathas not merely speak of the elect being thus "eager in bringing you songs of praise" but also hail their God and his Godhead:

"With these bounties, oh God (Ahura Mazda), may we never provoke your wrath, oh God, Right and the Good Mind, we who have been eager in bringing you songs of praise. Ye are they that are mightiest to advance desires and the Dominion of blessings" (Yasna XXVIII, 9).

CHAPTER VIII

THE SPELL OF VIRTUE

"HE is not mighty, oh Zoroaster, who is not mighty in righteousness; nor is he strong who is not strong in righteousness."

Thus speak the Nasks (Tahmura's Fragments, 103, 104) of the superior power of the good man; and in another place (Idem, 90);

"To obtain the treasures of the material world, oh Spitama Zoroaster, forego not the world of the spirit."

In these words, another of the Nasks (Westergard's Fragments, Vispa Humata, III, 1) laments man's weakness:

"All good thoughts, all good words, all good deeds— these do I willingly; all evil thoughts, all evil words, all evil deeds—these do I unwillingly."

Thus the sacred scriptures of the ancient Persians contrast the strength of virtue and the weakness of man when facing the temptations of life.

Elsewhere the Vendidad (Fargard XVIII, c. II, 17) puts into the mouth of the fiend of procrastination this soothing plea to the lovers of ease:

"Sleep on, poor fellow; the hour hath not yet struck. Fix not thy mind upon the three excellent merits, good thoughts, good words, good deeds! Rest rather thy mind now upon the three abominations, evil thoughts, evil words, evil deeds!"

Yet the Gathas (Yasna XLVIII, 4) urge that the prize and guerdon of the virtuous man are that he may be weak or strong, saying of such a man, that:

68

"Whoso, oh Lord (Ahura Mazda), makes his thoughts, now better and now worse, and likewise himself by action and word, and follows his own inclinations, wishes and choices, he shall in thy purposes be in a separate place at the last."

That is to say, his desires will lead him aright and astray, as his "inclinations, wishes and choices" may be pointed.

The Vendidad (Fargard X, 19) teaches that mastery as to this may be achieved by every man and enjoins it upon all, thus:

"Make thine own self pure, oh righteous man; every man in the world below can win purity for himself, by cleansing his heart with good thoughts, good words and good deeds."

And again (Fargard V, 21):

"With these words the Holy One, the Lord God (Ahura Mazda) cheered the holy Zoroaster, 'Purity is for man, next to life, the greatest good, that purity, oh Zoroaster, which is in the religion of God, for him who cleanseth his own soul with good thoughts, good words and good deeds!'"

Which purity, according to the Dadistan-i-Dinik (c. XCIV, 11) amounts to this:

"And this, too, was thus considered by them, that the man is most fortunate in whom are soundness of body, well-being and energy, who hath done such things that the last wish on departing this world is, 'These things will I strive yet more to do' and who shall have refrained from such things that the last wish when departing this world must be, 'These things I will strive to avoid; for had I done so, it would have been well with my soul.'"

In the same chapter it is urged that, when con-

fronted with the allurements of ease and of delight,
one must be mindful of his spiritual nature and of the
spiritual realities; the passage runs:

"It was also considered by them that every man
should bear in mind the things of the spirit at all times,
and the joys of heaven and the miseries of hell at the
very moment when comfort, happiness and pleasure
come to him" (Dadistan-i-Dinik, c. XCIV, 9).

That it is by counseling with others concerning what
is right and thereby being strong, that one attains the
impartial state which enables him to choose aright, the
Shayast-La-Shayast (c. X, 28) says in these words:

"The rule is, that an opinion upon whatever subject is to be formed by counseling with the good."

And also remarks, sagely, that:

"A knife of the keenest steel requires the whetstone
and the wisest man needs advice."

The Shayast-La-Shayast (c. XX, 8) enlarges upon
this idea, saying:

"This, too, that the walks of men are to be directed
chiefly to these three places, to the abode of the well-
informed, to the abode of the good, to the abode of the
Fire. To the abode of the well-informed that one may
become wiser and that religion may find lodgment
within him; to the abode of the good that, between
good and evil, he may eschew the evil and carry with
him the good; and to the abode of the Fire that the
Evil One may turn from him."

In the fragment of the Aögemaïde Nask (56) it is
shown that to be strong one must be wise, thus:

"Ignorance it is which ruineth most, ruineth them
that know not aright, both them that have perished
and them that are yet to perish!"

That which it is wisdom to learn and to know, another fragment of the Nasks (Tahmura's Fragments, c. XXV, 46) declares thus:

"Such an one, oh Spitama Zoroaster, shall arrive there as the strongest of the strong who here below most powerfully impelleth the righteous unto good works, think perfect thoughts, speak perfect words and do perfect deeds."

And in the Ormazd Yast (Introduction) strength is thus defined:

"I give praise unto well-thought, well-spoken, well-done thoughts, words and deeds; I embrace all good thoughts, good words and good deeds."

This is condensed also into the Persian grace, ever upon the Parsi's lips:

"Holiness is the best of all good."

By this is not meant self-righteousness; for that this is really weakness, the Nasks (Tahmura's Fragments, c. XXXVII and XXXVIII, 78-84) discerningly declare:

"He that in this world of the flesh, oh Spitama Zoroaster, deemeth overweening well of his own merit, all the time that he doeth it, his soul becometh weighed down with sin; but, if he deemeth justly of his own merit, or if he rate it lower than it is, then I, the creator, God (Ahura Mazda) will make his soul know joy and Paradise, eternal brightness, bliss beyond his desert and eternal happiness, while the wicked man is in torment."

The Dinkard rightly says of this:

"A man improves himself by humility when he rises in rank by his wealth and good deeds" (VII, 447).

The sort of knowledge one is duty bound to seek in order that he may be strong, is set forth in Shayast-La-Shayast (c. X, 27) as follows:

"The rule is that one is to proceed with great deliberation when he knoweth not if it be a sin or a good deed; in such cases, it is not to be done."

And again in this passage (c. X, 25):

"The rule is that when an action or an opinion is brought forward, and one knoweth not if it be a sin or a good deed, then, if it be possible, it is to be abandoned and is not to be done."

Also prudence and foresight should be the study of him who would be strong, of which the Aögemaïde Nask (53) says:

"Each day the living man ought to think that in the morning he is happy and of good repute; in the afternoon shame may come upon him."

And that to be anxious is cowardice and weakens the man, the Shayast-La-Shayast (c. XX, 12) enjoins, thus:

"This, too, that, as respects the world, anxiety is not to be suffered; the thing is not to be considered as anything whatever."

The very acme of that true wisdom which fortifies man, the Dadistan-i-Dinik (c. III, 19) is found in resignation and acceptance of one's lot, saying:

"A righteous man is the creature by whom is accepted that occupation which is provided for him, and is warily watchful in the world lest he be deluded by the Evil One."

The Dinkard says this of idleness:

"Idleness should be swept out of the world" (XII, 47).

All the machinations of Ahriman and all the allurements of sin Zoroaster esteemed to be pure delusion, mere negation of power. Thus in the Nasks (Aögemaïde, 31-36) it is declared:

"But without any reason men adhere to that evil guide, passion, creature of the demons, with the result that they think not of fate; and by the bent of their nature, they forget that they will die. They keep not in mind the passing of time and the temporal nature of the body; they ever wander about on the path of desire; they are tossed in doubt by evil passion; for the sake of that which perisheth away, they array themselves with hatred in the way of strife, one with another; in their youth they are intoxicated with pride; and in their age they will be full of remorse."

The Dadistan-i-Dinik (c. XCIV, 7) expatiates upon what constitutes the state of sin, as follows:

"And this too was their opinion that, when one shall do even that which he knoweth to be a sin, that is disobedience, and disobedience is of the nature of the adversary; when one shall omit to do that which he knoweth he ought to have done, that is greed and greed is the cunning of the adversary; and when one shall do that which he knoweth not to be that which he ought to do or to be that which he ought not to do, that is self-esteem if it be before it is fully revealed to his understanding, and self-esteem is the religion of the adversary."

That one repents, therefore, and seeks to throw off the shackles of his evil mind, is hailed by the Shayast-La-Shayast (c. IX, 6) as evidence of liberation from thraldom, thus:

"The good work of a man who hath relinquished a bad habit and through his good capabilities engageth in renunciation of sin, advanceth unto the future existence."

And the Dadistan-i-Dinik (c. XLI, 10) says of it:
"Renunciation should be during life; for it is said,

'Whoever when living, doth not become righteous, that is doth not atone unto the uttermost for his sin, for him when dead, there is no granting the best existence.' "

And in another place (c. XVI, 4) declares of the soul after death:

"That which is wicked, is then again desirous of its bodily existence, when it beholdeth these twain, the wonderfully constructed body which was its vesture and is now dispersed, and the soul that was the heart and life thereof; and is in distress on account of this, saying, 'Alas that in my bodily existence and course through the world there was no atonement for my sin and no accumulation of righteousness!' Also, in mourning over it, thus, 'In the days of my prosperity in the flesh, it would have been possible for me to atone for sin and thus to save my soul; but now am I separated from living men and from the joy of living, which is the great hope of the spirit's life to come; and I have fallen upon a perplexing account and a more serious danger.' "

The same book (c. XLI, 11) affirms, however:

"To commit no sin is better than retribution and renunciation of sin."

And the Nasks repeat (Tahmura's Fragments, c. XXVIII, 57):

"Of the mind, good thoughts; of the tongue, good words; of the hand, good works; these make the virtuous life."

And in another place (XLIII, 95) eloquently assert:

"One cannot for the wishing have the power of head of the household, of head of the borough, of head of the district, of head of the province; neither authority over brethren; nor a well set-up frame, and lofty stature; but one thing there is, oh Spitama Zoroaster, that every man in this world below may prize; he may prize virtue."

That virtue is indeed its own reward seems to be the burden of this text:

"The man who possesseth understanding, has promised to cling to the actions of the Good Mind and to the holy Piety, creator and comrade of the Right" (Yasna XXXIV, 10).

Self-mastery, as the very essence of this reward, is set forth in this saying of the Gathas (Yasna L, 9):

"With these prayers I would come and praise thee, oh God (Ahura Mazda), and thee, Right, with actions of the Good Mind. If I be master of my own destiny as I will; then will I take thought for the portion of the wise in the same."

The same idea of the close kinship of the rhythm of lofty verse with the rhythm of a benevolent and beneficent soul is also in this:

"With verses that are recognized as those of pious zeal, I will come before you with outstretched hands, oh God (Ahura Mazda), before you, oh Right, with the worship of the faithful man, before you with all the capacity of the Good Mind" (Yasna L, 8).

This possession of the soul in serene calmness of spirit involved eschewing the service of evil; and of this the poet and prophet speaks as follows:

"So this shall come to him through the Right, oh Lord (Ahura Mazda), which reward by this Dominion and Good Mind he promised, wheresoever by the power of his fate the neighboring possession prospers that now the liar holds" (Yasna XLIX. 3).

The great reward for this is that one possesses it; for he in very truth, possesses God.

And the great prayer is therefore for more abundant illumination through observation of the unvarying operation of the laws of nature, a prayer which in the Gathas runs thus:

"I beseech you twain, oh God (Ahura Mazda), and the Right, to speak what is after the thought of your will, that we may rightly discern how we may teach the religion that comes from thee, oh God (Ahura Mazda) (Yasna XLIX, 6).

It is the urgent need of this sense of the presence of God within the man which called forth the cry:

"May I obtain . . . abiding serenity for my soul" (Atas Nyasis, c. V, 12)!

Nothing but virtue can avail to secure this salvation. As the Shayast-La-Shayast puts it (c. XXII, 2):

"May the Good Mind grant thee wisdom, may the benefit of knowing the Good Mind be good thought, and mayest thou follow virtuous conduct to the salvation of the soul!"

And of the man who has lived the virtuous life and has encouraged others to do likewise, the Nasks declare:

"Such an one, oh Spitama Zoroaster, shall there arrive as the strongest of the strong, who here below most powerfully impelleth the righteous unto good works, to think perfect thoughts, speak perfect words and do perfect deeds" (Tahmura's Fragments, 45).

The Aögemaïde Nask (51) identifies man's virtue as his one permanent possession, thus:

"There cometh a day, oh Spitama Zoroaster, or a night, when the master quitteth his cattle, or the cattle quit their master, or the soul quitteth that body, full of lusts; but his virtue, which is of all that is his, the greatest, the best, the finest, never parteth from a man."

And in the pristine Gathas the question is asked, without doubting the answer:

"This I ask thee, tell me truly, oh God (Ahura Mazda), the religion which is the best for all that are, which in union with the Right should prosper all that is mine, will they duly observe it, the religion of my creed, with the words and action of Piety, in desire for thy future good things, oh Lord" (Yasna XLIV, 10)?

CHAPTER IX

WISDOM AND TRUST

"MAKE thy petition unto me, thou just man, unto me who am the Creator, the most beneficent of all beings, he who knoweth best, he who taketh most delight in answering the petitions that ascend to him. Make thy petition unto me, that thou mayst be a better man, that thou mayst be a happier man!"

Thus in the Vendidad (Fargard XVIII, c. I, 13) man is encouraged to lift his voice unto God for wisdom to make him better and happier.

In the Vistasp Yast (c. VI, 41) is found this discerning statement and command:

"Men with lustful deeds address the body; but all the night long do thou address celestial wisdom and call upon wisdom to keep thee wakeful."

The Dinkard says, "From trust in God (Ahura Mazda) arises a heroic heart" (XII, 69).

That man's ability to perceive what is right is from God and of God, in very truth an emanation of his own intelligence, the Gathas assert, in saying:

"When thou, oh God (Ahura Mazda), in the beginning did create beings and us by thy thought and intelligence, when thou didst make life clothed with body, when (thou didst make) actions and teachings whereby one may exercise choice at one's free will" (Yasna, XXXI, 11).

The Dadistan-i-Dinik echoes this thus (c. VII, 7):

"It is said in revelation that God (Ahura Mazda)

78

spake unto Zoroaster saying, 'Thou art to coöperate with the Good Mind, with thy pure, spiritual faculties, to the end that they may welcome him wholly, for when thou dost coöperate with the Good Mind, with thy pure spiritual faculties, thou shalt fully comprehend the two paths, that which is to do good and that which is to do evil!"

The Gathas (Yasna XLIII, 14) present God as actually, of his grace, instructing his devoted servant, thus:

"If thy provident aid, such as an understanding man with power would give his friend, comes to me through thy Dominion, through the Right, then to set myself against the foes of thy law, with all who are mindful of thy words."

The Shayast-La-Shayast (c. XXII, 3) echoes this by addressing this supplication:

"May Ardi-Vahista,[1] the glorious, grant thee understanding and insight!"

Another of the Gathas (Yasna XLVI, 19) puts it thus:

"These things wilt thou bring to pass for me, who best knowest how, oh God" (Ahura Mazda).

Both the supreme rôle of God in the opening of the human mind and that it is the divine Good Mind, his benevolent spirit, which operates, are set forth in this tribute to God, taken from the Gathas:

"Let your ears attend to those who in their deeds and utterances hold to your words, Lord (Ahura Mazda), and Right, to those of the Good Mind which are the first enlightener" (Yasna LI, 3).

This is not meant, however, to shift the responsibility from man to God, for man's remaining in ignorance; instead the command is:

[1] One of the angels.

"Take thou therefore counsel with thine own understanding" (Yasna LIII, 3).

The Dinkard says (VII, 441):

"God has given to all men sufficient ability to save themselves from sin as well as from Ahriman, the source of their sins and woes."

The Dinkard says of this as follows:

"Be it known that the man who is far-sighted . . . hopes to be saved from damnation by being in the good graces of the Almighty on account of his perfect veracity, his proper sense of justice, his fidelity to plighted word" (VII, 427).

The full consequence of failure to use one's faculties to acquire knowledge and to make use of it, are deplored in the Aögemaïde Yast (56) in these words:

"Ignorance it is which ruineth most, ruineth them that know not aright, both them that have perished and them that are yet to perish."

One of the Nasks gives what is doubtless a latter-day rendering of the doctrine that God somehow imparts wisdom, by affirming that this he does by means of man's study of his revealed word, in this passage:

"There be many words of wisdom that the soul may not conceive nor the tongue declare, without the Holy Word" (Tahmura's Fragments of the Nasks, XLV, 101, 102).

Zoroaster was not less insistent than was Socrates that reason, i.e. wisdom as the result of reasoning, is man's guide, which supplies infallible rules of conduct, if informed by a good purpose.

That man is a reasoning being is the foundation of morality, the very thing which makes him responsible.

Power brings accountability; that one may choose renders it incumbent upon him to choose rightly. In order so to choose, he must reason; in order to reason clearly and to use reason to produce right conduct, he must cultivate right intentions. Such is the doctrine; such also the clear truth of the matter.

Appreciation, as well as apperception, of God's law as revealed in nature constitutes this wisdom, according to the Zoroastrian scriptures; for in the Aögemaïde Nask (30) God (Ahura Mazda) is reported as saying:

"But, better and greater than all, I created the rightous man who hath truly received from me the praise of the Right in the good religion."

The same Nask (21) relates:

"There is a passage in which God (Ahura Mazda) spake unto Zoroaster, saying 'I created, oh Spitama Zoroaster, good report and salvation for the soul.' "

The Dinkard speaks of this:

"He in whose soul virtue dwells is well disposed toward others and desires, or is pleased with the happiness of others; thereby he becomes capable of preventing mutual injuries among men and of promoting the union of virtue among them" (V, 276).

The very foundation of the divine wisdom is considered by Zoroaster to be:

"Holiness is the best of all good."

This saying, ever upon the devout Parsi's lips, originated, says the Vendidad (Fargard XIX, c. III, 17, 18) with God himself, who gave directions for his worship, thus:

"Zoroaster inquired of God (Ahura Mazda) saying, 'Oh thou Maker of the good world, God, with what manner of sacrifice shall I worship, with what manner of sacrifice shall I make the people to worship, this creation of God?'

"God made answer and said, 'Go, oh Spitama Zoroaster, toward the high-growing trees, and before one of them that is beautiful, high-growing, and mighty, say thou these words, "Hail unto thee, oh good, holy tree, made by God! Holiness is the best of all good!" ' "

It is the more remarkable here since upon these plains such templed groves were infrequent; but perhaps this made them the more eligible as places of worship, though, as will be seen, the home, however humble, was and is the prime seat of devotion for this people.

The memorization and frequent recitation of the twenty sacred names of God constitute another way of coming into rapport with his wisdom, according to the witness of the Ormazd Yast (10-11); the passage runs thus:

"If thou desirest, oh Zoroaster, to destroy the malice of Daëvas and men, of the Yatus and Païrikas, of the oppressors, of the blind and of the deaf, of the two-legged ruffians, of the two-legged Ashemaöghas, of the four-legged wolves, and of the hordes with the wide front, with the many spears, with the straight spears, with the spears uplifted, bearing the spear of havoc, then recite thou these, my names, every day and every night."

The Zamyad Yast (c. II, 9-12) expresses in this formula for sacrificial ceremonies, the human heart-hunger for a life of active goodness unto the redemption of mankind:

"We sacrifice unto the awful, kingly glory, created by God (Ahura Mazda), most conquering, highly, working, that embraceth health, wisdom and happiness and is more powerful to destroy than all other creatures; that belongeth to God as (through it) God hath made the creatures, many and good, many and fair, many and wonderful, many and prosperous, many and bright.

"To the end that they may restore the world, which will (thenceforth) never grow old nor die, never decay and never perish, ever survive and ever increase and be master of its wish and, when the dead shall rise and when life and immortality shall come, the world will be restored at its wish.

"For then all creation will become immortal, the blest creation of the Good Spirit!"

That God is ever present with man upon the earth in the closest relationship, one of the Nasks (Tahmura's Fragments, c. XXCIII, 58) thus affirms:

"I, God (Ahura Mazda), am closer, oh Zoroaster, to that which all the world of the flesh thinketh, speaketh and worketh, than the nose is to the ears, or than the ears are to the mouth."

This doctrine of the presence, so precious to devotees of other religions, was implicit in all Zoroastrian conceptions of God.

Indeed, the very purpose of worship is given in the sacred writings of the Persians to be to draw near unto God, as is announced in this invocation from the Gathas:

"If ye are truly thus, oh God (Ahura Mazda), Right and the Good Mind, then give me this token, even a total reversal of this life, that I may come before ye again more joyfully with worship and praise" (Yasna XXIV, 7).

That God discerns clearly what has been, what is and what shall be and that he wills it, is the burden of this statement, also from the Gathas (Yasna XXIX, 4), as well as that it is the duty of man to learn his will in this way and to acquiesce with serene resignation:

"God (Ahura Mazda) knoweth best the purposes that have been wrought, already by demons and by mortals and that will be wrought hereafter. He, our God (Ahura Mazda), is the decider. So shall it be as he shall will."

The purpose in seeking to be near unto God is thus revealed, viz. to the end that man may see in the operation of God's laws in nature, that which is right and, thus discerning it, may do it.

That God himself is in, and of, the Right and in, and of, the Good Mind, "the same yesterday, to-day and forever," is declared in this passage from the Gathas:

"He that in the beginning, thought thus, 'Let the blessed realms be filled with lights'—he it is that by wisdom created the Right. Those realms that the Good Mind shall possess, God (Ahura Mazda) will prosper by thy spirit which, oh Lord, is ever the same" (Yasna XXI, 7).

In other words, through natural phenomena, one may trace the beneficence of God at work and know that which it becomes a man to do.

The Zoroastrian version is found in these words of the Gathas:

"Not to be deceived is the all-seeing God (Ahura Mazda)" (Yasna XLV, 4).

That is, he who desires only his own pleasure and is neglectful of his duty as his own eyes see it, deceives, not God, but his own, foolish self.

The Gathas represent the Almighty as the just God, visiting upon mankind the consequences of their deeds, whether good or evil; as for instance, in this:

"Even God (Ahura Mazda) who through his Dominion, appoints what is better than good for him that attendeth to his will but what is worse than evil

for him that obeyeth not, at the final end of life"
(Yasna LI, 6).

The Menuk-i-Khrat repeats this (19):

"And alms were given by thee to him who came
forth from near and him, too, who was from afar."

The Ahuna Vairya [2] echoes this, in speaking of the
selection of an earthly ruler, thus:

"Even as he (Zoroaster) is the Lord for us to choose,
so is he the judge, according to the Right, he that
bringeth the life-works of the Good Mind unto God
(Ahura Mazda), and Dominion unto the Lord, even
he whom they made shepherd of the poor."

The Shayast-La-Shayast, in the following remarkable passage (c. XV, 7, 8) also expresses the view that
man is made in the image of God, in this fashion:

"Whoever wisheth to propitiate the righteous man in
the world, wisheth to promote the things of God
(Ahura Mazda); and whoever he be, with whom God
abideth in every place, it is necessary that he should
propitiate the righteous man, in whatever hath happened and whatever happeneth to him, and should act
for his happiness, and afford him protection from the
wicked; for the righteous man is a counterpart of the
Lord God."

Here again is repeated the requirement that he who
would serve God, must serve good men, however poor
they be and therefore unable to return his generosity.

But the loftiest tribute unto God is that his own
All-Power is ever used for such ends; as is asserted in
this from the Gathas (Yasna LIII, 9):

"Thine, oh God (Ahura Mazda), is the Dominion
whereby thou canst give to the right-living poor man
the better portion."

[2] The most sacred invocation of the Parsis.

CHAPTER X

THE LIAR IS THE DIREST ENEMY

THE Persian religion is famous for its proscription
of the liar. It is the fact that, in the writings that are
clearly the earliest, the person that speaks falsely is
found the most despicable and is first condemned;
while it is only in later literature that most other forms
of sin are singled out and quite as roundly put under
ban.

It is this fact which has impressed the stranger and
which has been noted in the earliest sayings concerning Zoroaster; the fact that the liar is condemned, is
everywhere patent, and ever because he is the foe of
truth.

And all the passages in which the sin of reliance on
the false is plied with condemnation as being the opposite of the right, are found in the passages of the
Gathas, which are deemed much the earliest of the literature, mainly spoken by the mouth of Zoroaster
himself; as, for instance:

"When these two spirits came together at the beginning, then they set up Life and Not-Life; and at last
the worst shall be for them that follow the lie but the
best for them that pursue the Right. Of these two, he
that followed the lie chose to do the worst; the sanctified pursued the Right, he that clothed him with the
massy heavens as a robe" (Yasna XXX, 4 and 5).

Right, it should be premised, means first and foremost the truth; it may mean more, but always that at
least.

This religion seems to rest more upon these early writings than upon other and later scriptures; and, from its first appearance, to the men of other nations, it set forth the absolute fact that verity might be assumed when the Persian, of all men, spoke.

This has supplied to this day the reason why the Persian was, and the Parsi is in this day, so remarkably truthful and why that should be so big a feature in his religion.

That such is Zoroaster's meaning is clear from this passage:

"Mindful of your commands, we proclaim words, hard for them to hear who, on the command of the lie, aim to destroy the creatures of the Right but most welcome to them who give their hearts to God (Ahura Mazda)" (Yasna XXXI, 1).

And, in this passage, it is the person who, with knowledge of the truth, or, in any event, without knowledge of the falsity of what he says, plainly it may be spoken, is a liar:

"Then lifts up his voice the true speaker or the false, he that knows or he that knows not, in accord with his own heart and thought" (Yasna XXI, 12).

And again in the seventeenth verse, he speaks of it:

"Which is greater, the belief of the righteous or the belief of the liar? Let him that knows, tell to him that knows; let not him that knows not, deceive us longer."

And the fate of the perverter of the clear, undimmed truth in the affairs of men is thus set forth, in a later Gatha:

"For he is himself a liar who is good to a liar and he is a righteous man to whom the righteous man is dear; since thou, oh God (Ahura Mazda), has created men's souls from the beginning" (Yasna XLVI, 6).

And in another of the Gathas this question is finally set and remains unanswered:

"This I ask thee; tell me truly, oh God (Ahura Mazda), which of those with whom I would speak is a righteous man, and which is a liar" (Yasna XLIV, 12)?

It is thus seen that in the determination of this sort of evil man had his difficulties.

And yet the answer is unquestioned when the truth is clear, for then the upstart can be degraded and be opposed with full power; as Zoroaster elsewhere says, for himself:

"To the first inquiry, Zoroaster am I, a true foe to the liar, to the utmost of my power, but a powerful support would I yield to the righteous that I may compass the future things of the infinite Dominion, according, oh Lord (Ahura Mazda), as I praise thee and herald thee" (Yasna XLIII, 8).

Then it is the duty of every lover of the truth to be, as was Zoroaster, the foe of him who utters a lie; the duty commences when the light falls on the falsity and it appears. For clarity is sure to come and the falsehood is sure to be seen; then the true character of the lie shall appear. Therefore is it warned with zeal:

"Let none of ye attend the liar's words and demands. He leads house, clan, district and country into misery and destruction. Resist them, then, with weapons" (Yasna XXXI, 18).

And the liar may be recognized as having shunned the man who has particular friendship for the truth; for thus he comes to be the shower-up of the falsities about him. As the Gatha says:

"From this spirit have the liars fallen away, oh God (Ahura Mazda), but never the righteous; whether one be lord over little or of much, he is to show love toward the righteous but be ill toward the liar" (Yasna XLVII, 4).

Yet the lesson how to behave toward truth and toward falsehood is laid firmly down in the Gathas in these words:

"According as it is with laws that govern this life, so shall the judge deal most justly toward the man of the lie and toward the man of the Right, toward him in whom the false and the true balance.

"Whoso worketh ill for the liar, in word or thought or hands, or converts his dependents to the good— such men meet with the will of God (Ahura Mazda), to his satisfaction.

"Whoso is most good to the righteous man, be he a noble or a member of the community or of the brotherhood, oh God (Ahura Mazda), or with diligence cares for cattle, he shall forevermore be in the pasture of the Right and of the Good Mind" (Yasna XXXIII, 1-3).

The lie seemed a narrow basis for the opponent of God in the world and gradually there were other purposes added to that insistent wickedness of the foe which caused him to assume, both before and after, more the lineaments of Satan; as in this:

"And in this faith of ours, oh God (Ahura Mazda), the Right is laid down for blessings, to ruin us the heresy of the lie. Therefore I strive for the fellowship of the Good Mind and I forbid all intercourse with the liar" (Yasna XLIX, 3).

Indeed, in the burden of the liar and in the punishment set aside for him, it was necessary to apportion to him all the misconduct that the enemy of God would cherish; for his condemnation and punishment by men, blessings are given, as when:

"If mortals shall mark these commandments that

God (Ahura Mazda) hath ordained, of happiness and pain, blessings for the righteous and long punishment for the liars, then hereafter shall ye have bliss" (Yasna XXX, 11).

Again in the Gathas does this same condemnation of the false appear, as, for instance, here:

"What recompense thou wilt give to the two parties by thy red Fire, by the molten metal[1] give us a sign of it in our souls—even the bringing of ruin to the liar, and of blessedness to the righteous" (Yasna LI, 9).

And gladly will the prophet hear that such a sentence is passed upon him that leads men to listen to his falsehoods:

"Of those two things will I speak, oh Lord (Ahura Mazda)—for one may say a word to the wise—the ill that is threatened to the liar, and the happiness that clings to the Right. For he, the prophet, is glad for him who says this to the wise" (Yasna LI, 8).

And this sentence is theirs whose creed at its foundation is that evil for the right-living poor man exceeds their wealthy portion:

"To men of evil creed belongs the place of corruption. They that set themselves to condemn the worthy, despising the righteousness, forfeiting their own body —where is the righteous Lord who shall rob them of life and freedom? This, oh God (Ahura Mazda), is the Dominion, whereby thou canst give to the right-living poor man the better portion" (Yasna LIII, 9).

In this manner, then, they proceed to destroy for themselves the spiritual life:

"So it is in fact, ye men and women! Whatever happiness you look for in union with the lie shall be

---

[1] The molten metal is one of the tests laid down for the righteous to disprove attacks upon them.

taken away from your person. To them, the liars, shall be ill food, crying woe—happiness shall flee from them that despise righteousness. In such wise do ye destroy for yourselves the spiritual life" (Yasna LIII, 6).

And God, who has promised the best things to his humble follower, is asked whether the lover of the lie is to partake of them all, even without willing them, as follows:

"And all the best things which by this holy spirit thou hast promised to the righteous, oh Lord (Ahura Mazda), shall the liar partake of them without thy will, who by his actions is on the side of ill thought" (Yasna XLVII, 5)?

And he who refuses the help of him who would speak the word of God, the Good Mind and Right, is lost already:

"But whoso when thus approached should refuse his aid, he shall go to the abodes of the company of the lie. For he is himself a liar who is very good to a liar, he is a righteous man to whom a righteous man is dear" (Yasna XLVI, 6).

Yet, so much was in the dark concerning him whose chief evil was to tell a falsehood, that Zoroaster himself stood unaware of and accordingly himself calls for the utterance of God to tell him, saying:

"These things I ask of thee, oh God (Ahura Mazda), how it came about and how it will issue forth, that is the requitals that, in accord with the records, are appointed for the righteous and those, oh Lord, that are for the liars—how these shall be when they come to the reckoning" (Yasna XXXI, 14).

And Zoroaster, as his prophet, faces God impressively with this question, whether he has any duty in this difficult matter, saying:

"This I ask of thee; tell me truly, oh God (Ahura Mazda), whether I am to put the lie in the hands of Right, to be put down by the words of thy saying, to work a mighty destruction for the liars, to bring torments and enmities upon them, oh God (Yasna XLIV, 14).

Yet he faces God, again, in this matter; for in another Gatha he demands of him, this time with less question of his duty:

"Tell me, for thou art he who knoweth, oh Lord (Ahura Mazda), shall the righteous smite the liar ere the reprisals which thou hast conceived? That were, indeed, a message to bless the world" (Yasna XLVIII, 2).

And this language of the text is in line with this in the same Gatha, for it says:

"Who are they that will make peace with the bloodthirsty liars" (11)?

And there is much more than falsity in the liar, in fact, whose misdeeds are sufficient to make him, before the introduction of a Satan, the opposite of God, for in this passage he is held up for punishment:

"For ye have brought it to pass that men who do the worst things shall be called the beloved of the Daëvas, but excluded from the Good Mind, departing from the will of the Lord (Ahura Mazda), and from the Right. Thereby ye defrauded mankind of a happy life and immortality by the deed which he and the Bad Spirit, together with the Bad Mind and the Bad Word, taught you, ye Daëvas and liars, for the purpose of ruining mankind" (Yasna XXXII, 4 and 5).

But God, according to a further Gatha, himself called upon fire, upon his close resemblance on the earth, to clean the premises which had been occupied and degraded by the liars; for he speaks of it thus:

"Of thy Fire,[2] oh God (Ahura Mazda), that has the power of the Right, promised and mighty, we desire that it may be for the faithful man with manifested joy but for the foe with visible torment according to the pointings of the hand" (Yasna XXXIV, 4).

And the holiness of God is recognized in this action of the fire, by these words of his people:

"May he attain to that which is better than good, which teaches the straight paths to blessedness in this life here, of body and of thought, the true paths that lead to the world where God (Ahura Mazda) dwells, a faithful man, well-knowing and sacred like thee, oh God. Then shall I recognize thee as powerful and holy, Lord, when, by the hand in which thou thyself dost hold the destinies which thou wilt assign to the liar and to the righteous, by the glow of thy Fire who works with the Right, the might of the Good Mind shall come to me" (Yasna XLIII, 3 and 4).

[2] A test is here proposed, that by fire.

CHAPTER XI

EVIL IS DELUSION

"THEY, who by their evil purpose, make an increase of violence and cruelty with their tongues, the foes of cattle-nurture among its friends; whose ill deeds prevail, not their good deeds; these (shall be) in the house of the Daëvas (the place for) the very self of the liar."

Thus the Gathas (Yasna XLIX, 4) identify the maleficent, destroying spirit with the false faith, with the worship of evil spirits by the cruel, devastating enemies of peaceful, industrious herdsmen.

This evil deplores the prophet elsewhere, saying of it:

"The teacher of evil destroys the lore; he by his teachings destroys the design of life; he prevents the possession of the Good Mind from being prized. These words of my spirit I wail unto you, oh God (Ahura Mazda) and to the Right" (Yasna XXXII, 9).

In another place (Yasna XXX, 6) the same self-delusion is asserted of the evil spirits, themselves, thus:

"Between these the demons also chose not aright, for infatuation came upon them as they took counsel together, so that they chose the worst mind."

And in the same connection (Yasna XXX, 3) the prayer is uttered that this very thing may be true:

"Now the two primal spirits who revealed themselves in a vision as a twain, are the better and the worse in thought and word and action; and between these two may the wise ones choose aright, the foolish did not do it."

And again in yet another passage (Yasna XXIV, 8):

"Far from them that do not ponder the Right, is the Good Mind."

The prophet finds it far from reassuring that this be so; and in these words portrays the fate that awaits him who thus offends the divine Good Mind and Right:

"Thus the self of the liar destroys for himself the assurance of the right way; whose soul shall tremble at the revelation on the Sifting Bridge,[1] having turned aside with deeds and tongue from the path of the Right" (Yasna LI, 13).

For such a sin as this was Yima, the elder, involved by giving of the flesh of the ox to eat:

"In such sins as these, we know, Yima was involved, Vivahvant's son, who, desiring to satisfy men, gave our people flesh of the ox to eat. From these shall I be separated by thee, oh God (Ahura Mazda), at last" (Yasna XXXII, 8).

In illustration of this principle, the Bundahis (c. XVIII, 40) relates the following:

"Of the Evil Spirit are the law of foulness, the religion of sorcery, the weapons of fiendishness and the perversion of the works of God (Ahura Mazda); and his wish in this, 'Do not inquire about me nor understand me; for if ye inquire about me and understand me, ye will not follow me!' "

In another place (Mainyo-i-Khard, c. XL, 24-28) this idea is developed further as follows:

"The one thing that the Lord God (Ahura Mazda)

---

[1] The Sifting Bridge, to tell the righteous from the sinful, as shown hereafter.

desireth of them that follow him, is this, 'Ye shall understand what I am; for every one that understandeth me, followeth me and seeketh to please me'; and the one thing that Ahriman desireth of them that follow him, is this: 'Ye shall not understand me, what I am; for those whoso understandeth that I am evil, his deeds follow not after me and unto me neither advantage nor love cometh from that man.' "

One of the Yasts (XXII, c. XI, 42) describes thus vividly the method by which evil overcomes mankind:

"Here the fiendish Bushyast,ᵃ the longhanded, rusheth from the region of the north, speaking thus, lying thus, 'Sleep on, oh man! Sleep on, oh sinners! Sleep on, and live in sin!' "

The nature of evil, i.e. as a trap for slothful, inattentive men, is thus portrayed in the Gathas!

"But these that are of evil dominion, that is, of evil deeds, evil words, evil self and evil thought, liars, the souls go to meet them with foul food; in the house of the lie they shall be meet inhabitants" (Yasna XLIX, 11).

The heavy responsibility for deceiving another by bringing him under the delusion that wrong is right, and the punishment therefor, the Gathas (Yasna XXXI, 20) thus proclaim:

"Whoso cometh to the righteous, far from him shall be the future, long age, of darkness, of misery and crying of woe; such a life, ye liars, bring ye upon yourselves by your actions."

And that, however much it be illusion, evil is greatly augmented for the evil man into whose hands great power comes, is affirmed, thus:

"Whoso, oh God (Ahura Mazda) makes his thought

ᵃ A demon.

now better, now worse, and likewise himself by action and by word, and follows his own inclinations, wishes and choices, he shall in thy purpose be in a separate place at the last" (Yasna XLVIII, 4).

The fate that awaits these is also expressed, together with confidence that innocence protects, in a petition, to be found elsewhere in the Gathas (Yasna XLVI, 8):

"Whoso is minded to injure my possessions, from his actions may no harm come to me. Back upon himself may they come with hostility, unto his own flesh, all the hostile acts, to keep him far from the good life, oh God (Ahura Mazda), not from the evil."

The Vendidad (Fargard, VII, c. IX, 49) thus pointedly characterizes the consequences, as regards contagion and disease, of failure to enlarge one's knowledge of things:

"For people of small understanding who seek not for better understanding, the imps make these diseases stronger by a third."

Save in this negative sense, it is the Zoroastrian doctrine that evil and, therefore, of course the devil, has no real existence; of which it is said in Dadistan-i-Dinik (c. XIX, 2):

"Concerning Ahriman it is related that he hath no real existence."

The sense that this is true, is, doubtless, set forth in this passage from the Gathas (Yasna XXXII, 4):

"For ye have brought to pass that men who do the worst things shall be called beloved of the Daëvas, but excluded from the Good Mind, departing from the will of God (Ahura Mazda) and from the Right."

The Bundahis (c. I, 3) repeats this idea, with eloquence, thus:

"God (Ahura Mazda) and the place, the religion

and the time of God were and are and shall be, world without end; while Ahriman, in darkness, with backward understanding and desire to destroy, existed only in the abyss and it is he who shall not be."

And in the inspired Gathas God has answered, for with him the Good Mind and the Right are ever:

"To them God (Ahura Mazda) who is united with Good Mind, and in goodly fellowship with glorious Right, through Dominion, made reply: 'We make choice of your holy, good Piety; it shall be ours'" (Yasna XXXII, 2).

And, with this tribute to the Right, and this commendation of the Good Mind, is the prophet content to say:

"I will speak of him that is greatest of all, praising him, oh Right, who is bounteous to all that live. By the holy spirit let the Lord (Ahura Mazda) hearken, in whose adoration I have been instructed by the Good Mind. By his wisdom let him teach me what is best" (Yasna XLV, 6).

CHAPTER XII

TO DO GOOD AGAINST TO DO ILL

"EVER since the first being was created by us, I who am God (Ahura Mazda) have not rested at my ease, because of providing protection for them whom I created; and in like manner he (Ahriman) also hath not rested, because of contriving evil for them whom I created."

Thus the Bundahis (c. XXVIII, 3) represents the Almighty to have spoken to the effect that wickedness is doing ill to his creatures, is wronging them or injuring them; and that at this task the ingenuity of the Evil Spirit and of all evil spirits was taxed continually while God is constant in his protecting care of all beneficial creatures.

Of all the religions of the world, the Zoroastrian is peculiar in that its origin, its *raison d'être,* is not obscure.

It came into existence on the steppes, the great, elevated prairies, of western Asia and southeastern Europe.

It was founded by a leader who was himself primarily a husbandman and herdsman.

Its fundamental posit was that God (Ahura Mazda) is good, that he wishes the cultivation of land, that he desires the domestication and care of useful animals, that he favors the peaceful settlements of men; and, contrariwise, that evil is enmity unto God, that it would live by exploiting and despoiling others, that it rejoices in wanton slaying of dumb cattle and that its delight is to lay waste the settlements of the plains in an orgy of carnage, rapine and destruction.

From these conditions, not unlike those which are heralded to exist in the same, unlettered regions in this day, the untutored mind of the founder of this religion spelled out the right and wrong of these things and gave to the spirits which make for civilization and progress the name of God (Ahura Mazda) and to the spirits which would prosper by despoiling others, the name Ahriman, the devil.

The purpose to conserve all good and useful things and beings he pronounced blessed and divine, and the purpose to enjoy at others' cost and by the wasteful destruction of useful things and beings he pronounced fiendish.

Thus the Bundahis, in another passage (c. XXVIII, 39) affirms:

"Of the Evil Spirit are the law of vileness, the religion of sorcery, the weapons of fiendishness and the perversion of the creatures of God" (Ahura Mazda).

Zoroaster's own psalms, the Gathas, into which the very heart and soul of his teachings have been gathered, say of what took place among the evil spirits that:

"Between these two, the demons also chose not the Right, for infatuation came upon them as they took counsel together, so that they chose the worst mind. Then they rushed together to violence, that they might enfeeble the world of man" (Yasna XXX, 6).

The consequence of this evil choice on their part is said to be that they cannot rightly distinguish between right and wrong—that is, are affected with that singu-

lar purblindness regarding virtue which afflicts those in
all times who set their hearts upon building themselves
up by trampling upon others, whether it be with the
sword in hand or by compelling trade, instead of win-
ning it by the best service at the lowest cost.

This phase of it is referred to in another of the
Gathas (Yasna XXXI, 1) in marked contrast to the
recognition of the verities of the universe by them
whose purpose is to do good, in these words:

"Mindful of your commands, we proclaim words
hard for them to hear that, on the command of the lie,
destroy the creatures of the Right, but most welcome
to those that give their hearts to God (Ahura Mazda)."

Certain venal border tribes which were ever ready
to coöperate with marauding bandits were thus characterized by another of the Gathas (XLVI, 11):

"By their dominion the Karpans and the Kavis accustomed mankind to evil actions, so as to destroy
life."

Promise of God's favor and of leadership among
his fellows was given in these ancient psalms to the
man who should put the foe of the toiler to flight, in
these words:

"The liar stays the supporters of the Right from
prospering the cattle in district and province—in-
famous as he is, repellant by his actions! Whoso, oh
Lord (Ahura Mazda), robs him of dominion or of life,
he shall go forward and prepare the ways of the good
belief" (Yasna XLVI, 4).

Therefore was it within the power of God, himself,
to put forth his power to protect even the poor man as
Zoroaster says in this Gatha:

"Have ye Dominion and power, oh God (Ahura
Mazda), Right and Good Mind, to do as I urge upon

you, even to protect the poor man? We have renounced all robber gangs, both demons and men" (Yasna XXXIV, 5).

And questions yet more emphatically that it will bring us to more happiness in these words:

"Assured by you, oh God (Ahura Mazda), and Right, are the pointings of the hand—since you are well disposed to your prophet—which shall bring us to happiness, together with visible, manifest help" (Yasna L, 5).

That the victory will be unto the wise and good, filled with desire to benefit man, and not unto them who burn with thirst to destroy man, another of the Yasnas (XLVIII, II) in this passage affirms:

"Who are they that will make peace with the bloodthirsty liars? To whom will the love of the Good Mind come?"

The next stanza (12) of this immortal strain answers the question triumphantly in these ringing words:

"These shall be the deliverers of the provinces, who follow, after pleasing, oh Good Mind, by their actions, oh Right, depending on thy commands, oh God (Ahura Mazda). For these are they who shall be appointed the smiters of violence."

Help for man in opposing this aggression successfully and decisively was not looked for from above, however, by Zoroaster, save as it is inspired by God (Ahura Mazda); instead, by developing the resistance of the common man to assault upon this liberty and his rights, it was hoped and expected that the haughty foe would be overcome and overthrown. Of this the Gathas (Yasna XLV, 9) speak thus:

"Him thou shouldst seek to propitiate for us together with a Good Mind that at will maketh us weal or woe. May the Lord God (Ahura Mazda) by his dominion, bring us to work, to prosper our herds and men, so that we may, through the Right, have familiarity with the Good Mind."

The question is asked in all sincerity what brother it shall be whose conduct shall bring the community honor:

"And this let the Good Mind hear, oh Lord (Ahura Mazda); let the Right hear; do thou thyself listen, oh Lord, what man of the brotherhood, what noble it is, according to the law, who brings to the community good fame" (Yasna XLIX, 7).

And the Gathas always speak of the peace, life and strength which accompany him that does right, as in this passage:

"She will give us a peaceful dwelling, she will give lasting life and strength, she the beloved of the Good Mind. For it the Lord (Ahura Mazda) made the plants to grow at the birth of the first life, through the Right" (Yasna XLVII, 6).

Yet Zoroaster asked of God that he be told of all things:

"Tell me therefore what ye, oh Right, have appointed me as the better portion, oh Good Mind, for me to determine, to know and to keep in thought, which portion they envy me; tell me of all these things, oh God (Ahura Mazda), that shall not be or shall be" (Yasna XXXI, 5).

And the same prophet, calm in his assurance of his purpose, promises to revere their names, going before them in reverence:

"He, I ween, that the Lord (Ahura Mazda) knoweth, among all that have been and are, as one to whom in accordance with the Right the best portion falls for his prayer, these will I reverence by their names and go before them with honor" (Yasna LI, 22).

And Zoroaster in confidence affirms that none of these sins will the man of understanding commit with the foolish expectation of reaping a reward, since God knowest above all their issue:

"None of these sins will the understanding commit, in eagerness to attain the blessing that shall be proclaimed, we know, through the glowing metal—sins, the issue of which, oh God (Ahura Mazda), thou knowest best" (Yasna XXXII, 7).

And he orders in the Gathas precisely these consequences of man's choice of God or of Ahriman:

"Now the two primal spirits who revealed themselves in vision as twins are the better and the worst in thought and word and action; and between these two the wise one chose aright, the foolish not so" (Yasna XXX, 3).

And the wisdom of God in this he celebrates, thus:

"I conceived thee, Lord (Ahura Mazda), in my thought that thou, the first, art also the last; that thou art the father of the Good Mind for thus I apprehended thee with mine eye; that thou didst truly create the Right; and that thou art the Lord who should judge the actions of life" (Yasna XXXI, 8).

The ultimate futility of the deeds of evil men, as indeed of all evil in the universe, is thus proclaimed in the Dadistan-i-Dinik (c. XCIV, 8):

"And this too was held by them, that Ahriman would do all he could to injure God (Ahura Mazda) but that, when he hath done it, it harmeth himself and profiteth God."

CHAPTER XIII

THE GOOD MIND AND THE RIGHT FURNISH THE FORMATION FOR ETHICS

"For God (Ahura Mazda) reigneth, according as the Good Mind waxeth" (Tahmura's Fragments, c. V, 1).

"Oh, thou, the Right, shall I see thee and the Good Mind as one who knows" (Yasna XXVIII, 5)?

Thus, the prophet calls upon the Right and the Good Mind to help him and the Nasks proclaim that the Good Mind is the very essence of all good conduct, of God's (Ahura Mazda's) reign throughout the universe.

And again Zoroaster is shown petitioning for the wealth which is his when his life is in accord with the Good Mind:

"Grant me this, oh Piety—the destined gifts of wealth, the life of the Good Mind" (Yasna XLIII, 1).

And as if remembering that the Right and the Good Mind ever belong together, he gives this beautiful invocation to the Almighty that never shall they be divorced:

"I who would invoke thy obedience as greatest of all at the consummation, attaining eternal life, and the Dominion of the Good Mind, and the straight ways unto the Right, wherein God (Ahura Mazda) dwells" (Yasna XXXIII, 5).

And that God be not deceived, is the burden of this prayer:

"I will speak of what is best for this life. Through

the Right doth the Lord (Ahura Mazda) know it, who created the same as father of the active Good Mind, and the daughter thereof is Piety of the good deed. Not to be deceived is the all-seeing God (Ahura Mazda)" (Yasna XLV, 4).

The nature of the Right is shown clearly by the name which has been given to the quality; as this account of Zoroaster's statement will imply:

"Then show me the Right, upon whom I may call" (Yasna XLIII, 10).

Then, as if to further the claims of the Right to state the conditions and limitations of human conduct, he asserts the fatherhood of God (Ahura Mazda):

"He, even the Lord (Ahura Mazda) is the father of the Right" (Yasna XLVII, 2).

And, as regards men, who are answerable for evil actions, he spells the nature of Right aright when he says:

"From them the Right shrinks back far, as from us shrink the wild beasts of prey" (Yasna XXXIV, 9).

There is much to be gained by the way that men stand when they have lived uprightly as the Gathas say in this passage:

"They that live uprightly according to the Right among the many that look upon the sun, these when they stand in the judgment I will settle in the dwellings of the wise" (Yasna L, 2).

And there is much to be feared for those who, through hatred of God's commandments, dread to acknowledge them and so will not ponder the right, as the Gathas say:

"For by these sections they put us in fear, in which peril is for many, in that the stronger puts fear in me, the weaker one through hatred of thy commandment, oh God (Ahura Mazda). Far from them that do not ponder the Right shall the Good Mind be" (Yasna XXXIV, 8).

But Zoroaster appears before God, asking that the gifts of the Good Mind be given unto him and his forever:

"The best I ask of thee, oh the best, my God (Ahura Mazda), of a will consonant with the best Right, desiring them for the hero Frashaoshtra, myself and for them to whom thou wilt give them, the gifts of the Good Mind forever" (Yasna XXVIII, 8).

And it is beautifully said in the Dinkard (Bk. VI, v., X, 11):

"The essence of sin is excess and deficiency; whereas the essence of virtue is the mean."

The same is the burden of this prayer in the Gathas (Yasna XXIX, 10):

"Grant, oh God (Ahura Mazda), thou and the Right, might and sway unto these and the Dominion, oh Good Mind, by means of which he can make the dwelling-place good and peaceful. I have realized, oh God, that thou wert first to see this."

The Vendidad also (Fargard XVIII, c. I, 13) acclaims God (Ahura Mazda), "The most beneficent of all beings"; and in the Ormazd Yast (8) God is represented as saying, "My thirteenth name is the Most Beneficent."

Reference was had to this feature of the Almighty when this question was asked in the Gathas:

"Who is it, a faithful man he, who first taught that we honor thee as mightiest to help, as the holy, righteous Lord (Ahura Mazda) over deeds" (Yasna XLVI, 9)?

In other words, the mind to serve the universe

beneficently is identified with the very essence of God, himself, with that because of which he is God. Thus he is hailed elsewhere in the Gathas (Yasna XLIV, 7) as:

"I strive to recognize through this thee, oh God (Ahura Mazda), Creator of all through the holy spirit."

The distinguishing feature of the Zoroastrian conception of the ethical life is that it rests upon Good Mind and the Right, which are defined as the mind and principle to care for and protect all beneficent beings, men or beasts, and the conception of justice, which the good man shares with God.

Zoroaster, in the Gathas, derives this idea from the care of herds upon the plains, primarily, and contrasts this with the raids of bandits who, avoiding the toil of husbandry, swept down from the hills upon the plainsman, his settlement and his herd, pillaging, ravishing and slaying wantonly.

Something more, however, is necessary unto the Good Mind, and the Right, the sacred writings show, than mere good purpose; there must be intelligence and will, as well as benevolence and verity, to constitute beneficence and righteousness; there must be "good thoughts, good words, good deeds."

But all rests upon the Good Mind which is fundamentally the wish to do deeds of beneficence, to bless all creatures by real service, in unison with the Right.

For this benefit, it is recorded that Zoroaster's sweetheart, Jamaspa Hvogva, was a petitioner, saying:

"This Dominion they choose who have part in the Good Mind. This grant me, oh God (Ahura Mazda), that they may find thee, oh Lord, their protection" (Yasna LI, 18).

That conformity of the human mind, in thought,

word and deed, with the Good Mind of God (Ahura Mazda) is precisely that which leads man on to the other Holy Spirits and their ineffable blessings, is what is meant by this passage from the Gathas (Yasna XLV, 5):

"They who at my will offer him obedience, attain unto the twain, Well-Being and Immortality, through the deeds of the Good Mind."

To this, also, reference is made elsewhere in the Gathas (Yasna XLVI, 2) thus:

"I cry out before thee; see thou to it, oh God (Ahura Mazda), grant me support such as friend bestoweth upon friend. Mayest thou instruct me through the Right how to win the Good Mind."

What this reward should be, that is, both spiritual and material welfare, here and hereafter, is announced elsewhere in the Gathas, thus:

"I who would serve thee, oh God (Ahura Mazda), and the Good Mind, grant thou me, through the Right, the rewards of both worlds, that of the body and that of the mind, which set the faithful in felicity" (Yasna XXVIII, 2).

In the Nasks (Tahmura's Fragments, c. XXVII, 54, 55) it is said that God (Ahura Mazda) replied to the inquiry, as to how holiness is manifested, that it is "by good thoughts in perfect unity with sound reason."

This, then, is the Good Mind, supported by the Right.

From it they who would destroy the living of a good life, would seek to pervert the righteous by arguments to the contrary, as the Gathas say:

"It is they, the liars, who destroy life, who are mightily determined to deprive matron and master of the enjoyment of their heritage, in that they would pervert the righteous, oh God (Ahura Mazda), from the Good Mind" (Yasna XXXII, 11).

The Dadistan-i-Dinik (c. VII, 7) relates that God (Ahura Mazda) enjoined Zoroaster to cultivate the Good Mind to the end that he might "comprehend to the utmost the two ways, that which is good and that which is evil."

The fundamental character of evil is described as the ruin of the Good Mind, in this saying concerning Ahriman's activities:

"The teacher of evil destroys the love, he by his teachings destroys the design of life, he prevents the possession of the Good Mind from being prized" (Yasna XXXII, 9).

Whereas the divine office is thus characterized, elsewhere in Gathas (Yasna XXXI, 17):

"Which is greater, the belief of the righteous or of the liar? Let him that knows tell him that knows. Let not him that knows nothing deceive any more. Be thou unto us, oh God (Ahura Mazda), the enlightener of the Good Mind!"

Indeed, the Good Mind is asserted elsewhere to have been the very first effluence of God and that through which all good is effected, in this passage:

"First created he the Good Mind, by means whereof the progress of the creatures of God (Ahura Mazda) hath been achieved" (Bundahis, c. I, 23).

And, in one of the Gathas, the prophet declares: "He that would see life indeed, to him will he make known what in actions by the Lord's (Ahura Mazda's) ordinance is better during this existence" (Yasna LI, 19).

It is also identified in one of the Gathas as the

medium through which God's will is done among men and upon the earth, thus:

"What dost thou command? What wouldst thou we should do? What requirest thou of praise or sacrifice? Speak thou, oh God (Ahura Mazda), that we may hear what ordinances will be our destiny. Teach thou us, by means of the Right, the ways of the Good Mind that are blessed to go in" (Yasna XXXIV, 12)!

It is, second, the mind to bless and benefit that we are blessed to go in. The office of the Good Mind among men is identified with service of mankind, in this:

"To whom for help shall he who hath the Good Mind turn? I have faith, thou wilt thyself fulfill this for me, oh God (Ahura Mazda)" (Yasna XLVI, 3).

The Aögemaïde Nask (50) enlarges upon this, at the same time giving a most beautiful interpretation of religion, in this passage:

"Blind are they all who fail, while on this earth, to follow the religion of God (Ahura Mazda), to benefit living men and cherish the memory of the dead."

The Bundahis (c. IV, 2) echoing the Zend Avesta statement, represents God (Ahura Mazda) as saying, when he promised Zoroaster to mankind:

"I will produce for the whole world him who will preach carefulness," i.e. the loving care of all beneficent creatures.

On the contrary, complaint was made in the Gathas against Ahriman that he desires to keep man from developing the Good Mind, as in this passage in which he was described as he who "hath made the pious out as liars and desolates the pastures and lifts his weapon against the righteous man" (Yasna XXXII, 10).

The complete identification of these with the marauders and bandits who swept down the plains, sparing neither man nor beast, and the nature which their punishment will take in the after life, are seen in this pronouncement in the same Gatha:

"By their dominion the Karpans and the Kavis accustomed mankind to evil actions, thus to destroy life. Their own souls and their own selves shall torment them when they come where the Sifting Bridge[1] is, for all time dwellers in the house of the lie" (Yasna XLVI, 11).

And Zoroaster, in the Gathas, sets forth as learned when he came into this life, that failure to put in practice the rules of the Good Mind and the Right which he utters, will be woe throughout life:

"I will speak of that which God (Ahura Mazda) the all-knowing revealed to me first in this (earthly) life. Those of you that put not in practice this word as I think and utter it, to them shall be woe at the end of life" (Yasna XLV, 3).

And, in connection with his prayer for his father-in-law, Frashaöshtra Hvogva, he affirms that he knows that he will be forever blest, saying:

"To all eternity we would be thy beloved" (Yasna XLIX, 8).

And, rendering to himself the happiness and the self-satisfaction that attends him who bears the Good Mind and the Right ever his own, he proclaims:

"And with all these may I be in thy Dominion, oh Lord (Ahura Mazda)" (Yasna XLIX, 5).

And he addresses to God his earnest prayer that he be not parted from the company of the Right and the Good Mind:

"I know wherefore I am without success, oh Lord

[1] Where after death the evil souls are parted from the good.

(Ahura Mazda), because few cattle are mine, and for that I have but few folk. I cry unto thee, see thou to it, oh Lord, granting me support as friend gives to friend. Teach me by the Right the acquisition of the Good Mind" (Yasna XLVI, 2).

This Zoroaster asks, prefering his requests on the ground that the true judge is also the master who determines the two destinies for man:

"All this I ask, whether the husbandman shall find cattle in accordance with the Right, he that is perfect in actions, a man of understanding, when he prays to him who hath promised unto the upright the true judge, in that he is lord of the two destinies" (Yasna LI, 5).

CHAPTER XIV

THE PRINCIPLES OF THE RIGHT CONTROL

"HE careth not that holy Piety should be his; nor taketh his counsel with the Good Mind, oh Lord (Ahura Mazda)!"

Thus speak the Gathas (Yasna XLIX, 2) of the ruler whose government is evil; and in another place they identify evil government, in these words:

"When, oh Lord (Ahura Mazda) will the nobles understand the message? When wilt thou smite the filthiness of this intoxicant, by which the Karpans evilly deceive and the wicked lords of the land, with purpose fell" (Yasna XLVIII, 10).

In another Gatha such misuse of the cattle is recognized to be wrong:

"Have the Daëvas ever exercised good dominion? And this I ask of those who see how for the Daëvas' sake the Karpan and the Usij gave the cattle to violence, and how the Kavi made them continually to mourn, instead of taking care that they may make the pastures prosper through the Right" (Yasna XLIV, 20).

In another of the Gathas (Yasna XLVIII, 5) the prayer goes up:

"Let him that ruleth well, reign over us: let not him that ruleth ill, reign over us; let it be with the actions accounting to good lore, oh Piety."

This ambition was also such that the man who participated in upholding a righteous leader and ruler was on that account held separate and distinct:

"Yea, I do ask whether the understanding man who seeks to advance the Dominion over the dwelling, over the district, over the province, over the land, by the Right, will be one like thee, oh God (Ahura Mazda)— when will he be and how will he behave" (Yasna XXXL, 16)?

This rule, essentially of the Good Mind that protects useful men and useful beasts against the predatory, was also to be democratic, of the people, in order that it be the best and most effective; for of this, as has been seen, it is spoken in the Gathas:

"May the Lord (Ahura Mazda) by his Dominion bring us to work for prospering our beasts and our men, so that we may, through the Right, have familiarity with the Good Mind" (Yasna XLV, 9).

It was also a government of reason and of energy, as well as of good intentions—embracing all the components of the Good Mind—of which the Gathas were speaking; for the following are entrusted to the special keeping of God:

"And them, oh God (Ahura Mazda), into thy keeping in thy house I put them—men of the Good Mind, the souls of the Right and their worship, their Piety, and zeal, that thou mayest guard it, oh thou of mighty Dominion, with imperishable energy" (Yasna XLIX, 10).

In the Vistasp Yast (c. VII, 47-48) it is said of the good ruler:

"He wieldeth his power according to the will of God (Ahura Mazda), the spirit of good, and for the destruction of the spirit of evil, whichever of two rulers goeth quicker to perform the sacrifice; but if he would perform the sacrifice and prayer in not the right way, he doth not rightly wield the power and he may not reign. Such an one shall suffer ill in the next world, though he be the sovereign over a land, with brave steeds to mount and brave chariots to drive. Give thou, oh Zoroaster, the crown unto him who with a good will giveth the sway unto thy teachings!"

In the Nasks (Tahmura's Fragments, c. XIII, 13) the worst of evils for a people is thus set forth:

"Proclaim thou, oh Spitama Zoroaster, that the most excellent of all it is to have a ruler and a priest, for every man in this world below . . . that the worst of all evils is it to have no ruler and no priest or to have an evil ruler."

That this evil ruler is a ruler in the absence of the Good Mind, i.e. the good will, the intelligence and the energy requisite to rule in accordance with the principles of the Right, the Gathas affirm in this striking manner:

"At which goal thou wilt come with thy holy spirit, oh God (Ahura Mazda), with Dominion and with the Good Mind, by whose action the settlements shall prosper through the Right. Their judgments shall Piety proclaim, even those of the wisdom which none can deceive" (Yasna XLIII, 6).

The sacred writings do not fail to record that it is the Good Mind by virtue of which God himself rules, saying (Yasna XXXI, 6):

"To him shall the best come who as one that knows speaks to me Right's very word of Well-Being and Immortality, even that the Dominion of God (Ahura Mazda) which the Good Mind will render prosperous for him."

And that the ruler, worthy of his sway, is he who

protects the righteous against wrongdoers, the Shay-ast-La-Shayast (c. XV, 7) in this asserts:

"Whosoever wisheth to propitiate God (Ahura Mazda) in the world, wisheth to promote the things of God; and whoever he be with whom God abideth in every place, it is necessary that he should propitiate the righteous man in whatever hath happened and whatever happeneth to him and should act for his happiness and afford him protection from the wicked."

And earlier in his Gathas, he has taken a stand against violence and cruelty, decrying them:

"Violence must be put down; against cruelty take a stand, ye who would make sure of the reward of the Good Mind through the Right, to whose company the holy man belongs. His dwelling-places shall be in thy house, oh God (Ahura Mazda)" (Yasna XLVIII, 7).

And once more he affirms that God is with him:

"These things wilt thou bring to pass for me who best knowest how, oh Lord (Ahura Mazda)" (Yasna XLVI, 19).

And to the power of God, as shown by the Good Mind and Right, he pays the tribute that the reward of the wise, even thus with eyes open to all, is ever secure:

"To thee and to the Right we will offer the sacrifice with due service, that in thy established Dominion ye may bring all creatures to perfection through the Good Mind. For the reward of the wise man is forever secure, oh God (Ahura Mazda), among you" (Yasna XXXIV, 3).

CHAPTER XV

THE RIGHT IS THE WILL OF GOD

ZOROASTER conceived of the order of nature, with laws uniformly operating which it is the duty of a man to observe and learn, as God's (Ahura Mazda's) laws operating in nature, as the manifestation of the workings of the Good Mind of God, as the product of the rules of the Right and so of God.

The harmful and noxious things which he found, in inanimate nature or among living creatures, including man, were attributed to Ahriman (the devil), and his demons.

That these are also somehow parts of God's universal order, was dimly felt; but remained for him, as for all generations of men, a puzzle and a contradiction, to be overcome by faith in divine benignity.

The law of God (Ahura Mazda) which Zoroaster recognized and worshiped, was inimical to all that is destructive, and fostered beneficence everywhere.

"When may I know, oh God (Ahura Mazda), and Right, if by law ye rule over everyone whose destructiveness is a menace to me? Let the revelation of the Good Mind be confirmed to me; the future deliverer should know how his own destiny shall be."

Thus the psalmist beseeches the Almighty in one of the Gathas (Yasna XLVIII, 9) for a resolution of the question which has troubled man from the earliest dawn of his intelligence.

And in another of the Gathas, he is (Yasna XXXI, 7) proclaimed as:

"He that first conceived, 'Let the heavens be arrayed with stars,' lo, it is he, by his wisdom, who created Right. Those realms that the Good Mind shall possess, thou dost prosper, oh God (Ahura Mazda), by thy spirit which, oh God, is ever as now."

That is, it is he who is the God of law. This is re-echoed in another passage, already once quoted, thus:

"Of these two he that followed the liar chose to do the worst; the sanctified pursued the Right, he that clothed himself with the massy heaven as a garment" (Yasna XXX, 5).

And, also in the Gathas, he tells how God made deeds and creeds "whereby one may exercise choice at one's free will," saying:

"When thou, oh God (Ahura Mazda), in the beginning didst create beings and ourselves, by thy thought and intelligence—when thou didst make life clothed with body, when thou didst make deeds and creeds whereby one may exercise choice at one's free will" (Yasna XXXI, 11).

In another of the Gathas, the power to recognize God (Ahura Mazda) is thus ascribed to his immanence in nature:

"For with mine eye I clearly discerned it, that which is of the good spirit, of word and of deed, recognizing God (Ahura Mazda) through the Right" (Yasna XLV, 8).

God, everywhere in the Zoroastrian scriptures, is the God of law, "without shadow or turning," as it has been put—the God of the laws of the Medes and Persians, famous for their unswerving rigor and impartiality.

The Vistasp Yast (c. VI, 43) bespeaks this fate for the contemner of his law:

"He who hath little liking for the law, him place I down below to suffer."

That this law is the very consequence of effect upon cause which Isaac Newton referred to, when, after his labors to discern nature's laws and their operation, he said, "I do think the very thoughts of God," is made clear beyond the possibility of dispute by this passage from the Gathas (Yasna XLIII, 5):

"Yea, the holy one, I recognized thee, oh God (Ahura Mazda), when I saw thee in the beginning at the birth of life, when thou makest actions and words to have their results, evil to the evil and good fate to the good, through thy wisdom, as creation shall reach its goal."

And that this was deemed by Zoroaster the law of evolution of what is best and fittest, the law of progress, is clear from many passages, some of which have already been quoted.

Another of the Gathas (Yasna XXXIV, 13) puts this as follows:

"The course of the Good Mind, oh God (Ahura Mazda), which thou didst reveal unto me, on which way, well made by the Right, the souls of the future benefactors shall pass to the reward, that was prepared for them that are wise, which thou determinest, oh God."

The Dadistan-i-Dinik (c. III, 1, 2) gives this full and definite expression as the purpose for which all men were created, in the following question and answer:

"The second is that which you ask thus: For what purpose is a righteous man created for the world, and in what manner is it necessary for him to live in the world?

"The reply is this, that the Creator created all creatures for progress, which is his wish; and it is necessary for us to promote whatever is his wish that our wish may be realized."

And that man was created and exists for the purpose of progressing, to the end that the Good Mind may achieve a conquest over all evil, is set forth in this passage from the same book:

"The sixth question is that which you ask thus: Why are we men produced for the world, and what is it necessary for us to do therein? . . .

"All creatures are made for justice and the performance of what is acceptable unto the Creator . . . and that preparation arises from the complete predominance of the Creator and the non-predominance of Ahriman, as is said of it in revelation, thus, 'In that time I shall become completely predominant, I who am God (Ahura Mazda); in nothing whatever shall the Evil Spirit be predominant'" (Dadistan-i-Dinik, c. VII, 1-3).

The Gathas put this in the form of a prayer, indicating the Zoroastrian belief, also, that the will of God is that there shall be evolution to higher things, as follows:

"Through the Dominion, oh God (Ahura Mazda), assure us that mankind shall be capable in accordance with thy will" (Yasna XXXIV, 15)!

The Vendidad (Fargard VIII, c. III, 19) declares:

"The will of the Lord (Ahura Mazda) is the law of righteousness."

The Dadistan-i-Dinik in another place (c. LXXI, 1, 3, 4) discusses the old, old issue of fate and free-will thus illuminatingly:

" 'Is that which happens unto man through fate or through his act? Is his act destined or not destined? And does anything happen unto man save by fate, or what is the truth about it?' . . .

"The reply is this, that the high priests have said that there are some things through destiny, and there are some by one's act; and it is thus fully decided by them, that life, wife and child, authority and wealth are by fate, and that righteousness and wickedness, choice of priesthood, warfare and husbandry are by one's act. And this, too, they say, that that which is not destined for a man in the world, does not happen; and that which is destined—be it owing to his effort, will come forward—be it through sinfulness or sloth, he will be injured by that."

That the results upon conduct of effect, following cause, inevitable and in the regular order of things, are helpful, is declared in these words from the Gathas (Yasna XXVIII, 10):

"I also have realized thee, oh God (Ahura Mazda), as the first discoverer of this."

The Gathas, as has already been pointed out, thus connect knowledge of nature's uniform laws, the veritable will of God (Ahura Mazda), with virtue:

"Far from them who do not ponder the Right, is the Good Mind" (Yasna XXXIV, 8).

One of the Yasts gives this tribute to the law of God among men:

"The law of the worshipers of God (Ahura Mazda) is the truest giver of all good things, of all those that are the offspring of the good principle; such is the law of Zoroaster" (Srosh Yast Hadhokht, c. I, 3).

The famed invocations of the followers of Zoroaster reported in the Ormazd Yast (23) thus identifies the law that actually governs the universe as holiness and God's will:

"The will of the Lord (Ahura Mazda) is the law of holiness."

And in the Gathas this prayer of resignation is recorded:

"God (Ahura Mazda) knoweth best the purposes that have been wrought already by demons and mortals and will be wrought hereafter. He, our God, is the decider. So shall it be as he wills" (Yasna XXIX, 4).

The Ardibehist Yast (c. I, 3) thus acclaims the virtues of the Right as an attribute of God and component of the Godhead:

"I proclaim the Right. If I proclaim the Right, then easy is the way to the abiding-place of the other Amesha Spentas, which the Lord God (Ahura Mazda) maintaineth with good thoughts, with good words, and with good deeds."

The following invocation, taken from one of the Gathas (Yasna XXXIV, 12), shows that the universal laws were regarded as the expression of God's (Ahura Mazda's) benevolence for his creatures, of his Good Mind:

"Teach thou us, by the Right, the paths of the Good Mind, that are blessed to go in."

That evil things are done and that there are noxious things and malicious creatures, Zoroaster was far from denying; instead, they were recognized as opposites of God's will, existing in defiance of his will. This view was later modified, as the following passage from the Bundahis (c. XIX, 36) shows:

"God (Ahura Mazda) hath created nothing that is not useful; for all things are made for use."

The Arda Viraf echoes this sentiment with the following:

"Everyone who speaks correct and true, I honor and know" (Arda Viraf, 203).

And the Dinkard speaks as follows:

"The best thing is truth and the worst thing is falsehood" (XII, 40).

But the Sad Dar pays this tribute:

"One truthful man is better than the whole world speaking falsehood" (323).

And when the Right shall smite the lie, then his action shall exalt the man who humbly supplicates to God.

"When at the recompensings the Right shall smite the lie, so that what was long since made known, shall be assigned in eternity to Daëvas and men, then will it exalt with thy blessings, of God (Ahura Mazda), him who prays unto thee" (Yasna XLVIII, 1).

CHAPTER XVI

RIGHTS OF FELLOW MEN

"THIS I ask thee, tell me truly, oh Lord (Ahura Mazda), he that will not give that reward to him that earns it, even to the man, who fulfilling his word, gives him what he undertook—what penalty shall come to him for the same at this present? I know that which shall come to him at the last" (Yasna XLIV, 19).

The sentence which this passage presages is what the dictates of the Right indicates:

"That nature alone is good which shall not do unto another whatever is not good for its own self."

This saying in the Dadistan-i-Dinik (c. XCIV, 5) is like Jesus or, put negatively, like Confucius, and it is followed immediately by this which is like unto it:

"And this, too, was considered by them, that one should become the friend of every man, and this is thy nature; also should bring them forward into a good life, and this is thy wisdom; also think of them as thine own, and this is thy religion; and, through them, bring happiness unto thyself, and this is thy very soul."

The Dinkard speaks of this:

"Be it known that the duration of the soul is everlasting" (V, 301).

This elementary principle of moral conduct of man toward men is also found in this fragment of the Nasks (Aögemaïde Nask, 48):

"How is it that any mortal can wish for another

125

mortal the annihilation of his body or of his soul or death of his children or for his herd, if he knoweth enough to comprehend that he too is mortal?"

In this same fragment of the ancient writings, preserved unto this day, also appears the following (Aögemaïde Nask, 22-24):

"And in case of doubt we must consider as saved, him who, for all we have seen and know, hath been a believer in body and soul and hath done well in the sight of God (Ahura Mazda) and afflicted the Evil One, and him who hath had this for his chief purpose or hath caused this to flow from him, prosperity and joy for others, and that from him should not issue pain or injury for them."

The same fragment also proceeds (25):

"Oh thou, my perishable body, think good thoughts with thy mind! Oh thou, my perishable body, do good deeds with thy hand!"

This is explained in the Dadistan-i-Dinik (c. XXXVIII, 2):

"That every thought, word and deed, the consequence of which is joy, happiness and worthy recompense . . . is well-thought, well-said and well-done."

The Dinkard says:

"A man's body is protected in this world by philanthropy" (VII, 453).

Thus the ancient Persians and, following them, the Parsis have applied the fundamental principle of the Good Mind, so thoroughly exemplified by what their scriptures also say concerning care of man's lowly friends, the dumb beasts which he has tamed and domesticated, to the relations of men, one with the other.

Obviously the principle applies; equally obviously the sacred writings of Zoroaster so applied it.

The Good Mind, in which Zoroaster discovered the very essence of the divine, calls for loving care of all beneficent human beings, and as well, for the creation of conditions favorable to that care and to producing human beings that will exercise it.

In the first Sirozah (Bahman, 2) the power of the Good Mind, concentrated upon the thought of peace among men, is thus celebrated:

"To peace, whose breath is friendly and who is more powerful to destroy than all other created things."

To which the meaning, "Peace hath her victories no less than war," instead of the more obvious, "Where wealth accumulates and men decay," is to be attached.

To help the world forward, ever the ambition and struggle of noble minds, was also impressed upon followers of Zoroaster as a duty not to be shirked.

In the Gathas (Yasna XXX, 9) it is the very substance of the following prayer:

"So may we be those that make the world to advance."

In the Rashn Yast (c. I, 1) Zoroaster is represented as interrogating God (Ahura Mazda) concerning the scriptures:

"What of the Holy Word is created true? What is created progress-making? What is fit for man's comprehension? What is wholesome? What is wise? What is joyous?

To which God (Ahura Mazda) replied that this, indeed, is the subject of the Holy Word."

The duty of charity and hospitality toward good men is thus enjoined in the Nasks (Tahmura's Fragments, 105-109):

"He hath promoted nought, oh Zoroaster, nor shall he promote aught, who doth not fulfill the laws of perfect holiness, well-pondered in his heart, who hath not rejoiced and who rejoiceth not the righteous man that cometh within his gates; for they, oh Spitama Zoroaster, shall enter into Paradise, who are most generous to the righteous and who least vex their souls."

The Dinkard says of this:

"The heart and conscience of the generous man are warm and such a heart has the light of the holy fire . . . The generous man is exalted among men" (IX, 555).

And the follower of Zoroaster was not under any circumstances to exact interest for loans to others of the faith; as the Vendidad says:

"The religion of God (Ahura Mazda), oh Spitama Zoroaster, indeed taketh away from him who professeth it, the bonds of his sin; it taketh away breach of trust; it taketh away murdering one of the faith; it taketh away burying a corpse; it taketh away sins for which else there were no atonement; it taketh away the worst sin (i.e. the sin of usury); it taketh away any sin that may be committed" (Fargard III, c. IV, 41-42).

But this appears to have no application to him who was not of his own faith; which discrimination was not always observed, as appears from the following, from a commentary:

"He knows that it is lawful to take high interest, but he does not know that it is not lawful to do so from the faithful" (Commentary).

Thus the Zoroastrians were not originally personally ordered to deal with strangers.

And the condemnation of men as not righteous, who do not give of their store to the poor of the communion, is found in the Nasks (Tahmura's Fragments c. XLIV, 100).

"They seek not after righteousness; they seek not to succor and maintain the poor follower of the Holy Law."

The promise of a happy fate is, on the contrary, held out to them who come to the help of the needy among the servants of God, in this passage from the Vendidad (Fargard XVIII, c. II, 29):

"And whosoever shall give meat to one of the faithful, as much of it as the body of this Parodars bird of mine, I, God (Ahura Mazda), need not interrogate him twice; he shall go to Paradise."

The Dinkard says of our service to each other:

"When men love and help one another to the best of their power, they derive the greatest pleasure from loving their fellow men" (VIII, 454).

The following interesting chronicle of the unwilling testimony of the Druj, that neglect to feed the famishing poor is both a crime and a powerful encouragement of wickedness of all sorts, is found in the Vendidad (Fargard XVIII, c. III, 34-37):

"The Druj answered, 'Oh holy, well-formed Sraösha,[1] he is the first of my males who, being entreated by one of the faithful, doth not give him anything, be it ever so little, of the riches he hath treasured up. That man maketh me conceive progeny as other males make their females conceive by their seed.'

"The holy Sraösha, letting his club down upon her, asked the Druj: 'Oh thou wretched, worthless Druj! What is the thing that can undo that?' The Druj demon answered, 'Oh holy, well-formed Sraösha, this is the thing that undoeth it, namely, when a man, unasked, kindly and piously giveth to one of the faithful, something, be it ever so little, of the riches he hath treasured up.'"

[1] A powerful genius or angel.

The Vendidad is much more explicit about the fate of him who tightens his purse strings, in the following passage, which also exalts the humble tillers of the soil:

" 'Oh Maker of the material world, thou Holy One, who is the fifth that rejoiceth the earth with greatest joy?' God (Ahura Mazda) answered and made reply, saying, 'It is he who kindly and piously giveth to one of the faithful who tilleth the earth, oh Spitama Zoroaster!

" 'He who would not kindly and piously give to one of the faithful who tilleth the earth, oh Spitama Zoroaster, the Holy Power will throw him down into darkness, down into the world of woe, the world of hell, down into the deep abyss' " (Vendidad, Fargard III, c. III, 34, 35).

In the Nasks (Tahmura's Fragments, c. XXVI, 47) this beautiful reward for well-doing of that sort is set forth:

"Such an one, oh Spitama Zoroaster, shall there arrive, as the best of intercessors, who here below intercedeth for the poor man and the poor woman in their distress."

The Dinkard says of this:

"As far as possible, one should not partake of food till after feeding the needy" (IX, 638).

In the Vistasp Yast (c. V. 36) it is said of this:

"Thou art entreated for alms by the whole of the living world; and the holy law standeth ever at the door in the persons of thy brethren."

The Nasks (Tahmura's Fragments, c. XLIV, 100) identify charity with righteousness, saying of those who practice it not:

"They seek not after righteousness; they seek not

to succor and maintain the poor follower of the Holy Law."

And in another place (Tahmura's Fragments, XXXVI, 77) it speaks of "the holy generosity and bounty that reign between brethren in the faith."

The Vistasp Yast (c. V, 36) depicts this poignantly thus:

"Beggars stand ever at the stranger's door amongst them that beg for bread; ever will that bread be a burning coal upon thy head."

That is, the bread given by strangers to brethren in the faith who should have been aided by those of the faith.

Man's entire duty is thus explained by the Dinkard:

"That man has the worst desires, who thinks it right to amass the riches of this world" (III, 129).

Man's duty toward his fellows is set forth in the Shayast-La-Shayast (c. XX, 6) comprehensively, thus:

"The greatest concerns of men are these, to make him who is an enemy a friend, to make him who is wicked righteous, and to make him who is ignorant learned."

Certainly these appear to cover relations to pretty much all sorts of people to whom one is not attached by bonds which of themselves conclusively suggest his duties to them.

Waste, however, the most distinctive fault of our prodigal age, is condemned in the Vendidad (Fargard V, 60):

"God (Ahura Mazda), in sooth, doth not suffer us to waste anything that we may possess, not even so much as an asperena's weight of thread, not even so much as a maid lets fall in spinning."

CHAPTER XVII

RIGHTS OF ORDINARY MEN

NATURALLY, a religion which placed so much stress upon righteous and generous conduct would not tolerate despoiling others. Not only were robbery and theft condemned, but also forms of wronging others which are viewed by some peoples of ancient and of modern times who claim much for themselves respecting virtuous conduct, as venial and unimportant.

Thus the Vendidad (Fargard IV, c. 1) says of him who defaults in his promise to return what he has borrowed:

"He that doth not restore a loan unto him that hath lent it, stealeth the thing and robbeth the man. This he doeth every day, every night, so long as he keepeth in this possession the property of his neighbor, as if it were his own."

The reputation of the Parsis in India for fulfilling contracts is superior and excellent; and this good name has attached to the followers of Zoroaster since ancient times.

The fame of "the laws of the Medes and Persians" for strictness and severity, which was celebrated by the Hebrews upon their return from captivity, was in large part owing to the insistence of those laws upon performance of every obligation, promptly and in full, and the recognition of all sorts of fraud as heinous crimes, disgracing the perpetrators almost beyond redemption.

132

This duty, also, devolves upon a man, without regard to whether his agreements be with one of his community or with a stranger; for it is enjoined:

"Break not thy contract, oh Spitama, neither that which thou hast entered into with one of the unbelievers nor one that thou hast entered into with one of the faithful who is of thine own faith; for Mithra[1] standeth both for those of the faith and for those not of the faith" (Mihir Yast, c. I, 2).

The penance for breaking one's word was fixed by the Vendidad (Fargard IV, c. Ia) at six hundred stripes at the minimum and for breaking a contract regarding the land at not less than two thousand stripes.

Well could Herodotus (*Nat. Hist.*, I, 183) say of this people, "The basest thing with Persians is to lie; and next to it is to be in debt, for this reason, among many others, that he who is so, must needs sink to lying at last."

The Bundahis (c. XXIV, 24) says of the solid rewards of truthfulness:

"Of two men when they come together, he who is the wiser and the more truthful, will lead."

Yet the Gathas (Yasna XXXI, 13) limit that which man is at liberty to disclose, thus:

"What things are open or are secret, may be met with discretion, or what man for a little sin asks a severe penalty, these alike thou with thy flashing eye regardest by means of the Right."

It was not commanded, or even allowed, that one should spread all secrets and private matters abroad.

The unappeasable anger of the divine inquisitor,

---

[1] Mithra, an angel who guarded the truth and punished severely all forms of falsehood and breach of faith. In later times he was celebrated as a demigod.

Mithra, against him who speaks not the truth, is thus described in the Mihir Yast (c. V, 18-20):

"If the master of a house lieth unto him, or the lord of a borough or of a town or of a province, then cometh Mithra, angry and outraged, and breaketh asunder the house, borough, town or province and the masters of the houses or lords of boroughs, towns or provinces and the foremost men thereof. On whatever side there be one who hath lied unto Mithra, on that side Mithra standeth forth, angry and outraged, and his wrath is slow to relent. They who lie unto Mithra, however swift they run, cannot outrun; riding, they cannot outspeed; driving, they cannot outdrive."

The Vendidad (Fargard IV, c. IVb) says of him who is forsworn:

"Upon the very first time that this deed is done, without waiting until it is done again . . . down there the pain for it shall be as severe as any pain in this world—for this deed of him who, knowingly falsifying, standeth before the sulphur-laden, golden, truth-discerning waters, appealing unto Rashner,* with a lie upon his lips before Mithra."

The whole duty of man to his fellows is condensed in this from the Nask, (Aögemaïde, 50):

"Blind are they all who fail while on this earth to follow the religion of God (Ahura Mazda) to benefit living men and to honor the dead."

The Gathas, also, do not fail to celebrate this, nor to assign its reward; of this they say:

"Whoso is most good to the righteous man, be he a noble or a member of the community or of the brotherhood, oh God (Ahura Mazda), or with diligence cares for the cattle, he shall forevermore be in the

* The angel of truth.

pasture of the Right and the Good Mind" (Yasna XXXIII, 3).

And the Zend Avesta echoes this in the following:

"And I will bless thee with the fair blessing-spell of the righteous, the friendly blessing-spell of the righteous, that make the empty full and the full to overflow, that come to help him who faileth and make the sick whole again" (Vendidad, Fargard XXXI, c. 1).

The Dadistan-i-Dinik (c. VII, 1, 2) asks and answers a question concerning man's duty in the world in a manner, which covers both the duty to be beneficent and to refrain from being maleficent, thus:

"Why are we men produced in the world and what is it that we must do therein?

"The answer to this is . . . that man was created to do justice and to do for his Creator that which is acceptable unto him."

CHAPTER XVIII

RIGHTS OF INFIDEL FOES

This is recorded of the infidel foe and, on the contrary, his enemy, the saint:

"Thereupon unto him did I speak, 'To the first question, Zoroaster am I, a true foe to the liar to the utmost of my power, but a powerful support will I be to the righteous'" (Yasna XLIII, 8).

Yet the Vistasp Yast (c. VI, 44) rightfully ascribes this very view regarding the attitude which the believers should take toward the unbelievers, to Ahriman, the prince of darkness who is there reported as proposing:

"This is an unbeliever; let us cast him down below!"[1]

The Gathas, however, are militant against unbelievers, even unto persecution, commanding:

"Let none of you attend to the liar's words and commands; he leads house, clan, district and country into misery and destruction. Resist them, then, with weapons" (Yasna XXXI, 18).

This is repeated, with unction, thus:

"As the holy one, I recognized thee, oh God (Ahura

[1] This insistence of evil thought against infidels has not been practiced by the Parsis; concerning whose practice, its High Priest, Dhalla, in *Zoroastrian Ethics*, says: "The Parsi Mobad performed the Yasna ceremony and squeezed the Haöma plant, as his Hindu Brahman neighbor practiced his Yasna rites and pounded Soma. . . . The Hindu anathematises the *asuras* as the infernal beings, the Parsi pays his homage to the *ahuras* as the celestial beings" (p. 304).

Mazda), when the Good Mind came to me, when the still mind taught me to declare what is best. Let not a man seek, again and again, to please the liars for they make all the righteous enemies" (Yasna XLIII, 15).

The reason for this, at its inception, is, however, apparent and fully stated. It had reference to bandits, indulging in rapine and slaughter, who also followed gods that countenanced such a thing, not unknown in our own times; for delivery from these dreaded fiends Zoroaster offered up this prayer:

"Destruction is not for the right-living, not for the cattle-tender at the hands of the liars" (Yasna XXIX, 5)!

It was, indeed, for this, according to tradition, that he had been sent to a world, groaning with misery, of which the plainsmen and their herds suffering at the hands of the marauders constituted in their view a great part—he to whose coming God (Ahura Mazda) made reference in this:

"Then the Creator of the ox asked of the Right, 'Hast thou a judge for the ox that ye may be able to appoint him careful tendance as well as fodder? Whom do ye will to be his lord that he may drive off violence with followers of the lie' " (Yasna XXIX, 2)?

The Vendidad (Fargard XVI, c. III, 18) echoes and amplifies this sentiment in these words:

"The wicked, incarnations of the Druj, are contemners of the judge; they who contemn the judge, flaunt the King of Kings; they who defy the King of Kings, are the ungodly; all the ungodly are worthy of death."

The Gathas are not less emphatic, as in this passage, which also betrays the purpose of this severity:

"So they whose deeds were evil, let them be deceived and let them howl, abandoned to ruin" (Yasna LIII, 8).

Nonresistance was not a virtue among those who were exposed to the ravages of the Kurds of their day and generation.

This, according to Yasna (XLV, 7) is ever the desire of the holy man; it says of this:

"In immortality shall the soul of the righteous be joyful; its perpetuity shall be the torments of the liars."

That is, seek after the rewards of industry and to prevent spoliation and, therefore, resist and destroy the despoilers.

It is not only that the evil receive not the blessings which make the good happy, however, of which the Gathas speak; it is also that the good really seek to bring the wicked unbelievers to ruin.

Thus the Nasks (Tahmura's Fragments, c. XXXVI, 77) enjoin "the holy generosity and bounteousness that reign between brethren in the faith."

But in another place (Fragments Epatistan, Fargard I, First Part, 18) are found question and answer:

" 'He that refuseth food to the heathen and the sinner is he guilty?' 'He is not guilty unless he refuse it to the laborer in his service.' "

The Nasks also (Tahmura's Fragments, c. L, 110) declare:

"He who giveth unto the ungodly, violateth the Right"; and again (112), "He is himself unrighteous who is beneficent unto them that are unrighteous."

In Sad Dar a like sentence is found:

"Men of the good religion should give something to a man of different religion only in case of extreme necessity, lest it become a sin" (282).

Notwithstanding these harsh commands, it is strictly enjoined upon all his followers that they keep their contracts with those not of the faith to the very letter, as in this command of God to Zoroaster himself:

"Break not thy contract, oh Spitama, neither that which thou hast entered into with one of the unbelievers nor that which thou hast entered into with one of the faithful and who is of thine own faith; for Mithra stands both for the faithful and for them who are not of the faith" (Mihir Yast, c. I, 2).

The Gathas unquestionably require inexorably harsh treatment of wicked men, however, as when it is affirmed:

"Whoso worketh ill for the liar by word or thought or hand or converts his dependents to the good—such men meet the will of God (Ahura Mazda) to his satisfaction" (Yasna XXXIII, 2).

In the Nasks, also (Tahmura's Fragments, VIII, 4-6) the sentencing of malefactors unto death is thus enjoined:

"Hearken not to the law and the doctrine from the mouth of the unrighteous! He would bring into the house, the borough, the district and the country misfortune and death. Teach him with the thrust of the sword!"

All of this smacks rather of the hot rage of contending religions and creeds in the days of militant Christianity or of yet more militant Mohammedanism, than of the tolerance of the Medes and Persians, the first of the followers of Zoroaster to bulk big in the world's history, following a religion which caused them to liberate the Jews from captivity and rebuild their temple for them.

Yet this intolerance must have had its roots in the aloofness of the plainsmen and in their one contact with others, in early days, that is, in struggles to defend their settlements, their herds and their women and children—struggles which go on, now as then, upon these steppes, exposed to the incursion of men like the Kurds from the hills and the scarcely less feared and hated soldiery from the towns.

An interesting and very naïve instance of this attitude is afforded by the following specifications in the Vendidad of the test of skill in surgery, required before one could be permitted to practice upon the faithful:

"Oh Maker of the material world, thou Holy One, if a worshipper of God wish to practice the art of healing, on whom shall he first prove his skill? On the worshippers of God (Ahura Mazda) or on the worshippers of the Daëvas?

"God (Ahura Mazda) made answer and said, 'On worshippers of the Daëvas shall he first prove himself, rather than on worshippers of God. If he treat with the knife a worshipper of the Daëvas and he die; if he treat with the knife a second worshipper of the Daëvas and he die; if he treat with the knife for the third time a worshipper of the Daëvas and he die, he is unfit forever and ever. Let him then never attend any worshipper of God; let him never treat with the knife any worshipper of God, nor wound him with the knife. If he shall ever attend any worshipper of God, if he shall ever treat with the knife any worshipper of God, and wound him with the knife, he shall pay for his wound the penalty for willful murder.

"If he treat with the knife a worshipper of the Daëvas and he recover; if he treat with the knife a second worshipper of the Daëvas and he recover; if for the third time he treat with the knife a worshipper of the Daëvas and he recover; then he is fit forever and ever. He may henceforth at his will attend worshippers of God; he may at his will treat with the knife worshippers of God, and heal them with the knife" (Vendidad, Fargard VII, c. VIIa, 36-40).

It is to be noted, however, that the reward for successful treatment of the infidel was great and the loss if the treatment did not succeed was also great; accordingly, this must have secured the unbeliever against malpractice or wild experimentation.

In the early days, after Zoroaster's following was established and was dominant—not the earliest days, of course, when he had sore need for supporters—proselyting was all but proscribed.

Indeed this saying from one of the Nasks would indicate that it was entirely proscribed:

"He giveth a tongue to the wolf, that imparteth the Holy Word to a heretic" (Tahmura's Fragments, c. VII, 3).

But another passage (Fragments, Erpatistan II, Fargard I, First Part, 17) expatiates upon this in a way which rather weakens its force than actually removes its injustice, by calling for bare sustenance as the reward:

" 'Shall he teach a disciple, if he be a heathen or a sinner?' 'The righteous man in need, if he hath not wherewithal to sustain life, may in order to procure that with which to sustain life, teach for remuneration, but not without remuneration.' 'What remuneration?' 'That which correspondeth to what an ox ploughs; but he giveth a tongue to the wolf that imparteth the Holy Word to a heretic?' "

In later days when the faithful were oppressed and had need for powerful friends, it became a virtue to proselyte; of which the Dadistan-i-Dinik (c. XLII, 3) said:

"And every good work wrought in the good religion by them that are by him converted from a strange faith and irreligion, all that is wrought by them, after that, by virtue of the patience and praise of him who hath the shield of the religion, they have been saved from their irreligion, becometh his own, as though it had been set in motion by himself, and he hath the same praise and credit therefor."

The Bundahis (c. XXX, 11) relates how at the last judgment the follower of Zoroaster will be subject to the indictment of having failed to perform his duty of enlightening his neighbor who was not of the faith; the passage runs as follows:

"In that assembly whatever righteous man was a friend of a wicked one in the world, and the wicked man complaineth of him who is righteous, 'Why did he not make me acquainted, when in the world, with the good deeds he practiced, himself?' and if he who is righteous did not inform him, then it is necessary for that man to suffer shame accordingly in that assembly."

Yet, afar from these doctrines, the Gathas were to the contrary, as speaks this passage:

"If an understanding man shall be able to hold one who comes over from his vow and his ties of faith, himself having brought him thereto, and living after the ordinance, a righteous man converting a liar—then shall he tell it to the nobles, that they may protect him from injury, oh Lord (Ahura Mazda)" (Yasna XLVI, 5).

In any event, proselyting has for centuries been all but utterly forbidden among the Parsis:

For the apostate from the religion the condemnation was fierce and merciless. The Shayast-La-Shayast (c. XVII, 7) relates of the old saying concerning such:

"In one place it is declared that him that was begotten of the demons, him that committeth sodomy, and him that performeth the religious rites of an apostate, these three raise they not from the dead; for as much as he that was begotten of the demons is himself a demon, he that committeth sodomy becometh a demon and the soul of him that performeth the religious rites of an apostate will become a darting serpent."

In the Nasks (Fragments VI, Nirangistan I, Fargard II, 41) it is asked and answered:

" 'What is unbelief? What is impiety?' 'It is renouncing the religion of God (Ahura Mazda).' "

The Dadistan-i-Dinik (c. CLI, 3, 5) says of such:

"The reply is this, that an adult is worthy of death on account of the good religion he would abandon; on account also of the adoption of the strange faith he is worthy of death. . . . When he giveth up the ghost, without renouncing that sin, and impenitent, being still under that falsely conceived law, the place of his soul is in the worst state and his punishment is that of a multitude of transgressions, each worthy of death."

Yet the Shayast-La-Shayast (c. VI, 6) says of him who is merely not of the faith but no apostate, quoting a priest of high authority:

"Kushtano-Suged said that an infidel, if his good works are a single Tanupuhar more than his evil, is saved from torment."

The Vendidad (Fargard XVIII, c. I, 8, 9) reports this conversation:

"Zoroaster besought the Lord (Ahura Mazda) inquiring, 'Oh thou Creator of the material world, thou Holy One, what is it that bringeth on us the unseen power of death?' God made answer and replied, 'It is he that teacheth a wrong religion.' "

This also, in the same book (Vendidad, Fargard XV, c. I, 1, 2) is included as the first of five sins, "that, being committed, but not confessed or atoned for, make him that hath committed them, a Peshotanu," but it is there limited to one who leads his fellow astray, "with a full knowledge and appreciation of his sin."

The duty of hating the infidel is again urged here:

"Whoso therefore in the future lightly esteemeth the Daëvas and those mortals who lightly esteem him, even all others save that one who highly esteemeth him, unto him shall the holy self of the future deliverer as Lord of the house, be friend, brother, father, oh God (Ahura Mazda)" (Yasna XLV, 11).

In contemplating this appalling fervor of hatred of one's fellow men, one needs continually to be reminded that it was at the time, hate against hate, persecution against persecution, directed against peoples who made destruction, or what in modern days has been aptly termed "frightfulness," a virtue, worshiping gods that looked upon their awful deeds with approval. Of such, the Gathas say:

"They who by their evil purpose make increase of violence and cruelty with their tongues, the foes of cattle-nurture among its friends, whose ill deeds prevail, not their good deeds; these shall be in the house of the Daëvas, the place for the very self of the liar" (Yasna XLIX, 4).

That one must resist such to the uttermost and must refuse to yield unto them the supremacy, another of the Gathas thus affirms:

"This I ask what penalty is for him who seeks to achieve kingship for a liar, for the man of ill deeds, oh God (Ahura Mazda), who finds not his living without injury to the husbandman's cattle and men, though he does him no harm" (Yasna XXXI, 15)?

It was thus the theory that the good religion had been known to primitive man, but had been lost.

Even the power and sway of unbelief, however, did not cause the faithful to fear that this would again come to pass; for in the Gathas, it is promised:

"Never shall the false teacher destroy the second life, the liar, in perversion by his tongue, unto evil belief" (Yasna XLV, 1).

CHAPTER XIX

RIGHTS OF THE MARRIED

"Earnestly will I lead her to the faith, that she may serve her father and her husband, the farmers and the nobles, as a righteous woman serves the righteous. The glorious heritage of the Good Mind . . . shall the Lord (Ahura Mazda) give to her good self for all time" (Yasna LIII, 4).

Thus speaks Jamaspa in the Gathas concerning a bride of Zoroaster.

Life, and the actual living of it, Zoroaster identified very particularly with the family and with the perpetuation of mankind.

Unto the Amesha Spenta, Piety, were committed "virtuous women" (Shayast-La-Shayast, c. XV, 4) and the same book (c. XXII, 5) contains this prayer:

"May Piety grant thee credit and honor among men through thine offspring and bestow upon thee, as wife, a woman from a strong race!"

The family, therefore, became the special care of Piety and the morals of sex were thus raised into a prominence rarely, if ever, equaled in other ancient religions.

The ethical import of sexual conduct was judged severely by their consequences or, more accurately stated, by the consequences fairly to be expected.

The Vendidad (Fargard III, c. 1) records this reply of the Almighty to Zoroaster's question:

" 'Oh Maker of the material world, thou Holy One,

146

which is the second place where the earth feels most happy?'

"God (Ahura Mazda) made answer and said, 'It is the place whereon one of the faithful erecteth a house with a priest within, with cattle, with a wife, with children, and good herds within; and wherein afterwards the cattle continue to thrive, virtue to thrive, the dog to thrive, the wife to thrive, the child to thrive, the fire to thrive, and every blessing of life to thrive.' "

The same Fargard (c. III, 24) refers to the hardships of the spinster's lot, childless and without a husband, thus:

"Unhappy is the land that hath long lain unsown with the seed of the sower and wanteth a good husbandman, like unto a well-shapen maiden that hath long gone childless and wanteth a good husband."

Zoroaster and his followers condemn celibacy utterly and find no warrant for it in nature; the unmarried of both sexes are looked on with disfavor and there is no celebration of continence as purity.

The Vendidad (Fargard IV, c. IIIb, 47) proclaims this in these words:

"Verily say I unto thee, on Spitama Zoroaster, he that hath a wife, is far above him that liveth in continence; he that maintaineth a household, is far above him that hath none; he that hath children, is far above him that hath no child."

The Menuk-i-Khrat says of the wife who is correct in her conduct:

"The woman who is young, who is properly disposed, who is faithful, who is respected, who is good-natured, who enlivens the house, whose modesty and awe are virtuous, a friend of her own father and elders, husband and guardians, handsome and replete with animation is chief over the women who are her own associates."

The Bahman Yast (c. II, 13) relates that Zoroaster told God (Ahura Mazda) of his dream:

"I beheld a rich man without children and he was not exalted in mine eyes; and I beheld a poor man with many children and he was exalted in mine eyes."

The Ashi Yast (c. X, 59) declares that the third wailing of Ashi Vanguhi, when contemplating the evils of the world, was:

"This is the worst deed that men and despots commit, when they deprive maids, who have long been unfruitful, of marrying and bringing forth children."

And the same Yast (c. X, 39) relates that unto Vayu, the genius of the air and of fruitfulness, "did maidens, whom no man had known, offer up a sacrifice on a golden throne, under golden beams and a golden canopy, with bundles of baresma and offerings of boiling milk, begging of him a boon, 'Grant us, oh Vayu who dost work on high, that we may find a husband, young and beautiful in person, who will treat us well our whole lives long and bless us with offspring.'"

The Bahman Yast (c. III, 22) which threatens the unbelievers that those of the faith "will slay, so that a thousand women can, after that, see and kiss but one man," was not, by this language, offending against any Zoroastrian precept concerning the family, for both polygamy and concubinage were allowed. Even now, if his marriage yield no child that is worthy and a surviving male, there is allowed another marriage while the former one continues.[1]

The Shayast-La-Shayast (c. XII, 14) repeats the

---

[1] "Each one of them married several legitimate wives and acquired for himself yet several more concubines." See Rapp, *Religion and Customs of the Persians*, pp. 298-300; *Herod.* I. 135; Strabo, p. 733, etc.

ancient rule "that it is well that any of those that take a handmaid as a concubine and have offspring from her, accept all male children as their sons," excusing the overwhelming failure to accept girl children as of "no advantage."

Modern Parsis, however, permit plural marriage in any case only if it be that sons are not born and survive, and a second marriage, otherwise, only in case of divorce of the wife for her adultery.

This passage from the Ashi Yast (c. II, 10) indicates, however, very liberal tolerance of polygamy in those days:

"They whom thou dost attend, oh Ashi Vanguhi, have their ladies that sit on their beds, waiting for them. They lie on the cushions adorning themselves . . . with square-bored earrings and a necklace of gold, saying, 'When will our lord come? When shall we enjoy in our bodies the delights of love?' "

The holier and spiritually more intimate relationship, however, which arises in monogamic marriage, appears to be recognized in the Shayast-La-Shayast (c. XII, 30) as follows:

"The rule is that, when a man hath performed his form of worship and his wife hath not performed it, it is extremely necessary to perform the suitable form of worship . . . so that they may become such as are dwelling more closely together in the spiritual existence."

This is indicated also in somewhat vague language in another chapter (LIV) of the same book.

And a further passage of another book runs, so that one might suspect that monogamy was meant, but it has the other meaning, that a man is only to marry *such* a woman:

"Let your love ever be for a foresighted and modest woman and marry such a one only" (Andarz-i-Ataport i Marashand).

The Aban Yast (c. XXI, 87) represents maidens as calling upon the goddess to supply husbands for them:

"The maids of barren womb, longing for a lord, will beg of thee a strong husband.

"Women, on the point of bringing forth, will beg of thee a good delivery.

"All this wilt thou grant unto them, as it lies in thy power, oh Ardvi Sura Anahita."

For a peculiar and very fanciful reason, the Shayast-La-Shayast (c. X, 19) makes it out to be yet more incumbent upon a woman to marry than upon a man, saying of this:

"The rule is that when a man marrieth not a wife, he is not therefore deserving of death; but when a woman marrieth not a husband, she is therefore deserving of death, since for a woman there is no offspring save by lying with a man and else no progeny cometh from her, but for a man though he have no wife, if he recite the Zend Avesta, there may flow, as the Vendidad sayeth, descendants (in the faith), stretching onward into the great hereafter."

That is to say, he may have spiritual progeny. This is very evidently an invention to avoid too crushing condemnation of celibacy or barrenness.

The Dinkard says of a man:

"Every man that has a material body should regard his own marriage as a good work incumbent on him to perform. . . . And he should promote the marriages of others (IX, 609).

The duty of the father to provide his daughter a husband of the faith, the Vendidad thus proclaims:

" 'He shall, in a godly and pious manner, give in marriage unto one of the faith a virgin, whom no man hath known, to redeem his own soul.' 'Oh thou Creator of the material world, thou Holy One, what sort of virgin?' God (Ahura Mazda) made answer and said, 'His sister or his daughter, of full age, with earrings in her ears, past her fifteenth year' " (Fargard XIV, 15).

It was also held that wife and child should be educated, as in the following:

"Do not refrain from educating your wife and children, your countrymen and yourself" (Andarz-i-Atarhat-i-Maruspand 2).

That the first duty of the bride is to live in accordance with the Good Mind, she is thus admonished by the Gathas (Yasna LIII, 5):

"Say them to heart and learn to get them within your very hearts with earnest attention to the life of the Good Mind."

In the Vistasp Yast (c. VII, 50) lust is condemned in woman, thus:

"The fiend is powerful to distress and to dry up the milk of the woman who indulges in lust."

Though in the Vendidad (Fargard XV, c. IV, 46-49) there is a circumstantial account which seems to attest that mongrelism, a sort of "melting-pot," would produce the strongest and best progeny, the followers of Zoroaster were, in point of fact, of quite the contrary view, viz. that to breed true to strain, is best in the case of man, as in the case of beast.

It was but natural that these herdsmen should, as the result of experience, so conclude as regards their herds; and the aloofness of settlements and the perpetual feuds with the hillmen also powerfully encouraged intermarriage among them. The non-propagandist type of their faith and the recommendation to marry within the faith also militated to increase the intensity of interbreeding.

The Parsis have limited next-of-kin marriage to marriage of first cousins, which they yet favor.

It was, however, already, when the Zend Avesta was compiled, so recognized a valid duty to intermarry that (Vendidad, Fargard VIII, c. II, 13) much could be forgiven "a man or woman who hath married the next-of-kin," meaning thereby a man or woman who is father or mother, a brother or sister, or another who is closely related.

In the Zend and Pahlavi books, however, many instances of, and many arguments for, marriage of brother and sister and even of father and daughter, quoting, as an example of the former, the wedding of the first parents of mankind and, as an example of the latter, the fabled intercourse between Ahura Mazda and his daughter, Vohu Manah.[2]

It is also not necessary thus to explain away this tenet, since such was also the rule in Egypt of old where the marriage of brother and sister was ever very especially favored.

Next-of-kin marriage was deemed so holy that the Shayast-La-Shayast related that Ahriman could not touch it in any way (c. XVIII, 1-3) and the Bahman Yast records (c. II, 58):

[2] "Pure Zoroastrianism never advocated it; it was practiced by non-Zoroastrian Persians; it was advocated at least during the Sassanian and early Arab periods by a Magianized priesthood; it appears to have been a theoretical ideal, prompted by the religious and political situation of the period; it was constantly resisted (even as an ideal) by a large—and doubtless, ever increasing—body of the faithful; it has disappeared." Hastings, *Encyc. of Ethics and Religion.*

"God spake unto Zoroaster, saying, ' . . . the most perfectly righteous is he that is steadfast in the good religion of the worshippers of God (Ahura Mazda) and continues the pious practice of next-of-kin marriage in his family.' "

Notwithstanding which, it was also, in the books, being firmly adhered to; for the Dadistan-i-Dinik (c. LXXVII, 4-6) says:

"The man and woman were by him (Ahura Mazda) also made to lust and thereby became father and mother of mankind upon the earth. . . . And the law and the religion authorized this as a proper desire; so long as in those who are related, but not in those who are not related, and with them who form next-of-kin unions through their own sense of duty and desire for more progeny, the entire progress of the world is joined and will flow therefrom until the end of the world."

According to Menuk-i-Khrat, next-of-kin marriage was the second of the good works (26) and its dissolution fourth in heinousness (71).

The equal social position of woman, so different from that which exists among the near-by peoples of the Orient, is indicated in this from the Nasks (Erpatistan, Fargard I, first part, 5):

" 'Which of the two shall officiate as priest, the mistress or the master of the house? And, if either is better fitted to carry on the farm, which shall go forth? 'If the master of the house carry on the farm, the woman shall go forth; if the woman carry on the farm, the master of the house shall go forth.' "

The Yast (XXII, c. II, 18) speaks of the virtue of a wife thus, "the saintly woman, rich in good thoughts, good words and good deeds, well-principled and obedient to her husband"; and at another place (V. 36) of "the devilish woman, rich in evil thoughts, evil words and evil deeds, evil religion, ill-principled and disobedient to her husband."

The Dinkard (IX, 639) says of the frequency of propagation:

"Frequent repetition of the act of propagating the offspring is an act of great worth."

The Menuk-i-Khrat (12) demands abstinence from adultery, saying:

"Thou shouldst be an abstainer from the wives of others; because all these three would become disregarded by thee, alike wealth, alike body and alike soul."

CHAPTER XX

RIGHTS OF THE SEXES

"Therefore, let the people learn by heart this holy text, 'He that doth not eat, hath not strength to perform the arduous labor of a holy life, hath not strength to do the work of husbandry, hath not strength to beget children.' "

Thus speaks the Vendidad (Fargard III, c. III, 33) like a modern work on biology.

Here is another passage, connecting overnutrition and propagation in a manner which would do credit to a modern zoölogist, discussing the multiplication of unicellular organisms and making his deductions therefrom:

"Quadrupeds walked forth on the land, fish swam in the waters and birds flew about in the air; in every pair of them, at the time good feeding was enjoyed, a longing arose therefrom, pregnancy and birth" (Selections of Zad-Sparam, Appendix to Bundahis, c. IX, 9).

The duty, above all things, to defend and protect every expectant mother, whether woman or beast, the Vendidad (Fargard XV, c. IIb, 19) enjoined upon every human being, saying:

"It is incumbent upon those of the faith to watch over every pregnant female, two-footed or four-footed, two-footed woman or four-footed beast."

And, as regards the pregnant beast, it is elsewhere recorded (Vendidad, Fargard XV, c. III, 45):

"Atar,[1] the son of God (Ahura Mazda) watches over her as well as over a woman."

The Sirozah Murdad (I, c. XI, 7) mentions among the objects of the sacred sacrifices:

"We sacrifice . . . unto the females that bring forth flocks of males."

The Shayast-La-Shayast (c. XII, 3) commends and commands those comforts which make for higher birth-rate:

"The rule is that they keep a fire in the house because, from not keeping the fire properly, there arise less pregnancy of women and lamentations for men's loss of virility."

In the same book (c. XII, 7) this is said of childbirth:

"The rule is this, that the labor of childbirth is not to be accomplished at night, except while with the light of a fire, or the stars and moon upon it; for great opposition is connected with it and, in the twentieth of the Husparam Nask, it is shown that over the soul of him who works in the dark, there is more predominance of the evil spirit."

In the Bundahis (c. XVI, 1, 2) instructions are given for birth control, not for preventive purposes, but to produce a larger birth rate, as follows:

"On the nature of generation it is saith in revelation, that a woman when she cometh out from menstruation, during ten days and nights, when they go near unto her, readily becometh pregnant. When she is cleansed from her menstruation, and when the time for pregnancy hath come, always when the seed of the man is the more powerful, a son arises from it; when that

[1] Atar, the god of fire.

of the woman is more powerful, a daughter; when both seeds are equal, twins and triplets."

The Bundahis (XIV, 31) offers this explanation, a sort of forecast of modern views of natural selection, for the great impulse, so overmastering, to procreate:

"Many are created in all species of beings, to the end that, when one shall perish through the Evil Spirit, another shall remain."

In a more poetical and less direct fashion, scarcely hinting the truth about it, the Vendidad (Fargard XXI, c. IIIa, 6, 7) makes all the productive powers of the earth servitors of the unborn, thus:

"Of thee, oh child, will I cleanse the birth and growth; of thee, oh woman, will I purify the body and powers. I will make thee rich in progeny and in mind; rich in seed, in milk, in fat, in marrow, and in offspring. I will bring thee a thousand pure springs running to the pastures that give good for the child's support."

The Ashi Yast (c. X, 57, 58) records concerning abortion and adultery:

"The first wailing of the great Ashi Vanguhi [2] is her wailing about the courtesan who destroyeth her fruit. Stand thou not near her; sit thou not upon her bed. . . . The second wailing of the great Ashi Vanguhi is her wailing about the courtesan who bringeth forth a child begotten by a stranger and presenteth it to her husband."

The Zoroastrian scriptures are apparently unusually considerate, however, of the wife who has yielded to temptation and who bears a child for her paramour; for in the Commentary upon Fargard XV of the Vendidad, it is provided that her child shall be received

[2] A demigoddess or angel.

into the family and that the invader of the sanctity of the home shall not be held too strictly to account for his weakness. Of this, the text runs:

"If there hath been no sin in her and if a man, knowing her shame, wisheth to take it off of her, he shall call together her father, mother, sisters, brothers, husband, the servants, the menials and the master and mistress of the house, and he shall say, 'This woman is with child by me, and I rejoice in it'; and they shall answer, 'We know it, and we are glad that her shame is taken off of her'; and he shall support her as a husband doth."

The Dinkard speaks of this:

"That woman should be considered free and innocent who has committed adultery with a stranger but who is proved to have received no aid from other people to save her from the faithless man" (VII, 441).

All the Zoroastrian authorities were by no means so tolerant.

Thus the Dadistan-i-Kinik (c. LXXVIII, 3) urges of adultery that:

"Its modes of theft or spoliation are just as much more heinous than other theft and spoliation, as a man and that which arises from his procreation of his kind are greater in importance than possessions."

Other grounds for reprobating such conduct are there named in part as follows:

"One is this, that it is important to consider the loose life of the adulteress and the evil character assuredly and unquestionably involved. . . .

"One is this, that it may be that she will become pregnant from such intercourse and will feel obliged to commit abortion.

"One is this, that by coming into intercourse with a

man, while she is pregnant, the living child in her womb may die in consequence of that intercourse.

"One is this, that in case she become pregnant through such intercourse and, upon signs thereof, she taketh a drug, in her shame and dread.

"One is this, that a foreign and infidel woman may become pregnant by that intercourse, and give birth to a child, which remaineth in its foreign habits and infidelity, but groweth up to maturity with a child which is recognized to belong to the woman's husband" (Dadistan-i-Dinik, c. LXXVIII, 4-8).

In the Nasks, the behavior of the man who takes the wife of another is thus characterized:

"If the man take her with him to enjoy her body, he is a highwayman, if he do this openly, and a despoiler, if he do it in secret" (Erpatistan Nask, Fargard I, 6).

It is noteworthy that Zoroaster and his followers, though so far from favoring celibacy that they attribute greatly superior virtue to the conjugal state, condemned, as in the foregoing, sexual promiscuity more unsparingly than most other ethical teachers of ancient times.

In the Vistasp Yast (c. VII, 50) already once quoted, is found this condemnation of lust in a woman, coupled with a warning as to consequences:

"The fiend is powerful to distress, and to dry up the milk of, the woman who indulges in lust."

In the Vendidad, the offenses of the promiscuous courtesan are thus reprehended:

"Zoroaster inquired of God (Ahura Mazda) saying, 'Who is it that giveth thee the sorest grief? And who that paineth thee with the keenest pain?'

"The Lord God made answer and said, "It is the

courtesan, oh Spitama Zoroaster, who within her min-gleth the seed of the faithful and of the infidel, of the worshippers of God and the worshippers of demons, of the wicked and the righteous.

"One glance from her drieth up, oh Zoroaster, a third part of the mighty torrents that course down the moun-tains; one glance withereth a third part of the glorious, golden, thriving plants, oh Zoroaster; one glance put-teth to nought, in the man of the faith, a third part of his good thoughts, of his good words and of his good deeds and a third part of his strength, of his trium-phant power and of his holiness.

"Verily say I unto thee, oh Spitama Zoroaster, such beings ought to be slain even more than gliding ser-pents, than howling wolves, than the wild she-wolf that fatteneth upon the fold or the she-frog that descendeth upon the waters with her thousandfold spawn" (Ven-didad, Fargard XVIII, 61-65).

This is more in accord with Eastern practices in this regard than the more merciful rule set up in the Com-mentary and already set forth in these pages, that much is forgiven the erring woman if her paramour come forward to claim her.

Another saying, attributed to a lost passage of the Vendidad, is "that a woman that hath in a single day given up her body unto two men, is sooner to be slain than a lion or a serpent" (Old Rav. 59b).

In the Ashi Yast it is seen, however, that the nega-tive virtue of chastity, even of the very young of both sexes, was so far from being highly regarded by the ancient Persians, that, instead, its possessors, until they tasted the joys and responsibilities of marriage, were classed, as respects their being proper persons to offer the sacrifices, with persons condemned on the ground of sexual misconduct. Of this it says (c. X, 54).

"And the great Ashi Vanguhi said, 'No libation will be acceptable unto me that is offered up to me by a man who is impotent, by a courtesan who produces untimely issues, by young boys or by maidens who have not known man.' "

The chief thing in all sexual intercourse, according to the sacred books of Zoroaster, is that the seed should not be wasted, nor the child destroyed.

In the Vendidad (Fargard XV, c. IIb, 15-16) neglect to support a betrayed woman, with the result that her child is lost, is identified with the crime of murder, thus:

"If a man come near unto a woman, either dependent upon the head of a household or not so dependent, either married or unmarried, and she conceive by him, so long shall he support her, until the child is born. If he shall not support her and on that account the child shall come to grief, he shall for his crime pay the penalty of willful murder."

In the same Fargard (c. IIa and b, 9-13) the guilt of destruction of progeny is further discussed:

"If a man come near unto a woman, either dependent upon the head of a household or not so dependent, either married or unmarried, and she conceive by him, let her not, being ashamed before the people, produce the menses in herself, against the course of nature, by means of water and of plants.

"And if the woman, being ashamed before the people, shall produce the menses within herself against the course of nature, by means of water and plants, it is a fresh sin, as grievous as the first.

"If a man come near unto a woman, either dependent

upon the head of a household or not so dependent, either married or unmarried, and she conceive by him, let her not, being ashamed before the people, destroy the fruit in her womb; and if the woman, ashamed before the people, shall destroy the fruit in her womb, the sin is upon both the man and herself; the murder is both upon him and upon her; both he and she shall pay the penalty for willful murder.

"If a man come near unto a woman, either dependent upon the head of a household or not so dependent, either married or unmarried, and she conceive by him, and she say unto him, 'Lo, I have conceived by thee!' and he answer, 'Go, then, unto the beldame and ask her for a drug that she may procure thee a miscarriage,' and the woman goeth unto the beldame and asketh her for a drug that may procure for her a miscarriage, and the beldame giveth her banga or shaëta, a drug that killeth in the womb or expelleth from the womb, or some other drug that causeth miscarriage, and he say unto her, 'Cause thou thy fruit to perish!' and she cause her fruit to perish, the sin is then upon the heads of all three, the man, the woman and the beldame."

This is really indistinguishable from the modern view of these matters; it proceeds, however, in the Zoroastrian teaching, from the fundamental proposition that to waste the seed is in itself wicked—that any form of birth control, not excepting continence, is evil.

The Dadistan-i-Dinik (c. LXXVII, 11) says of a man who practices it:

"He that wasteth seed, useth to cause the death of progeny. If this were practiced in every case, producing a foul cessation of the procreation of mankind, all human life would come to an end; and certainly conduct, which if indulged in by all, would depopulate the world, is, and furthereth, the dearest wish of Ahriman."

This, also, helped to bring about the utter reprobation of sodomy which the Persians, unlike the more dissolute Greeks, viewed with horror and inexpressible disgust.

The Zend Avesta most explicitly excoriated this crime, saying:

"The Lord God (Ahura Mazda) made answer and said, 'He that lieth with mankind as man lieth with womankind or as a woman lieth with mankind, is a person that is essentially a demon. Such a man is a worshipper of demons, a male paramour of demons, a female paramour of demons, a wife unto a demon. Such a man is as evil as a demon and is in his whole being a demon. Such a man is a demon before he dieth and becometh after death one of the invisible demons. Such is he, whether he hath lain with mankind as mankind or as womankind.'" (Vendidad, Fargard VIII, c. V. 32).

In this connection (Fargard VIII, c. VI, 27) in response to an inquiry concerning atonement for voluntary sodomy, it is related that:

"The Lord God (Ahura Mazda) answered and said, 'For that deed there is nothing that can pay, nothing that can atone, nothing that can wash it away. It is a sin for which there is no atonement forever and ever.'"

The Vendidad (Fargard I, 12) attributed the origin of unnatural vice to Ahriman himself, saying:

"Thereupon came Ahriman, who is all death, and he countercreated a sin for which there is no atonement, the unnatural sin."

CHAPTER XXI

RIGHTS OF THE LAND

"Unhappy is the land that hath long lain unsown with the seed of the sower and wanteth a good husbandman, like unto a well-shapen maiden that hath long gone childless and wanteth a good husband."

Thus speaks the ancient Persian scriptures (Vendidad, Fargard III, c. III, 24) concerning the land's use for tillage—tillage which is one of the most important acts of conformity with the requirements, perhaps the very earliest of man's adjustments to nature's laws and of man's manipulation of nature's forces for his advantage.

In the first chapter of the same Fargard (4) this question is asked and answered:

" 'Oh thou Creator of the material world, thou Holy One, which is the third place where the Earth experienceth the most joy?' God (Ahura Mazda) made reply and answered, saying, 'It is the place where one of the faithful soweth most corn, grass and fruit, oh Spitama Zoroaster, where he irrigateth soil that is dry or draineth soil that is too wet.' "

Agriculture, then, was seen to be a sacred duty to be performed, with devout care, as coöperation with God, himself.

Tradition, as handed down by the Gathas (XXXI, 10) has it that:

"Of these two chose the cow, for herself, the cattle-tending husbandman as its lord according to the Right, the man that advances Good Mind."

It was, according to another of the Gathas (Yasna LI, 14) interference with tillage, in part, which characterized and condemned the marauding Karpans, as guilty of grievous violation of God's law.

"The Karpans will not obey the statutes and ordinances concerning husbandry."

This is also a part of the indictment of the evil-doer in another of the Gathas (Yasna XXXII, 10).

"He that would thus destroy my teaching . . . desolates the pastures and lifts his weapon against the righteous man."

This civilization, which began upon the steppes of Asia and of Europe, centered in the plains settlements, patriarchal in form, with wandering herds and little, protected plots of land, cultivated with care and unflagging application. The duty of the well-meaning man to do his share in this was, therefore, inculcated as a thing of religious and moral import, a part of his service of mankind, and in conjunction with the divine forces, uniformly operating.

The close relationship to this sacred duty of the care of flocks and herds is indicated in the following:

" 'Oh thou Creator of the material world, thou Holy One, which is the fourth place where the Earth experienceth the most joy?' God (Ahura Mazda) made reply and answered, saying, 'It is the place where flocks and herds do most increase' " (Vendidad, Fargard III, c. I, 5).

The duty of fertilization, restoring productiveness to the soil, is enjoined in this passage which follows in turn:

" 'Oh, thou Creator of the material world, thou Holy

One, which is the fifth place where the Earth experienceth the most joy?' God (Ahura Mazda) made reply and answered, saying, 'It is the place where the flocks and herds yield the most dung' " (Idem c. I, 6).

Thus was the duty of diversified farming, such as furnishing fuel and replenishment of the soil, urged upon these plainsmen, as primarily religious and fundamentally ethical—duties sadly neglected even unto, and indeed into, these times, to the impoverishment of many lands, despite our much broader and deeper scientific knowledge of the consequences of neglect to the land.

The Gathas celebrated this sacred service by praying for special blessings upon him who tended herds and tilled the soil:

"Thou art the holy father of this spirit which has created for us the luck-bringing cattle and for its pasture to give it peace, hast created Piety when he had taken counsel, oh God (Ahura Mazda), with the Good Mind" (Yasna XLVII, 3).

This applied likewise and indeed very particularly to the well-to-do; their wealth imposed upon them all the greater obligation.

Thus, as regards hunting as a sport, it is brought down to us through the Shayast-La-Shayast (c. VIII, 3) that:

"It is not allowable that, because of their dexterity as horsemen, men may hunt nor for others to hunt for game, unless their wealth is smaller than three hundred stires."

The origin of plants is thus accounted for in the Zend Avesta:

"These plants, I, God (Ahura Mazda), do rain down upon the earth, to bring food unto the faithful and fodder to the beneficent cow—to bring food to my people, that they may thrive thereon, and fodder to the beneficent cow" (Fargard V, c. IV, 20).

The legend was that, until the Evil One made his countercreations, all the plant life of the earth was for sustenance or for healing.

Thus the Bundahis (c. XXVII, 1) repeats this idea, succinctly as follows:

"Of the nature of plants, it saith in revelation that, before the coming of the destroyer, vegetation had no thorn or bark about it; but, afterwards, when the destroyer came, it became coated over with bark and thorns, for antagonism mingled with every single thing; owing to that cause, vegetation is also much mixed with poison."

When it is recalled that evil, to the mind of Zoroaster, is that which destroys and good that which protects and preserves, this becomes not unlike the modern, scientific method of accounting for such devices, viz. that they were developed as a means of protection against the evil foe without and therefore, in a very real sense, owed their existence to the existence of that foe.

Nowhere, in this holy writ, are the merits of productive industry and the holiness of labor celebrated to better effect than in this famous passage of the Vendidad (Fargard III, c. III 25-29):

"He who shall till the earth, oh Spitama Zoroaster, with the left arm and the right, with the right arm and the left, unto him will she bring forth plenty of fruit; even as were it a lover resting with his bride upon her bed, the bride would bring forth children, so shall the earth also teem with fruit for him!

"He who shall till the earth, oh Spitama Zoroaster,

with the left arm and the right, with the right arm and the left, unto him thus the earth speaketh, 'Oh thou man, who dost till me with the left arm and the right, with the right arm and the left, here shall I ever go on, bearing, bringing forth all manner of good, bringing first unto thee my grain.'

"He who doth not till the earth, oh Spitama Zoroaster, with the left arm and the right, with the right arm and the left, unto him thus the earth speaketh, 'Oh, thou man who dost not till me with the left arm and the right, with the right arm and the left, ever shalt thou stand at the door of the stranger among them that beg for bread; the refuse and the crumbs of bread shall be given unto thee, given by them that have a plenteous store.' "

In the same connection and immediately following this passage, the following question is asked and answered:

" 'Oh thou Creator of the material world, thou Holy One, what food is that, wherewith the religion of God is filled?'

"God (Ahura Mazda) made reply and answered, saying: 'He that soweth corn, soweth also righteousness; he maketh God's religion to go forward, he nourisheth the religion of God, as much as could he with the feet of a hundred men, with the breasts of a thousand women—yea, with ten thousand sacrificial ceremonies.

" 'When barley was created, the demons were startled; as it grew, the demons' hearts failed within them; as the bloom came, the demons groaned; and as the ear formed, the demons fled aghast. In that house dwell the demons where wealth decays; if there be a store of grain, it is as if red-hot iron were turned about in their throats.

" 'Therefore, let the people learn by heart this holy text, "He that doth not eat, hath not strength to perform the arduous labor of a holy life, hath not strength to do the work of husbandry, hath not strength to beget children. It is by eating that every creature in this world hath life and, by failing to eat, it dieth soon away." ' "

The Shayast-La-Shayast (c. X, 18) in this naïve passage accounts for famines, at the same time ascribing to them depopulation, not merely because of too many deaths but also because of too few births:

"The rule is this, that, when in any land they put their trust in a false judge and maintain him over them, in that land, owing to the wrong and injustice which that judge committeth, the clouds and showers become deficient, a portion of the deliciousness, fatness, wholesomeness and milk of all cattle and goats fails and many children are destroyed in their mothers' wombs."

This connection, when not interrupted by conscious birth control, between a liberal diet and an increase of population, which has been deemed a discovery of Adam Smith as regards humanity and political economy and, as regards all life, a modern scientific hypothesis, was not unknown, then, in the days of Zoroaster nor by them unappreciated.

It is significant that his notion of the right is that there should be both the plenty and the increase and that virtue is to be found in that which makes for the preservation and proliferation of human beings. This, it will later appear, is really a cardinal principle in the ethics of Zoroaster.

In the Aban Yast (c. I, 1) it is related that God (Ahura Mazda) spake unto Zoroaster, saying:

"Offer thou up a sacrifice, oh Spitama Zoroaster, unto
this spring of mine, Ardvi Sura Anahita, the wide-
spreading and health-giving, that hateth the demons
and obeyeth God's laws; that is worthy of sacrifice in
the material world and worthy of prayer in the material world; the life-increasing and holy, the wealth-
increasing and holy, the land-increasing and holy, the
herd-increasing and holy, the fold-increasing and holy;
that purifieth the seed of all males, that purifieth the
wombs of all females for bearing, that maketh all
females to bring forth with safety, that putteth milk
into the breasts of all females in right measure and
richness."

That this religion of the preservation of human life,
and of the fructifying power of the earth to that end,
declared what is right for all men in all times, is implied
in this famous passage of the Vendidad (Fargard I):

"Lo, I have made every land dear unto its people,
though it possess no charm whatever!"

And in this answer which, according to the Zend
Avesta, God also vouchsafed Zoroaster, the life of the
diligent husbandman is given its due meed of praise,
as one of true piety, in words very nearly duplicating
a passage already quoted:

" 'Oh, thou Maker of the material world, thou Holy
One, who is the fourth that rejoiceth the earth with
greatest delight?'

"God (Ahura Mazda) made answer and said, 'It is
he that planteth most corn, grass and fruit trees, oh
Spitama Zoroaster, who watereth the ground when dry
or draineth the ground when too wet' " (Vendidad,
Fargard III, c. III, 23).

In such esteem was the husbandman held that one
refused alms to one of the faith of them who were in

distress, at the peril of his soul; for of such the Vendidad says:

"He who hath not with kindness and humility given of his bounty unto one of the faith that tilleth the earth, oh Spitama Zoroaster, life will surely cast him down into darkness, down into torment, into hell, into the bottomless abyss (Fargard III, c. III, 35).

CHAPTER XXII

RIGHTS OF THE HERD

The Good Mind, which underlies all morality, is then not merely the exercise of reason pure and simple, but its exercise to forward the fostering care of every beneficial creature, the "carefulness" which it was Zoroaster's expressed mission to promote.

It was, accordingly, the prime essential of the Zoroastrian creed that unless the fall of a sparrow was beneath the benevolent notice of God, and, what is more to the purpose, that its loving care is the plain duty of man, he must not leave the exercise of this Good Mind toward God's creatures to their creator, alone, but must do his part in all regards, with intelligence and eager willingness.

This religion, as has been said, sprang up in very primitive days among the herdsmen on the plains of Asia, which are now in Persia or in Russia, or near there, about the Caspian Sea.

It found its very conatus in the protection of these settlements and their herds of cattle from marauders who sallied forth from mountain fastnesses to prey upon the possessions of the husbandmen and who left a trail of pillage, of rapine and of ruthless destruction of men and beasts behind them. Against these would-be "supermen" of that day, with the "will of power," the herdsmen asked succor from the beneficent forces of the universe, crying unto God:

"Can my soul count on anyone to shelter? Who is there found for my herd, who for myself a protector indeed, save as I apply to the Right and to thee, oh God (Ahura Mazda) and to the Good Mind" (Yasna L, 1)?

The first contrast of sorts of human conduct, therefore, among the denizens of the plain was between banditry and husbandry, between the wanton destruction of herds and their care. Thus the Gathas proclaim:

"Thine was Piety, thou the Ox-Creator, even wisdom of spirit, oh God (Ahura Mazda), for thou gavest the cattle their choice whether to depend on a husbandman or on one who is no husbandman" (Yasna XXXI, 9).

That is, by what was, in fact, directed natural selection, the cattle prospered under the care of the herdsmen.

The selection of Zoroaster as the prophet of God is ascribed by the Gathas (Yasna XXIX, 1-3) to the cry of the cow for a defender against the brigand, in this passage:

"Unto thee, the soul of the ox cried, lamenting, 'For whom madest thou me? Who hast created me? Violence and rapine hast oppressed me, outrage and might. Other than thee, herdsman have I none. Prepare for me then the blessings of pasture?' Thereupon, the Creator of the ox asked of the Right, 'Hast thou a judge for the ox that ye may be able to appoint him zealous tendance as well as fodder? Whom do ye will to be his lord that he may drive off violence, with the followers of the lie.' To him the Right made answer, 'There is for the ox no helper that can keep harm from him. Those yonder have no knowledge how right-doers act toward the lowly.' "

That is to say, the masterful, who mistake possession

of the riches created by those whom they despoil, for real blessings, yet prey upon God's creatures, failing to discern that his plan is that all be blest by that which alone can bless them, service of one another and of all of God's beneficent creatures.

This conception, that God in the world stands for beneficence and for the protection of the beneficent against the maleficent, finds utterance again in the Gathas in the piteous appeal of the ox, when apprized that Zoroaster, a mere mortal, had been deputed to defend her (Yasna XXIX, 9).

"Thereupon the soul of the ox lamented, 'That I must be content with the ineffectual word of an impotent man for my guide when I wish for one that commands with might. Whenever shall it be that one shall give me the best of help?' "

What their herds meant to this people of the plain, the Bahman Yast (c. XX, 61) puts in these words:

"In the ox is our strength, in the ox our reliance; in the ox our boasting, in the ox our victory; in the ox our food, in the ox our raiment; in the ox tillage that causeth food to come forth for us!"

That this must have been no overstatement, is clear from the fact that among these primitive people of the plain, scarcely any domestic animal, other than cattle and the plainsman's dog, is mentioned. Horses or even asses they seem to have been mostly unacquainted with, pigs utterly so and sheep very nearly so. The cattle meant meat, milk, cheese and butter for man's support; hides for raiment, shoes, tents, water-bottles, drayage, transportation, ploughing, even dung for his fire—no small matter on the arid plain where other fuel was often unobtainable—and for fertilization.

Cattle were, therefore, a large part of the wealth of

the plainsman, sometimes his all. To him, also, their helplessness against assaults by marauders appealed for aid to him as their master, as the helper ordained by nature to protect the herd.

There was no escape from the conclusion that, whether he acted out of a sense of responsibility or merely to protect his own interest and from motives of selfishness purely, it was his duty to defend these dumb brutes against the spoiler.

That righteous rule begins with, and is based upon, defense and preservation of the herds, is thus cele- brated in the Gathas:

"Let him that ruleth well, reign over us! Let not him that ruleth ill, reign over us! Let it be with the actions according to good lore, oh Piety. Perfect thou for man, oh thou most good, the future birth and for the cow—skilled husbandry. Let her grow fat for our nourishing" (Yasna XLVIII, 5).

This fostering care the Shayast-La-Shayast (c. XV, 10) enjoins upon the man who would propitiate the divine Good Mind, that he "should keep them (the kine) in a warm place"; that "in summer he should provide for them a store of straw and grain, to the end that it be not necessary to turn them out to graze in the winter"; and that "he should not separate them from their young nor bar their young from their udders; for they are the counterpart in the world of the divine Good Mind."

Zoroaster, in accepting his mission, including provision for cattle, prayed that he might be equal to the burden laid upon him, saying:

"With outspread hands in petition for that help, oh God (Ahura Mazda), first I will pray for the works of the holy spirit, oh Right, that I may please the will of the Good Mind and the ox soul"(Yasna XXVIII, 1).

And this joint supplication is found elsewhere in the Gathas (Yasna XXIX, 5):

"To God (Ahura Mazda) with outspread hands, we twain would pray, my soul and that of the pregnant cow, so that we twain urge God with entreaties. Destruction is not for the right-living nor for the cattle-tender, at the hand of the liars."

In the Gathas, also, this appeal against the marauders is made unto God:

"This I ask, what penalty is for him who seeks to achieve kingship for a liar, for the man of ill deeds, oh God (Ahura Mazda) who finds not his living without injury to the husbandman's cattle and men, though he does him no harm" (Yasna XXXI, 15).

For the despoilers quick destruction was petitioned for in these words:

"So they whose deeds are evil, let them be the deceived; let them all howl, abandoned in ruin" (Yasna LIII, 8).

The Vistasp Yast (c. VI, 41) enjoins care of cattle upon the faithful, fostering care even in times when no danger threatens, saying:

"Three times each day rise and go look after man's benefactors, the cattle."

And the Gathas prophesy thus an evil fate for them who destroy these dumb friends of humankind:

"The Karpans will not obey thy statutes and ordinances concerning husbandry. For the pain they inflict on the cattle, fulfill upon them, through their actions and judgments, that judgment which at the last shall bring them to the house of the lie" (Yasna LI, 14).

On the contrary, the poet and prophet of the Lord would shield from harm the cowherds of the plain, saying of this (Yasna XXXIII, 4):

"I who by my worship would keep far from thee, oh God (Ahura Mazda), disobedience and bad thought, heresy from the nobles, and from the community the lie that is most near, and from the brotherhood the slanderers and from the pasture of the cattle the worst herdsman."

CHAPTER XXIII

RIGHTS OF THE DOG

"If those two, my dogs, the shepherd dog and the watch dog, pass any house of mine, let them not be driven upon it; for upon the earth created by God (Ahura Mazda) could no house abide, were it not for these two, my dogs, the shepherd dog and the watch dog."

Thus the Zoroastrian scriptures (Vendidad, Fargard XIII, c. IX, 49) enjoin, as a prime duty, the exercise of the Good Mind, of the benevolent disposition, of fostering care, toward that other faithful friend and companion of the plainsman, his dog. He seems, next to the herd, the first of their claimants upon man.

In another place in the same Fargard (c. II, 8) the following warning is given against beating one of these friends of man:

"Whosoever shall strike a shepherd dog, a house dog, a stray dog or a hunting dog, when the soul of that man shall pass into the other world, it shall go howling louder and grieved more sorely than goeth the sheep in the great forest where the wolf rangeth."

In another place (Vendidad, Fargard XIII, c. VI, 39) the following account of the virtues of the dog is ascribed to God, himself:

"The dog, oh Spitama Zoroaster, I, God (Ahura Mazda), have created self-clad and self-shod, watchful and wakeful, sharp-fanged, born to accept his sustenance at the hand of man and to safeguard the goods of man. I, God, have made the dog mighty in strength against the evil-doer, when of sound disposition, and watchful over man's goods; and neither the thief nor the wolf shall, without an alarm, fetch aught from the house of the man who arouseth at the dog's outcry. Nay, the wolf shall be beaten and torn; he hasteneth away, he melteth away like the snow."

And in yet another place (Fargard XIII, c. X, 50) the Vendidad says:

"He that killeth a water dog bringeth about a drought which drieth up the pastures."

The Vendidad (Fargard XIII, c. V, 35-37) commands thus, even as regards a dog which, by reason of sickness, has become transformed from a beneficent friend of man into a maleficent being:

" 'Oh, thou Creator of the material world, thou Holy One, if there be in the house of a worshipper of God (Ahura Mazda) a cross dog, who hath lost his scent, what shall thy worshippers do in respect to him?' God answered and made reply, saying, 'They shall attend him to heal him as they would do in respect to one of the faithful.' "

It is also provided that, if the dog cannot be healed, he is to be protected against injuring others or himself and that, in case, for want of that protection, he shall come to grief, the persons responsible for his unguarded state shall be "Peshotanus" or outlaws, until purified by penitence and penances.

The dog, however, was also held to strict accountability for injury to innocent passers-by, as well as those responsible for his unguarded state; and provision for this was also made, thus:

" 'Oh thou Creator of the material world, thou Holy One, if there be in the house of a worshipper a cross

dog that biteth without barking, what shall thy worshippers do in respect to him?' God (Ahura Mazda)
answered and made reply, saying, 'They shall place
about his neck a collar of wood and thereto fasten a
muzzle. . . . If they shall not do this and the dog shall
bite without barking, falling upon a sheep or wounding
a man, the dog shall suffer for the wound he inflicted
as for willful murder'" (Vendidad, Fargard XIII, c.
V, 29-31).

The obedience of the dog and his dependence upon
the will of man and the consequent duty of man toward
this faithful friend and helper are set forth by the Vendidad in this connection (Fargard XIII, c. IV, 28) in
these words:

"For in this material world, oh Spitama Zoroaster, it
is the dog, of all the creatures of the Good Mind, that
most quickly becometh old, not eating, though beside
people eating, and guarding goods, none of which he
receiveth. Bring ye milk and flesh, fat and lean, unto
him; this is food fit for the dog."

And again in the same chapter (20) the question is
asked and answered:

" 'Oh thou Creator of the material world, thou Holy
One, if a man give unto a shepherd dog bad food, of
what sin doth he make himself guilty?' God (Ahura
Mazda) answered and made reply, saying, 'He maketh
himself guilty of the same sin as though he should
serve bad food to a master of a house of the first
rank.' "

The duty of man, not merely to avoid giving bad or
poisonous food to a dog, but also to watch carefully
that the food is not dangerous to him because of sharp
bones, such as chicken or fish bones, or because too hot,
is enjoined in this:

"If the bones stick in the dog's teeth or clog his throat or if the food, being too hot, burn his mouth or tongue, he may come to grief thereby; and if he come to grief thereby, the man who hath done the deed becometh a Peshotanu" (Vendidad, Fargard XV, c. I, 4).

It is well worthy of note that, despite the emphasis laid upon good purpose everywhere in the Zoroastrian scriptures, good intention must accord with the exercise also of good sense, in order that the Good Mind, which is the cardinal virtue, be truly exercised; therefore the careless act, which results in injury, is judged by its consequences and condemned as gravely wrong.

The Good Mind not merely means well, but also really takes care; else it is not accepted as genuine.

The later writings give an account of creation, not out of accord, also, with certain passages, yet extant, of the older writings, which ascribe certain forms of life to the Evil One; thus the Bundahis (c. III, 15) says of Ahriman:

"And noxious creatures were diffused by him over the earth, biting and venomous, such as the snake, scorpion, toad and lizard."

And again (c. XIX, 30) says of this:

"The conclusion is this, that of all beasts and birds and fishes, every one is created over against some noxious creature," i.e. for the purpose of overcoming the evil done by that creature as, for instance, the vulture overcomes the evil done by the bacilli of disintegration.

The evil of these noxious creations of Ahriman consists, however, in their evil mind, that is their disposition to injure and their cunning in inflicting injury; and they are judged sharply thereby as in this concerning hybrids between the shepherd dog and the wolf:

" 'Oh thou Creator of the material world, thou Holy one, which of two wolves deserveth more to be slain, he that a he-dog hath begotten upon a she-wolf or he that a he-wolf hath begotten upon a she-dog?' God (Ahura Mazda) answered and made reply, saying, 'Of these two wolves, the one that a he-dog hath begotten upon a she-wolf deserveth more to be slain than the one that a he-wolf hath begotten upon a she-dog" (Vendidad, Fargard XIII, c. VII, 41, 42).

The reason ascribed is that such offspring "are more murderous, more malicious, more destructive to the folds" than any others, be they dogs or wolves.

The necessity for ascribing to the Evil One the creation of beings possessed of an evil mind, because indeed the evil mind is the very essence of the Evil One and because, if not possessed of it, no creature, however lowly, is evil, caused the Bundahis to make this declaration (c. XIX, 36) which is really one of confession and avoidance:

"God (Ahura Mazda) hath created nothing that is not useful; for all things are made for use."

CHAPTER XXIV

MAN'S RIGHTS IN EATING AND DRINKING

THE Zoroastrian scriptures are extraordinarily silent concerning habits of eating or of drinking, except that so far is fasting from being enjoined that it is roundly condemned as evil. Yet it is said that before the millennium mankind will gradually wean itself from eating until able to subsist without it.

There is no food, fit for human consumption, that is treated as taboo.

Since conversation and gayety usually go with feasting, it may well be that the following from the Dadistan-i-Dinik, if well enforced, rendered all other expostulations unnecessary:

"It is commanded, before eating, when the mouth is not soiled with food, that the mouth proceed to utter a silent prayer of praise. Thereafter, being duly seated and having duly eaten, one is to cleanse the mouth with a toothpick and water; and, at the close of the meal, before speaking, the praise of sacred beings is again celebrated by the mouth so cleansed. And between the grace before eating and the grace after eating, one is not to speak and if during the meal the mouth shall utter a word, the grace to be said, before eating and after, must be repeated. Every individual organ hath one function but two functions are connected with the mouth, speaking and eating; and because so connected, they are antagonistic, one to the

183

other, for speaking is from the thought within to the instruction without and eating fetcheth food from without to sustain life within. As the ancients have said, where one organ hath two functions, it is particularly true that two operations, such as speaking and eating, should not both be performed at the same time. In order that those operations be kept distinct, one from the other, it is decreed to be inconsistent with virtue that the practice of uttering praise and glorification of sacred beings, while the mouth is in the act of eating and until it hath been cleansed of food, be indulged in" (c. XL, 7-12).

This practice perhaps illustrates the tendency of later Parsi teachers to meet new issues by inferences as to what nature's law calls for, and what could be more natural than that an organ, such as the mouth, fitted to perform two functions, to eat and to speak, should at a given time be devoted to one of them to the exclusion of the other?

Concerning wine, there is an utter absence of reference to it in the older Zoroastrian scriptures, as if the use of it, or in any case the abuse of it, had been almost, or totally, unknown among the dwellers on the plains, as indeed may well have been the case.

As the famous passage in the Rubaiyat indicates, the Persians, perhaps because, owing to their lighter and more equable temperament, less prone to excesses than other races about them, have not been disposed to take too seriously the prohibition of wine drinking by the rules of the religion which has, by brutal force of arms, displaced that of Zoroaster in their land.

In the Dadistan-i-Dinik, written after contact with other peoples, having other habits and other views of ethics, had made the question an important one, the

subject is treated, with great moderation, but in a way
intended to be exhaustive, as follows:

"The fiftieth question is that which you ask, thus:
As to one of the good religion who drinks wine immoderately, and loss and injury happen to him owing
to that immoderate drinking, what is then the decision
about him? And how is the measure of wine drinking
which, when they drink, is then authorized for them?

"The reply is this, that whoever through the influ-
ence of opportunity drinks wine immoderately, and is
adult and intelligent, through every loss and injury
which thereupon come to him from that immoderate
drinking, or which occasion anything unto any one, is
then causing such pollution to the creatures, in his
own pleasurably varied modes, that the shame owing to
it is a help out of that affliction.

"And even he who gives wine authorizedly unto any
one, and he is thereby intoxicated by it, is equally
guilty of every sin which that drunkard commits owing
to that drunkenness.

"And concerning that drunkenness, what is said is
that that is to be eaten through which, when one eats
it, one thinks better and acts better; and such even is
the food by which, through having drunk wine, one
becomes more virtuous, or does not become more vicious, in thought, word, and deed. When an experiment
as regards its being good is tried, so that having drunk
it in that proportion one becomes better, or does not
become worse, then it is allowable to drink it.

"When an untried person, for the sake of being tried,
has drunk a mingled portion, first of one drinking cup,
secondly of two drinking cups, and thirdly of three
drinking cups, and through 'drinking it he becomes
more virtuous, or does not become more vicious, in

thought, word or deed, he may increase the drinking
cups, and the experiment is allowable unto those tested
just so far as the proportion is such that he becomes
better, or does not become worse. To those tested, it is
authorizedly given to that amount through which the
experimenting that is mentioned has extended; and
to him who, it is proved, will become worse through
the drinking of wine, that amount, through the drinking of which, when given in the experiment, it was seen
that he became worse, is not authorizedly given" (Part
II, c. LI).

The right and wrong of wine selling also could not
fail to come forward for discussion, when the trade
came to be viewed as disgraceful because of the growing number of those who found evil in the abuse of intoxicants; for the followers of Zoroaster have ever
prided themselves upon their adherence to those things
which are of good report and upon eschewing all conduct which falls under just condemnation.

Accordingly, the Dadistan-i-Dinik also takes this
subject under consideration, with the following exceed-
ingly moderate and just observations:

"The fifty-ninth question is that you ask thus: If
they should sell wine unto foreigners and infidels, what
is then the decision about it?

"The reply is this, that there is very vehement danger of grievous sin, and it would be an evil occupation,
except if through the operation of that wine selling of
theirs the wine is kept more away from those who
become worse through immoderate drinking of wine,
and comes to those who drink wine in moderation—
whom they cause to become better through drinking
the wine" (Part II, c. L).

Whatever may be thought about the wisdom of preventing, so far as that is possible, the manufacture, sale and use of intoxicants as a measure of precaution against the demoralization of men or on hygienic grounds, there can be little question that, as a matter of ethics, this is much sounder than the extravagant assertions, often indulged in, regarding the inherent sinfulness of the use, manufacture or sale of that, which is often a danger, but which may also be safely enjoyed if in strict moderation.

In any event, these are good ethical rules for those who use wine or who sell it; and they were rules made for them and for their guidance, only.

CHAPTER XXV

EARTHLY REWARDS AND PUNISHMENTS

"Even that way of the Good Mind, oh God (Ahura Mazda) of which thou didst speak to me, whereon, a way well made by the Right, the souls of the future benefactors shall pass to the reward prepared for the wise as thou determineth, oh God."

Thus the Gathas (Yasna XXXIV, 13) give assurance of real blessings for them who live good lives upon the earth.

That this is true while yet in the flesh, as well as after death, the Shayast-La-Shayast thus inculcates (c. XX, 10):

"This, also, that he whose deeds are for the spirit, the world is his and the world of spirit yet more is his; while he whose deeds are for the body, is subject to the will of the world of spirit which snatches from him this world, whether he will or no."

The same notion, i.e. that the man who is blinded by material things cannot divine the spiritual, though he be thwarted by it constantly, is set forth in the Nasks (Tahmura's Fragments, c. XLV, 101, 102):

"There be many works of wisdom that the soul may not conceive nor any tongue declare, without the Holy Word."

That is, without thought upon, and insight into, revealed truth.

Zoroaster in no wise commended fasting or emaciation. Of this the Vendidad speaks thus:

188

"And of two men, he that filleth himself with meat, receiveth in him the Good Mind much better than he who doth not so. The latter is all but dead; the former is above him by the worth of an asperena, by the worth of a sheep, by the worth of an ox, by the worth of a man.

"This man can strive against the onsets of Astovidhotu; he can strive against the well-darted arrow; he can strive against the winter fiend, with thinnest garment on; he can strive against the wicked tyrant and smite him on the head; he can strive against the ungodly, fasting Ashemaögha (Vendidad, Fargard IV, c. IIIb, 48, 49).

In the Zoroastrian scripture (Gathas, Yasna LI, 1) appears this promise:

"The good, the precious Dominion, as a most surpassing portion, shall the Right achieve for him that zealously does what is best with his deeds, oh God (Ahura Mazda). This will I bring about for us at every now."

This best is, both here and hereafter, doubtless that which the Nask (II, Zend Fragments, 4) promises, saying:

"Good renown here below and long bliss unto the soul."

As regards the hereafter, it is the pronouncement of God, recorded in another of the Nasks (Tahmura's Fragments, XXV, 45) that:

"Such an one, oh Spitama Zoroaster, shall there arrive as the strongest of the strong, who here below most powerfully impelleth the righteous unto good works."

As regards this life on earth, the Bundahis (c. XXIV, 30) affirms:

"The conclusion is this, that everyone who performeth a great duty, hath then much value."

And the Nasks (Tahmura's Fragments, XL, 90) say of this, most aptly:

"To obtain the treasures of the material world, oh Spitama Zoroaster, forego not the world of spirit."

In another place (Tahmura's Fragments, c. XLII, 94) the Nasks thus celebrate the wisdom of "seeking according to right," by this declaration:

"All these things, that one is in accordance with the Right procureth, oh Spitama Zoroaster; it procureth all good things, food and drink—however great, however good, however to be desired."

It is written in the Gang-i Shayigan of charity:

"Nay even the kingship of the kings of this world and the wealth that accompanies it will not last; but the deeds of charity done by one in his good times will be everlasting and indestructible."

The promise of God (Ahura Mazda) unto the pure in heart, who call upon the sacred name in time of trial, is thus recorded in the Srosh Yast (Hadhokht, c. I, 4, 5):

"And he who should pronounce that word, oh Zoroaster, either a man or a woman, with a mind all intent on holiness, with words all intent on holiness, with deeds all intent on holiness, when he is in fear either of high waters or of the darkness of a rainy night;

"Or at the ford of a river, or at the branching-off of roads;

"Or in the meeting together of the faithful, or the rushing together of the worshippers of the demons;

"Whether on the road or in the law he has to fear, not in that day nor in that night shall the tormenting fiend, who wisheth to torment him, prevail to throw upon him the look of his evil eye, and the malice of the thief who carrieth off cattle shall not reach him."

It is, notwithstanding their reliance upon nature's unchanging order, upon the event of providential interference, so far reaching as this, that the Vendidad (Fargard IV, c. IV, a, 46) prescribed the trial of an accused by ordeal, in these words:

"Before the boiling water, publicly prepared, oh Spitama Zoroaster, let no man be so bold as to deny having received the ox or the garment that is in his possession!"

Of this the Nasks (Tahmura's Fragments, c. LIV, 116, 117) say:

"And, though he may bribe the judge, he cannot bribe the ordeal and escape it."

The Dinkard thus speaks of it:

"And robbery is this: whoever speaks about the wealth which is not his own, thus, 'Would that it were mine'" (XII, 3)!

The protection of God was not withheld, either, according to the Zoroastrian scriptures, from the man who, by reason of his dire poverty, had not been able to perform all the services of devotion; of this the Nirangistan Nask (III, 52) says:

"If a worthy man,

"Working hard and teaching the Holy Wisdom,

"Have no sufficient living

"And dream of getting sufficient meat;

"If such a one only recite (the prayers),

"He who celebrates the festival cannot charge him with non-celebration;

"For as far as he recites (the prayers), he has celebrated the festival."

The Zoroastrians, as time went on, were evidently

more and more put to it to account, on this theory, for the greater prosperity in this world of many who were not of their faith or whose lives, by their canons, were openly evil. Accordingly, the Dadistan-i-Dinik thus discusses that problem:

"The fifth question is that you ask thus: Why doth evil always happen more to the good than to the evil?

"The reply is this, that not at every time and every place, and not to all the good, doth evil happen more— for the spiritual welfare of the good is certainly greater. ... This, too, is more particularly such as the ancients have said, that the labor and trouble of the good are much more in the world, and their reward and recompense are more certain in the spiritual existence; and the comfort and pleasure of the bad are more in the world, and their pain and punishment in the spiritual existence are more severe; and this, too, is the cause, that the good, through fear of the pain and punishment of hell, should forsake comfort and ease in the world, and should not think, speak, or do anything improper whatever and, through hope for the comfort and pleasure in Heaven, they should accept willingly, as their yoke, much trouble and fear in the practice of virtue in thought, word, and deed.

"The bad, through being provided with the temporary enjoyment—even that enjoyment of improprieties for which eventually there is hell—then enjoy themselves therein temporarily, and lustfully on account of self-gratification; those various actions also, through which there would be a path to Heaven, they do not trouble themselves with; and in this way, in the world, the comfort and pleasure of the bad are more, and the anxiety, vexation, despondency and distress of the good have become greater. The reason is revealed by the stars" [1] (c. VI, 1-9).

The Aögemaïde Nask (82) offers this briefer but clearer statement of the difference between the rewards:

"The wicked acquire cattle, the wicked acquire horses, the wicked acquire sheep and corn, but the wicked tyrant doth not acquire a store of good deeds!"

The most ancient writings, however, troubled themselves not at all about these things; but cried triumphantly, as in this from the Nasks:

"There is only the path of righteousness. All other paths are no paths. It is religion, the exterminator of Ahriman, that rendeth in pieces the demon worshippers, the men who live in sin" (Sundry Fragments, 2).

And Zoroaster, speaking of life's close, as distinguished from the mere appearance of things at its noonday, thundered in the Gathas the warning unto all mankind:

"They who will not fulfill this command, as I both conceive it and declare it—for them shall the last of life be misery" (Yasna XLV, 3)!

On the other hand the blessings of happiness and prosperity were definitely promised the righteous, in this world as in the future life. Thus Ashi Vanguhi, the goddess of piety, celebrated as a daughter of God (Ahura Mazda), was fabled to bring to them who served God, fortune and prosperity.

Accordingly, the great Ashi Yast pays this effluence of God, a most enthusiastic and eloquent tribute (c. I, 1-3, 6) from which these passages are taken to show

---

[1] This, from one of the later books, is one of the very few references to astrology in Parsi literature.

what reward for living lives in accord with the divine law, the followers of Zoroaster were led to expect:

" 'We sacrifice to Ashi Vanguhi, who is shining, high, tall-formed, well worthy of sacrifice, with a loud-sounding chariot, strong, welfare giving, healing with fullness of intellect, and powerful;

" 'The daughter of God (Ahura Mazda), the sister of the Amesha Spentas, who endoweth all the Saöshyants [2] with the enlivening intelligence. She also bringeth heavenly wisdom at her wish, and cometh to help him who invoketh her from near and him who invoketh her from afar, and worshippeth her with offerings of libations. . . .

" 'Ashi is fair, Ashi is radiant with joy; she is far-piercing with her rays. Ashi giveth good glory unto those men whom thou dost follow, oh Ashi! Full of perfumes is the house in which the good, powerful Ashi Vanguhi putteth her . . . feet, for long friendship.

" 'They whom thou dost attend, oh Ashi, are kings of kingdoms, that are rich in horses, with large tributes, with snorting horses, sounding chariots, flashing swords, rich in aliments and in stores of food, well-scented, where the beds are spread and full of all the other riches that may be wished for. Happy the man whom thou dost attend: Do thou attend me, thou, rich in all sorts of desirable things, and strong!

" 'They whom thou dost attend, oh Ashi Vanguhi, have houses that stand, well-laid up, rich in cattle, foremost in universal order, and long-supported. Happy the man whom thou dost attend! Do thou attend me, thou rich in all sorts of desirable things, and strong!

" 'They whom thou dost attend, oh Ashi Vanguhi,

[2] Who are to usher in the millennium.

have beds that stand well-spread, well-adorned, well-made, provided with cushions and with feet inlaid with gold. Happy the man whom thou dost attend! Do thou attend me, thou rich in all sorts of desirable things, and strong!

" 'They whom thou dost attend, oh Ashi Vanguhi, have their ladies that sit on their beds, waiting for them; they lie on the cushions, adorning themselves . . . with squared-boned earrings and a necklace of gold, saying, "When will our Lord come? When shall we enjoy in our bodies the delights of love." Happy the man whom thou dost attend! Do thou attend me, thou rich in all sorts of desirable things, and strong!

" 'They whom thou dost attend, oh Ashi Vanguhi, have daughters that sit . . . thin is their waist, beautiful is their body, long are their fingers; they are as fair of shape as those who look on, can desire. Happy the man whom thou dost attend! Do thou attend me, thou rich in all sorts of desirable things, and strong!' "

The Gathas also (Yasna XXXIII, 10) offer up this prayer to God:

"All the pleasures of life which thou holdest, those that were, those that are, those that will be, oh God (Ahura Mazda), by their good thou wilt apportion them."

CHAPTER XXVI

RENUNCIATION, AURICULAR CONFESSION, PENANCE AND ABSOLUTION

"THESE things I ask thee, oh God (Ahura Mazda), how will it come about and how this will issue—the requitals that in accord with the records are appointed for the righteous and those, oh God, that belong to the liars, how these shall be when they come to the reckoning."

Thus the Gathas (Yasna XXXI, 14) put the world-old question. The Vendidad answers it in the two ways in which man has, perhaps, ever answered it.

First (Fargard X, 19):

"Make thine own self pure, oh righteous man! Every man in this world below can obtain purity for himself, by cleansing his heart with good thoughts, good words and good deeds."

And, second (Fargard V, c. V, 26):

"The priest hath power to remit him one-third of his penalty; if he hath committed aught other sin, it is remitted also by his repentance; if he hath committed no other sin, he is absolved by his repentance for all time to come."

In the same book (Fargard VIII, c. V, 30) this power of purification is ascribed to the Zoroastrian religion, thus:

"In the same way, oh Spitama Zoroaster, the religion

of God (Ahura Mazda) cleanseth the faithful from every evil thought, word and deed, as a swift-rushing, mighty wind cleanseth the plain. Let, therefore, all the deeds he doeth be henceforth good, oh Zoroaster; a full atonement for his sin is made by means of the religion of God."

This is repeated in another place (Fargard III, c. IV, 41-42) preceded by these explanatory details:

"The religion of God (Ahura Mazda), oh Spitama Zoroaster, indeed taketh away from him who professeth it, the bonds of his sin; it taketh away breach of trust; it taketh away murdering one of the faith; it taketh away burying a corpse; it taketh away sins for which else there were no atonement; it taketh away the worst sin (i.e. the sin of usury); it taketh away any sin that may be committed."

The reward for performing the services requisite for purification is, in some cases, very considerable; as, for instance, this for cleansing a man who is tainted with corruption (Nasu) through contact with a dead body:

"Zoroaster inquired of God (Ahura Mazda) saying, 'Oh thou Maker of the material world, thou Holy One, what shall be the reward of that man, after his soul hath left his body, who hath cleansed from the Nasu the man defiled by the dead?' God made answer and said, 'The bliss of Paradise canst thou promise to that man as his reward in the other world'" (Vendidad, Fargard IX, c. II, 43-44).

This reward, however, as all other rewards for this spiritual cleansing, be they temporal or eternal, is not for every man, but only for him who is prepared for this sacred office by learning the rites and ceremonies.

Thus the Vendidad (Fargard IX, c. III, 47) sets

forth the evil consequences when unskilled hands are applied to this task, in the following colloquy:

" 'O thou Maker of the material world, thou Holy One, if a man that knoweth not the rites of cleansing in accordance with the law of God (Ahura Mazda) offer to cleanse the unclean, how shall I then oppose the Druj that from the dead rusheth upon the living? How shall I oppose the Druj that from the dead defileth the living?' God made answer and said, 'Then, oh Spitama Zoroaster, the Druj, Nasu, appeareth to wax stronger than she was before; stronger, then, are sickness and death and the forces of the demon than they were before.' "

In other paragraphs (51-52) of the same Fargard, this question concerning that matter is asked and answered:

" 'Who is the man, oh God (Ahura Mazda), that threateneth to deprive the world of its fullness and increase and to bring unto it sickness and death?' God made answer and said, 'It is the ungodly Ashemaögha,[1] oh Spitama Zoroaster, who in this material world cleanseth the unclean without knowing the rites of purification according to the law of God.' "

The Yasts urge the necessity for making gifts to the priests, as a means to salvation, thus:

"He that wisheth to obtain the celestial reward, obtaineth it by giving unto him that maintaineth the law before us in this world here below" (Vistasp Yast, c. IV, 30).

That a man should be prepared to offer up his all, is indicated in this dialogue (Vendidad, Fargard XIX, c. V, 26):

"Zoroaster inquired of God (Ahura Mazda) saying,

[1] Infidel.

'Oh, thou All-Knowing God, ought I to urge upon the godly man, ought I to urge upon the godly woman, ought I to urge upon the wicked worshipper of demons, living in his sins, to give the earth made by God, the corn in the fields and all else that they possess?' God made answer and said, 'This shouldst thou, oh holy Zoroaster.' "

The Vendidad (Fargard IX, c. II, 37-40) gives the following information concerning ancient prices for absolution:

"Thou shalt purify a priest for a blessing of the just.

"Thou shalt purify the lord of a province for the value of a camel of high value.

"Thou shalt purify the lord of a town for the value of a stallion of high value.

"Thou shalt purify the lord of a borough for the value of a bull of high value.

"Thou shalt purify the master of a house for the value of a cow three years old.

"Thou shalt purify the wife of the master of a house for the value of a ploughing cow.

"Thou shalt purify a menial for the value of a draught cow.

"Thou shalt purify a young child for the value of a lamb.

"These are the heads of cattle—flocks or herds—that the worshippers of God (Ahura Mazda) shall give to the man who hath purified them, if they can afford it; if they cannot afford it, they shall give him any other value that may make him leave their houses well pleased with them and free from anger.

"For if the man who hath purified them leave their houses displeased with them, and full of anger, then the Druj, Nasu, entereth them from the nose (of the dead), from the eyes, from the tongue, from the jaws, from the sexual organs, from the hinder parts."

The Nasks, however, advise that poverty maketh no man unrighteous and that salvation is free, thus:

"If he have no means, his poverty shall not be accounted unto the godly man for unrighteousness" (Tahmura's Fragments, c. XII, 12).

It was, according to tradition, the early practice for a priest to receive gifts only, the priest asking these by beggings alms if necessary, but doing no work but that of priest; considerable departures were, of course, made from this, such as, for instance, are set forth in this passage from the Dadistan-i-Dinik (c. XLVI, 5):

"But indeed, when they do not obtain a daily livelihood from priestly duty, and the good do not give them selected gifts suitable for it, and they do not let them obtain any from the next of kin or the wicked even by begging, a livelihood may be requested for the paid performance of ceremonies, management of all religious rites and of other duties therein of a priestly disciple. When even by these they do not obtain it, they are to seek a livelihood by agriculture, sheep rearing, penmanship, or other proper employment among priests; and when it is not possible for them to live even by these, they are to seek it by bearing arms, hunting, or other proper employment in the profession of a virtuous warrior. And when it is not even possible for them to maintain their own bodies, which are kept in hand as required, by that which in half-starvation is consumed, they are authorized to beg a suitable gift as an effectual remedy."

The absolute necessity, as a condition to salvation, for a man to submit to the authority of the priests, the

Shayast-La-Shayast (c. XVII, 8) sets forth in this fashion:

"This, too, is revealed by the Avesta, that God (Ahura Mazda) spake thus, 'Give ye up the persons of all men, with the submissiveness of worshippers, to that man to whom the whole Avesta and Zend is easy, so that he may make you acquainted with duties and good works; because men go to hell for this reason, when they do not submit their persons to priestly control and do not become acquainted with duties and good works.'"

In another place (c. VIII, 2) the same book urged the necessity for auricular confession of sin, saying of this:

"The sin of him that is worthy of death, is to be confessed unto the high-priests and he is to surrender his body—save to the high-priests, he is not to surrender it."

Full absolution and indeed something very like plenary indulgence is promised in this remarkable passage also taken from the same book (c. VIII, 23):

"Ataropad, son of Maruspend, said that it is always necessary to be more diligent in performing one's worship of God (Ahura Mazda) at a time when many mortal sins are being committed; since all sins may be purged by renunciation, when one shall atone by complete self-sacrifice and shall engage in radical renunciation of his sin, he becometh free from the sin, in renunciation of which he engageth, for God will not abandon his own creatures unto the Evil Spirit unless on the ground of non-renunciation."

The Shayast-La-Shayast, however, is also authority (by hearsay, as in the case just mentioned) for quite the contrary view, that is:

"Saöshyants said that to enter into that best life it is not necessary to perform the ceremony; for when a man's good works are one tanapuhar more than his sin, he attains that best life and no account is taken whether or no he performed the ceremony, for the reason that in Heaven it is not necessary to perform ceremonies, for an excess of good works is requisite to attain Heaven. Saöshyants also said that in Heaven he that is below is exalted unto him that is above" (c. VI, 4, 5).

The religious ceremonies of cleansing are described in the Vendidad (Fargard VIII, c. III, 19) as commencing in the following impressive manner:

"A priest shall first proceed along the road and speak aloud these triumphant words: 'The will of the Lord (Ahura Mazda) is the law of righteousness.' 'The gifts of the Good Mind are the deeds done in this world for God (Ahura Mazda).' 'He who relieveth the poor maketh God (Ahura Mazda) king.' "

The simpler elements of the formulas of the ceremony are given in the following passage from the Vendidad (Fargard XI, 4-7):

"If thou desirest to purify the house, say these words aloud, 'As long as the sickness lasteth, my great protector is he who teacheth virtue to the perverse.'

"If thou desirest to purify the Fire, say these words aloud, 'Thy Fire, first of all, do we approach with worship, oh Lord God (Ahura Mazda)!'

"If thou desirest to purify the water, say these words aloud, 'Waters we worship, the Maëkaïnti waters, the Hebvaïnti waters, the Fravazah waters.'

"If thou desirest to purify the earth, say these words aloud, 'This earth we worship, this earth with the women, this earth which beareth and those women who are thine, oh God (Ahura Mazda)!'

"If thou desirest to purify the cow, say these words aloud, 'The best of all works we will fulfill while we order both the learned and the unlearned, both masters and servants, to secure for the cattle a good resting-place and fodder.'

"If thou desirest to purify the trees, say these words aloud, 'For him, as a reward, God made the plants to grow.'

"If thou desirest to purify the faithful man or the faithful woman, say these words aloud, 'May the vow-fulfilling Airyaman² come hither, for the men and women of Zoroaster to rejoice, for the Good Mind to rejoice, with the desirable reward that religion deserveth. I solicit for holiness that boon which is vouchsafed by God!'"

² A demigod or angel.

CHAPTER XXVII

DEPARTURE FROM THIS WORLD

" 'Oh thou Maker of the material world, thou Holy One, doth water slay?' God (Ahura Mazda) made answer and said, 'Water slayeth no man. Asto-Vidhotu[1] bindeth him and, thus bound, Vayu[2] carrieth him away. The tide casteth his body upon the beach and the birds feed upon it. When he goeth away, it is by the will of fate that he goeth.'

" 'Oh thou Maker of the material world, thou Holy One, doth fire slay?' God made answer and said, 'Fire slayeth no man. Asto-Vidhotu bindeth him and, thus bound, Vayu carrieth him away. The fire consumeth the flesh and the limb. When he goeth away, it is by the will of fate that he goeth.' "

Thus the Vendidad (Fargard V, 8, 9) declares the Zoroastrian view of the phenomenon of death.

It was not a dissolution—that followed, as regards the body, in order of time—but a withdrawal of that which had, out of particles of food, water and air, built up the body after its own design and had ordered it and commanded it throughout its existence in such manner as seemed serviceable and useful.

This is echoed in this saying of the Vistasp Yast (c. IV, 32), "When his soul goeth out of his body through the will of fate."

[1] One of the demons.
[2] The angel of death.

The inevitability of death is celebrated in the Nasks, thus:

"For if there were, or could be, any escape from death, the first of the world, Gayomard, king of the mountain (would have escaped) who for three thousand years kept the world free from death and old age, from hunger, thirst, and evil. Yet when death came over him, he delivered up his body and could not struggle with death" (Aögemaïde Nask, 85-87).

In the same connection (70-76) this Nask thus beautifully characterizes both the approach and the ruthlessness of the fell destroyer:

"To every one cometh the unseen, deceiving angel of death,

"Who accepteth neither cajolement nor bribe,

"Who is no respecter of persons,

"And ruthlessly maketh men to perish;

"And this glorious one must go the way he never went,

"See what he never saw,

"And discourse with him (Ahura Mazda) whom no one can deceive or mislead."

Yet the Zend Avesta encourages man to call upon the clouds to send down the cooling rain to heal, crying unto them:

" 'Come, come, ye clouds, from up above, down to the earth, by thousands of drops, by myriads of drops,' thus call, oh holy Zoroaster, 'to destroy sickness, to destroy death, to destroy the sickness that slayeth, to destroy death that slayeth' " (Vendidad, Fargard XXI, c. II, 2)!

And also authorizes exorcism by the following words, used as a formula:

"To thee, oh sickness, say I 'Avaunt!' To thee, oh

fever, say I 'Avaunt!' To thee, oh evil eye, say I 'Avaunt' " (Vendidad, Fargard XX, c. I, 7)!

In another place, the same idea is put forward in this form:

"And I will bless thee with the fair blessing-spell of the righteous, the friendly blessing-spell of the righteous, that maketh the empty swell to fullness and the full to overflowing, that cometh to help him who is ailing, and maketh the sick man sound again" (Vendidad, Fargard XXII, c. I, 5).

The same is also included in this prayer in the Bahram Yast (33):

"Give unto that man brightness and glory, give him health of body, give him sturdiness of body, give him victorious strength of body, give him full welfare of wealth, give him a virtuous offspring, give him long, long life, give him the bright, all-happy, blissful abode of the Holy Ones!"

Prayer for rescue from destruction, not merely for an individual, but for a nation and a race, is in this, together with confidence that it will be granted:

"We sacrifice unto Verethraghna,⁸ created by God (Ahura Mazda), who maketh virility, who maketh death, who maketh resurrection, who possesseth peace, who hath a free way.

"Unto him did the holy Zoroaster offer up a sacrifice (asking) for victorious thinking, victorious speaking, victorious doing, victorious addressing, and victorious answering.

"Verethraghna, created by God, gave him the fountains of manliness, the strength of the arms, the health of the whole body, the sturdiness of the whole body,

⁸ A genius or angel.

and the eyesight of the Kara fish, that liveth beneath
the waters and can measure a rippling of the water,
not thicker than a hair, in the Tigris whose ends lie
afar, whose depth is a thousand times the height of a
man. . . .

"The Lord God (Ahura Mazda) said, 'If men sacrifice unto Verethraghna, created by God, if the due sacrifice and prayer is offered unto him, just as it ought to
be performed in the perfection of holiness, never will
a hostile horde enter the Aryan countries, nor any
plague, nor leprosy, nor poisonous plants, nor the
chariot of a foe, nor the uplifted spear of a foe' "
(Bahram Yast, c. XI, 29 and 48).

In the Ram Yast (c. IV, 14-16) it is related that
Yima, the shepherd, offered such a supplication to
Vayu, angel of the air, who is the very genius of death
itself and who summons the spirit from earth, and that
it was accorded him in the following manner, in accordance with the custom:

"I will sacrifice to the waters and to him that divid-
eth them.

"To this Vayu do we sacrifice, this Vayu do we invoke . . .

"Unto him did the bright Yima, the good shepherd,
sacrifice from the height Hukaïrya, the all-shining and
golden, on a golden throne, under golden beams and a
golden canopy, with bundles of baresma and offerings
of full-boiling (milk).

"He begged of him a boon, saying, 'Grant me this, oh
Vayu, who dost labor on high, that I may become the
most glorious of the men born to behold the sun; that
I may make in my reign both animals and men undying, waters and plants undying, and the food for eating creatures never failing.'

"In the right of the valiant Yima there was neither cold wind nor hot wind, neither old age nor death, nor envy, made by the demons."

That these were veritable prayers, also, expected to elicit the favor of the celestial powers and not merely empty formulas, is indicated by this endorsement of physical healing, taken from the Ardibehist Yast (c. II, 6):

"One may heal with Holiness, one may heal with the Law, one may heal with the knife, one may heal with herbs, one may heal with the Holy Word; amongst all remedies this one is the best-healing one that heals with the Holy Word; this one it is, that will best drive away sickness from the body of the faithful; for this one is the best healing of all remedies."

The Zend Avesta, itself, is full warrant, likewise, for this view; since it speaks of the matter in this fashion:

"If several healers offer themselves together, oh Spitama Zoroaster, namely, one who heals with the knife, one who heals with herbs, and one who heals with the Holy Word, then this man is the best healing of all healers who heals with the Holy Word. He will best drive away sickness from the body of one of the faith" (Vendidad, Fargard VII, c. VIIb, 44).

By the "Holy Word" was meant the Zend Avesta, especially the Gathas, and the process was by intoning, reading or reciting passages aloud, with earnest prayers for healing.

Yet the Zoroastrian scriptures, from the earliest to the latest, celebrate the virtues of healing plants and the goodness of God in creating them for the ministration of relieving sickness and disease.

The Bundahis (c. IX, 3, 4) thus epitomizes it:

"On the whole earth plants grew up like hair upon the heads of men. Ten thousand of them grew forth of one special description, for keeping away the ten thousand species of disease which the Evil Spirit produced for the creatures; and from those ten thousand, the one hundred thousand species of plants have grown forth."

The Vendidad (Fargard XX, c. I, 4) represents God as declaring:

"I, God (Ahura Mazda), brought down the healing plants, which by many hundreds, by many thousands, by many myriads, grow up all around the one White Haöma." *

The Bahman Yast (c. II, 53) gives this prophecy concerning the greatly augmented efficacy of means of physical healing, as the end of the world approaches:

"In that millennium . . . mankind will become so versed in medicine and will keep and put so much in use effective physic and other remedies that, when they are confessedly at the point of death, they do not thereupon die."

Moreover, the spiritual means of causing one's life to continue did not fail here, as elsewhere, to degenerate into seeking to employ such means for shortening the lives of enemies.

Thus in the Nasks is found this supplication:

"May he perish, within the year, within the month! I, worshipper of God (Ahura Mazda) would make him to perish through my spells" (Westergard's Fragments, I, c. VIII, 1)!

That one should be prepared for life's ending, is an obvious lesson from the certainty of death and the

* A fabled growth at the bottom of the sea said to possess miraculous powers of healing.

uncertainty of life, which the Zoroastrian scriptures did not fail to deduce.

Thus the Aögemaïde Nask (39) puts it:

"For if one say, 'On this earth of the seven Karshvares there is somebody going to die,' everybody ought to think, 'Perhaps it is I.'"

And in the same connection (41-47) expatiates upon it, thus:

"Now when a man setteth forth upon a journey, he taketh provisions with him;

"If it be for one day's march, he taketh provisions for two days;

"If it be for two days' march, he taketh provisions for three;

"If it be for ten days' march, he taketh provisions for fifteen;

"And he thinketh that he will come back in health to his well-beloved, friends, parents, and brethren.

"How then is it that men take no provisions for that unavoidable journey, on which one must go once for all, for all eternity?"

The Zoroastrians, like most other Orientals, have a prescribed period of mourning, notwithstanding their confidence that death is but release from the flesh—mourning for the deprivation of companionship discernible by the senses, because, as the poet has it, "he put our lives so far apart, we cannot hear each other speak."

The Vendidad in the following passage (Fargard XII, 1-7) by singular reasoning, makes this mourning period twice as long for a wicked man as for a righteous man:

"'If one's father or mother die, how long shall they stay in mourning, the son for his father, the daughter for her mother? How long for the righteous? How long for the sinners?' . . .

"God (Ahura Mazda) made answer and said, 'They shall stay thirty days for the righteous, sixty days for the sinners.'

" 'If the master of the house die, or if the mistress of the house die, how long shall they stay? How long for the righteous? How long for the sinners?'

"God made answer and said, 'They shall stay six months for the righteous, a year for the sinners.' "

The spirit, with which one should encounter death, is admirably set forth in the Aögemaïde Nask (103-104) in these words:

" 'I am thankful unto the Lord God (Ahura Mazda)!' Thus think I in a grateful spirit, 'The beast of burden doth not cast off his burden. Fate hath come upon me; it cannot be cast off!' "

This Nask, which is a treatise that "inculcates a serene resignation to death," as an authority upon the Zoroastrian scriptures has put it, proposes as the motto for men about to die (1):

"We come, we rejoice, we submit."

The Zend Avesta, itself, however, gives solace to the yet living in this world-famous passage, of unmatched eloquence and poetical insight:

"If death come after noon, may healing come at eve!

'If death come at eve, may healing come at night!

"If death come at night, may healing come at dawn!

"And showers shower down new water, new earth, new plants, new healing powers and new healing" (Vendidad, Fargard XXI, c. II, 3)!

CHAPTER XXVIII

DISPOSAL OF THE DEAD BODY

Soil, the cultivation of which was accounted so sacred a thing, could not, of course, lightly be exposed to contamination; accordingly, the Zend Avesta commands, as regards the bodies of the dead:

"And two men, strong and agile, having changed their garments, shall lift the body from the clay or the stones, or out of the plastered house, and they shall lay it down at a place where they know that there are always corpse-eating dogs and corpse-eating birds" (Vendidad Fargard VIII, c. II, 10).

That the Parsis expose the bodies of their dead to be consumed by vultures is, of course, well-known. In olden times it was either to the beasts or birds.

Three reasons for this, each persuasive in a high degree, could be assigned, viz. that such a course accords best with the economy of the universe since it makes the most obvious use, that of food, of a beneficent material, instead of permitting it to become noxious; that to do so reminds one most powerfully that this is not, and never was, his friend; and that thus the horrors of disintegration by corruption and the possibility of infection of living beings are avoided.

The suggestion that, instead, there be recourse to the funeral pyre could not be tolerated by followers of Zoroaster, who, as has been seen, regarded fire as essentially divine and not to be profaned in this fashion.

Moreover, such a course prevents the use of the material in accordance with the universal scheme of things and merely dissipates it.

The greatest stress is placed in the Zoroastrian scriptures upon the necessity for avoiding the spread of contagion. The living forces of corruption were recognized to be of the evil mind, i.e. intent upon destroying beneficent forms of life. To permit the body to corrupt was, therefore, to set these forces at work. To expose the body to beasts and vultures was, instead, to solve the problem by means of the Good Mind, i.e. intent upon preserving beneficent forms of life.

In the Zend Avesta this question was asked and answered, to show that the bacilli of disintegration are at work as soon as the breath has quit the body:

"Zoroaster inquired of God (Ahura Mazda) saying, 'Oh Lord God, Most Beneficent Spirit, Maker of the material world, thou Holy One, when a man dieth, at what moment doth the Druj, Nasu, rush upon him?'

"God made answer and said, 'Immediately after death and as soon as the soul quitteth the body, oh Spitama Zoroaster, the Druj, Nasu, cometh and rusheth upon him from the regions of the north, in the shape of a raging fly, with knees and tail protruding, droning endlessly, and like unto the foulest vermin' " (Vendidad, Fargard VII, c. I, 1, 2).

The Dadistan-i-Dinik (c. XVII, 16, 17) thus explains the reasons for the rule that the body should be exposed as food for carrion-eating birds and beasts:

"But it is not proper to recount the devouring of the noxious creatures, for the spirit of the body is troubled when it observes the alarmed manifestations of life which was in the bodies of those destroyed, the noxious creatures upon the goodly forms, and the mode and strangeness of the disintegration and destruction. And so it then becomes the more remedial way, when, as it is ordered in revelation, the body, fraught with corruption, is placed on the ground of a clear mountain-spur and, in order not to convey it to the water, plants, and men of the plain, it is fastened in the customary manner, so that the corpse-eating beasts and corpse-eating birds, which are not subject to the hand of men, and are likewise not entertained as food, shall yet not drag any of it away for man's eating of dead matter."

The revelation, referred to, which instructs how the body is to be disposed of, is doubtless this passage of the Zend Avesta, narrating the replies which God vouchsafed Zoroaster when he inquired concerning this matter:

" 'Oh Maker of the material world, thou Holy One, whither shall we bring, where shall we lay, the bodies of the dead, oh God?'

"God (Ahura Mazda) made answer and said, 'On the highest summits, where they know there are always corpse-eating beasts and corpse-eating birds, oh holy Zoroaster!

" 'There shall the worshippers of God fasten the corpse by the feet and by the hair, with brass, stones, or clay, lest the corpse-eating beasts and the corpse-eating birds shall go and carry the bones to the water and to the trees.' . . .

" 'Oh Maker of the material world, thou Holy One, whither shall we bring, where shall we lay, the bones[1] of the dead, oh God?'

"God made answer and said, 'The worshippers of God shall make a receptacle out of the reach of the dog, of the fox, of the wolf, and wherein rain water cannot stay.

[1] That is, after the flesh has been stripped from them .

" 'They shall make of it, if they can afford it, with stones, plaster, or earth; if they cannot afford it, they shall lay down the dead man on the ground, on his carpet and his pillow, clothed with the light of heaven, and beholding the sun' " (Vendidad, Fargard VI, c. V, 44-51).

The process of dealing with the hut or tent within which a dog or man has died, is thus described in the Zend Avesta:

" 'If a dog or a man die within a hut of wood or a tent of felt, what shall the worshippers of God (Ahura Mazda) do?'

"The Lord God made answer and said, 'They shall search for a Dakhma, they shall look all about for a Dakhma. If they find it easier to remove the dead, they shall do so and permit the house to stand and shall fumigate it with garlic or benzoin or aloes or pomegranate or some other pungent plant. If they find it easier to remove the house, they shall do so, leaving the dead lying upon the spot, and shall fumigate the house with garlic, or benzoin, or aloes, or pomegranate, or some other pungent plant' " (Vendidad, Fargard VIII, c. I, 1-3).

In case the death takes place in winter, when the cold will preserve the body and when the corpse-eating creatures may not be available, the following procedure is allowable, according to the Zend Avesta:

" 'Oh Maker of the material world, thou Holy One (Ahura Mazda), if the summer is past and the winter hath come, what shall the worshippers of God do?'

"God made answer and said, 'In every house, in every borough, they shall raise three[a] rooms for the dead.'

[a] One for men, one for women, one for children.

" 'Oh Maker of the material world, thou Holy One, how large shall be these rooms for the dead?'

"God made answer and said, 'Large enough not to strike the skull of the man, if he should stand erect, or his feet or his hands stretched out; such shall be, according to the law, the rooms for the dead.

" 'And they shall let the lifeless body lie there, for two nights, or for three nights, or a month long, until the birds begin to fly, the plants to grow, the hidden floods to flow and the wind to dry up the earth.

" 'And as soon as the birds begin to fly, the plants to grow, the hidden floods to flow, and the wind to dry up the earth, then the worshippers of God shall lay down the dead, his eyes toward the sun.

" 'If the worshippers of God have not within a year, laid down the dead, his eyes toward the sun, thou shalt prescribe for that trespass the same penalty as for the murder of one of the faithful until the corpse hath been rained upon, until the Dakhma hath been rained upon, until the unclean remains have been rained upon, until the birds have eaten up the corpse' " (Vendidad, Fargard, V, c. III, 10-14).

This practice of exposing bodies was adopted by all followers of Zoroaster; of it the Aögemaïde Nask (VIII, 54, 55) says:

"Every day the living body is thrown, for their food, to the birds that wheel in the empty sky. This is the way with things of this earth."

The Dadistan-i-Dinik (c. XVII, 1, 2, 7) discusses the practice and gives reasons for it in the following:

"What is the purpose of giving up a corpse to the birds?

"The reply is this, that the construction of the body of those passed away is so wonderful that two co-

existences have come together for it. . . . The injury
of the destroyer to the body of those passed away is
contaminating: the Nasu rushes on it and, owing to its
violence, when it becomes triumphant over the subconscious mind of the righteous man, and frightens it from
the place of the catastrophe and puts itself into its
place in the body, that body is then, for that reason,
called dead matter."

This is understood to mean that the destroying
demon usurps the place of the subconscious mind which
had departed, and with glee superintends the awful
work of disintegration, carried on by the foulest
processes.

The Dadistan-i-Dinik (c. XV, 1) also inquires:
"Doth the extinction of life result from the gnawing
of dogs and of birds upon the body?" and (c. XV, 4)
answers this as follows: "Death cometh once and once
only unto the righteous and the wicked; . . . but the
gnawing by dogs and by birds happeneth not unto
each and every one."

In a subsequent chapter, it asks and answers the
following question:

"When the dogs and birds tear it, doth the soul
know it, and doth it occur uncomfortably for it, or
how is it?

"The reply is this, that the pain occasioned by the
tearing and gnawing would so gall the body of a man
that, though the soul were abiding with the body, such
soul, which one knoweth is happy and immortal, would
then depart from the body, along with the animating
life, the informing consciousness and the remaining
manifestations of life. The body, however, of itself
is inert, unmoving, and not to be galled; and at last
no pain whatever galleth it, nor is perceived. And the

soul, with the life, standeth outside the body and is not uneasy as regards the gnawing, though, through spiritual perception, it seeth and knoweth it" (Dadistan-i-Dinik, c. XVI, 1, 2).

For obvious reasons, the plainsmen would view with suspicion the bearing of a dead body forth by one man, alone, since this would be the resort of the murderer in order to conceal his crime. The Vendidad accordingly, independent of what reason for the lone man's action there might be, attached guilt to the very act itself and imposed therefor lifelong defilement, thus:

"Let no man alone by himself carry a dead body. If a man alone by himself beareth forth a dead body, the Nasu rusheth upon him to defile him, from the nose of the dead man, from his eye, from his tongue, from his jaws, from his sexual organs, from his hinder parts. This Druj, Nasu, falleth upon him, even to the tip of his nails and he is unclean thenceforth for ever and ever" (Fargard III, c. III, 14).

His banishment was indeed decreed and ultimately his execution, as the essential condition to his final absolution and salvation.

In another place (Fargard IX, c. II, 41), the Vendidad declares:

"It grieveth the sun, forsooth, oh Spitama Zoroaster, to shine upon a man defiled by a corpse; it grieveth the moon; it grieveth the stars."

That this condemnation was associated with the idea of the foul bacilli which attack the newly deserted body and does not apply after such are no longer present, is shown by this question and its answer:

" 'Oh Maker of the material world, thou Holy One (Ahura Mazda), shall the man be clean who hath touched a body that hath been dried up and extinct more than a year?'

"God made answer and said, 'Yea, he is clean. The dry mingleth not with the dry. Were the dry to mingle with the dry, soon all this, my material world, would be one vast Peshotanu, bent upon the destruction of righteousness and with a soul, crying out and bewailing, so numberless are the beings that perish upon the face of the earth" (Vendidad, Fargard VIII, c. VI, 33, 34).

Unlike the man who has alone borne a dead body, he who has only touched it, whether when newly dead or putrid, can be cleansed; of this the Vendidad says:

" 'Oh Maker of the material world, thou Holy One (Ahura Mazda), can the man be made clean that hath touched the corpse of a dog or the corpse of a man?'

"God made answer and said, 'He can, oh holy Zoroaster!' "

" 'How so?'

" 'If the Nasu hath already been expelled by the corpse-eating beasts or by the corpse-eating birds, he shall cleanse his body with gomez³ and water, and he shall be clean. If the Nasu hath not been expelled by the corpse-eating beasts or by the corpse-eating birds, then the worshippers of God shall dig three holes in the ground, and he shall thereupon wash his body with gomez, not with water' " (Vendidad, Fargard VIII, c. VII, 35-37).

If the corpse, however, were of an infidel, contact with it cannot contaminate; this for a fanciful reason which is given in the Vendidad by question and answer as follows:

" 'Oh Maker of the material world, thou Holy One (Ahura Mazda), if the dead hath been a wicked, two-footed ruffian, such as an ungodly infidel, how many

³ The urine of the bull, deemed by Zoroastrians to have special purifying qualities.

of the creatures of the good spirit doth he indirectly defile?'

"The Lord God made answer and said, 'No more than doth a frog whose venom hath dried up, and who hath been dead longer than a year. Whilst living, oh Spitama Zoroaster, a wicked, two-legged ruffian, such as an ungodly infidel, directly defileth the creatures of the good spirit and indirectly defileth them. Whilst living he afflicts the water, whilst living he extinguishes the fire, whilst living he carrieth off the cow, whilst living he striketh the man of the faith a deadly blow that parteth soul from body; not so will he do when dead' " (Fargard V, c. V, 35-37).

The following lengthy passage from the Zend Avesta is given in full, in order to show how Zoroaster regarded sepulture of the body, the nature of his objections to it, his abhorrence of "Dakhmas," that is, raised places for the deposit of bodies until they can be consumed by beasts and birds and, above all, the sanitary reasons given for this abhorrence:

" 'Oh Maker of the material world, thou Holy One (Ahura Mazda), how long after the corpse of a dead man hath been laid down on the ground, clothed with the light of heaven and beholding the sun, is the ground clean again?'

"God made answer and said, 'When the corpse of a dead man hath lain on the ground for a year, clothed with the light of heaven and beholding the sun, then the ground is clean again, oh holy Zoroaster!'

" 'Oh Maker of the material world, thou Holy One, how long after the corpse of a dead man hath been buried in the earth, is the earth clean again?'

"God made answer and said, 'When the corpse of a dead man hath lain buried in the earth for fifty years, oh Spitama Zoroaster, then the earth is clean again.'

" 'Oh Maker of the material world, thou Holy One,
how long after the corpse of a dead man hath been laid
down on a Dakhma, is the ground, whereon the
Dakhma stands, clean again?'

"God made answer and said, 'Not until the dust of
the corpse, oh Spitama Zoroaster, hath mingled with
the dust of the earth. Urge every one in the material
world, oh Spitama Zoroaster, to pull down ' Dakhmas'! . . .

"God further answered and said, 'Those Dakhmas
that are built upon the face of the earth, oh Spitama
Zoroaster, and whereon are laid the corpses of dead
men, these are the places where there are demons,
these are the places whereon troops of demons rush together; whereon troops of demons come rushing along;
whereon they rush together to kill their fifties and their
hundreds, their hundreds and their thousands, their
thousands and their tens of thousands, their tens of
thousands and their myriads of myriads.

" 'On these Dakhmas, oh Spitama Zoroaster, those
demons take food and void filth. As you men in the
material world, as you cook meal and eat cooked meat,
so do they. It is, as it were, the smell of their feeding that you smell there, oh men!

" 'For thus they go on revelling, until that stench is
rooted in the Dakhmas. In those Dakhmas arises the
infection of diseases, itch, fever, naëza, rickets, chill
and hair untimely white. At those Dakhmas congre-
gate the worst destroyers from the hour when the sun
goeth down' " (Vendidad, Fargard VII, c. VIII, 45-
53, 56-58).

The feeble powers of imagination of the average
man, his inability to perceive the thing which is real

⁘ I.e. After they have fulfilled the purpose for which they are
made.

unless his senses apprise him of it and his disregard of what is reason should make him to know beyond a shadow of a doubt, is surely that which enables great communities to go on, poisoning the earth with decaying flesh, which, by being covered out of sight, but contaminates the more and longer. This contamination and its living, though evil, nature, the Persian prophet appreciated to the full and so provided by means of the religion which he taught, severe penance for the worshiper of God who sinned in this respect.

This condemnation, the Vendidad ascribes to God, himself, in its narration of the following conversation of Zoroaster with the Almighty:

" 'Oh Maker of the material world, thou Holy One (Ahura Mazda), if a man shall bury in the earth either the corpse of a dog or the corpse of a man, and if he shall not disinter it within half a year, what is the penalty that he shall pay?'

"God made answer and said, 'Five hundred stripes with the Aspahe-astra,⁵ five hundred stripes with the Sraösho-Karana.'⁶

" 'Oh Maker of the material world, thou Holy One, if a man shall bury in the earth either the corpse of a dog or the corpse of a man, and if he shall not disinter it within a year, what is the penalty that he shall pay?'

"God made answer and said, 'A thousand stripes with the Aspahe-astra, a thousand stripes with the Sraösho-Karana.'

" 'Oh Maker of the material world, thou Holy One, if a man shall bury in the earth either a corpse of a dog or the corpse of a man, and if he shall not disinter it within the second year, what is the penalty for it?

⁵ Whip used in administering retributive punishment.
⁶ Also a whip used in punishment.

What is the atonement for it? What is the cleansing from it?'

"God made answer and said, 'For that deed there is nothing than can pay, nothing that can atone, nothing that can cleanse from it; it is a trespass for which there is no atonement, for ever and ever.' "

" 'When is that so?'

" 'It is so, if the sinner be a professor of the religion of God, or one who hath been taught in it; but he be not a professor of the religion of God, nor one who hath been taught in it, then his sin is taken from him, if he maketh confession of the religion of God and resolve never to commit again such forbidden deeds' " (Vendidad, Fargard III, c. IV, 36-39).

The very contact of the dead body with the earth, through death taking place upon it, contaminated it, according to Zoroaster's view; the following from the Vendidad shows this and how long a time must elapse before the ground is purified:

" 'How long is a piece of ground to lie fallow upon which dogs or men have died?'

"God (Ahura Mazda) made answer and said, 'A year shall the piece of ground lie fallow on which dogs or men have died, oh holy Zoroaster; a year shall no worshipper of God sow or water that piece of ground whereon dogs or men have died' " (Fargard VI, c. I, 1-2).

As is yet the view of men, this contamination does not continue so long in the case of water, especially running water, as follows:

" 'Oh Maker of the material world, thou Holy One (Ahura Mazda), what part of the water in a pond does the Druj, Nasu, defile with corruption, infection and pollution?'

"God made answer and said, "Six steps on each of the four sides. As long as the corpse hath not been taken out of the water, so long shall that water be unclean and unfit to drink. They shall, therefore, take the corpse out of the pond, and lay it down on the dry ground, and of the water they shall draw off the half, or the third, or the fourth, or the fifth part, according as they are able or not;[7] and after the corpse hath been taken out and the water hath been drawn off, the rest of the water is clean, and both cattle and men may drink of it at their pleasure, as before.' . . .

" 'Oh Maker of the material world, thou Holy One, what part of the water of a running stream doth the Druj, Nasu, defile with corruption, infection and pollution?'

"God made answer and said, 'Three[8] steps down the stream, nine steps up the stream, six steps across. As long as the corpse hath not been taken out of the water, so long shall the water be unclean and unfit to drink. They shall, therefore, take the corpse out of the water, and lay it down on the dry ground. After the corpse hath been taken out and the stream hath flowed three times, the water is clean, and both cattle and men may drink of it at their pleasure, as before' " (Vendidad, Fargard VI, c. III, 30-32, 39-41).

That in that early day Zoroaster and his plainsmen followers should have recognized the derivation of a long list of physical disorders from the infection of a dead body and because of this should have reprehended burial or exposure, whether under, upon, or over the surface of the earth, in such a manner as to prevent

[7] Indicating an opinion, not wholly erroneous, that putrefactive poisons rise toward the surface.

[8] A peculiar disproportion, if the numbers are correct.

the scavenger beasts and birds consuming the flesh before corruption reduced it to a festering mass, must surely be taken as evidence of his clear-sightedness.

His conviction in the matter was withal so strong that he places above all other services to the soil from which we derive our sustenance, this service, attributing the command to God, himself:

" 'Oh Maker of the material world, thou Holy One (Ahura Mazda), who is the first that rejoiceth the earth with greatest delight?'

"God made answer and said, 'It is he that disinterreth most dead bodies of dogs and men.'

" 'Oh Maker of the material world, thou Holy One, who is the second that rejoiceth the earth with greatest delight?'

"God made answer and said, 'It is he that levelleth most of the Dakhmas* upon which the dead bodies of men are laid' " (Vendidad, Fargard III, c. III, 12, 13).

The Vendidad also gives this account of the origin of these offenses, in which it declares both to be unpardonable sins:

"Thereupon came Ahriman, who is all death and he counter-created a sin for which there is no atonement, the burying of the dead. . . . Thereupon came Ahriman, who is all death, and he counter-created a sin for which there is no atonement, the cooking of corpses" (Fargard I, 13, 17).

Since these cannot be atoned for, cannibalism cannot be visited with worse; but the same book pronounces upon it a like sentence in the following:

" 'Oh Maker of the material world, thou Holy One

* This, notwithstanding that the erection and use of these "towers of silence" are enjoined as a religious duty; of course, it refers to demolition of those which are no longer required.

(Ahura Mazda), can he become clean again who hath eaten of the carcass of a dog or of the corpse of a man?'

"The Lord God made answer and said: 'He cannot, oh holy Zoroaster! . . . The fiend Nasu falleth upon him and taketh hold of him even to the end of the nails and he is unclean thenceforth for ever and ever' " (Vendidad, Fargard VII, c. IV, 23, 24).

CHAPTER XXIX

THE SOUL IMMEDIATELY AFTER DEATH

THE Dadistan-i-Dinik (c. XXXVII, 21) thus sets forth the only requisites in order to secure immortal life, requisites calling alone for a clean and upward-tending life:

"To make the good creatures again fresh and pure, and to keep them constant and progressing in pure and virtuous conduct, is to render them immortal."

The following interesting legend, purporting to show how impossible it is for any man to become an immortal, until after death, and for the wicked to achieve immortality at all, is extracted from the Bahman Yast (c. II, 1-3):

"In the Vohu Manah Yast commentary, it is declared that Zoroaster asked for immortality from God (Ahura Mazda) a second time, and spoke thus, 'I am Zoroaster, more righteous and more efficient among these, thy creatures, oh thou Creator, if thou wilt make me immortal, as the tree opposed to harm, and Gopati-shah, Gosti Fryan, and Kitrokmiyan, son of Vistasp, who is a Peshotanu,[1] were—if thou wilt make me immortal, they of thy good religion will believe that the upholder of religion, who receives from God his pure and good religion of the worshippers of God, will become immortal; then they will believe in thy good religion.'

[1] Three men, mentioned in Zoroastrian traditions as having become immortal, while living in the flesh.

"God made answer and said, 'If I should make thee immortal, Zoroaster, the Spitaman, then Tur-i Bradarvash, the Karap, will also become immortal; and if Tur-i Bradarvash, the Karap, should become immortal, the resurrection and future existence would not be possible.' "

The following beautiful account is given in the Yast (XXII, c. II, 1-36) of the experience of the soul, already immortal, when it issues forth from the body:

"Zoroaster inquired of God (Ahura Mazda) saying, 'Oh Lord God, Most Beneficent Spirit, Maker of the material world, thou Holy One, when one of the faithful departeth this life, where doth his soul abide on that night?'

"The Lord God made answer and said, 'It taketh its seat near the head, singing the Ustavaïti Gatha and proclaiming happiness, "Happy is he, happy the man, whoever he be, to whom God giveth the full accomplishment of his wishes!" On that night, his soul tasteth as much of pleasure as the whole of the living world can taste.'

" 'On the second night where doth his soul abide?'

"The Lord God made answer and said, 'It taketh its seat near the head, singing the Ustavaïti Gatha and proclaiming happiness, "Happy is he, happy the man, whoever he be, to whom God giveth the accomplishment of his wishes!" On that night his soul tasteth as much of pleasure as the whole of the living world can taste.'

" 'On the third night doth his soul abide?'

"The Lord God made answer and said, 'It taketh its seat near the head, singing the Ustavaïti Gatha and proclaiming happiness, "Happy is he, happy the man,

whoever he be, to whom God giveth the accomplishment of all his wishes!" On that night his soul tasteth
as much of pleasure as the whole of the living world
can taste."

" 'At the end of the third night, when the dawn
appeareth, it seemeth to the soul of the faithful one
as if it were brought amongst plants and perfumes; it
seemeth as if a wind were blowing from the region of
the south, a perfume-laden wind, sweeter than any
other wind in this world. And it seemeth to the soul
of him of the faith as if he were inhaling that wind
with the nostrils, and he thinketh, "Whence doth that
wind blow, the sweetest-scented wind I ever inhaled
with my nostrils?"

" 'And it seemeth to him as if his own conscience
were advancing to him in that wind, in the shape of a
maiden fair, bright, white-armed, strong, tall-formed,
high-standing, thick-breasted, beautiful of body, noble,
of a glorious seed, of the size of a maid in her fifteenth
year, as fair as the fairest thing in the world. And the
soul of the faithful one addresseth her, asking, "What
maid art thou, who art the fairest maid mine eyes have
ever beheld?"

" 'And she, being his own conscience, answereth him,
"Oh thou youth of good thoughts, good words, and
good deeds, of good religion, I am thine own conscience!

" ' "Everyone did love thee for that greatness, goodness, fairness, sweet-scentedness, victorious strength
and freedom from grief, in which thou dost appear
to me;

" ' "And so thou, oh youth of good thoughts, good
words, and good deeds, of good religion, didst love me

for that greatness, goodness, fairness, sweet-scented-ness, victorious strength, and freedom from grief in which I appear to thee.

" ' "When thou wouldst see a man deriding and performing deeds of idolatry, or rejecting (the poor) and shutting his door, then thou wouldst sit singing the Gathas and worshiping the good waters and Atar, the Son of God, and rejoicing the faithful that would come from near or from afar.

" ' "I was lovely and thou madest me still lovelier; I was fair and thou madest me still fairer; I was desirable and thou madest me still more desirable; I was sitting in a forward place and thou madest me sit in the foremost place, through this good thought, through this good speech, through this good deed of thine; and so henceforth men make obeisance unto me for my having long sacrificed unto and conversed with God."

" 'The first step that the soul of the faithful man maketh, placeth him in the Good-Thought Paradise; the second step that the soul of the faithful man maketh, placeth him in the Good-Word Paradise; the third step that the soul of the faithful man maketh, placeth him in the Good-Deed Paradise; the fourth step that the soul of the faithful man maketh, placeth him in the Eternal Light.

" 'Then one of the faithful, who had departed before him, asketh him, saying, "How didst thou depart this life, thou holy man? How didst thou come, thou holy man, from the abodes full of cattle and full of the wishes and enjoyments of love, from the material world, into the world of spirit? From the world of corruption into the world of incorruption? How long did thy felicity last?"

" 'And the Lord God maketh answer for him, saying, "Ask him not what thou asketh him who hath just trod the dreary way, full of fear and distress, where the body and the soul part from one another. (Let him eat) of the food brought to him, of the oil of Zaremaya; [2] this is the food for the youth of good thoughts, of good words, of good deeds, of good religion, after he hath departed his life. This is the food for the saintly woman, rich in good thoughts, good words, and good deeds, well-principled and obedient to her husband, after she hath departed this life." '

"Zoroaster also inquired of God, saying, 'Oh Lord God, Most Beneficent Spirit, Maker of the material world, thou Holy One, when one of the wicked perisheth, where doth his soul abide on that night?'

"The Lord God made answer and said, 'It rusheth and sitteth near the skull, singing the Kima Gatha, [3] oh holy Zoroaster (which runneth), "To what land shall I turn, oh God? To whom shall I go with my praying?"

" 'On that night his soul tasteth as much of suffering as the whole of the living world can taste.'

" 'On the second night where doth his soul abide?'

"The Lord God answered and said, 'It rusheth and sitteth near the skull, singing the Kima Gatha, oh holy Zoroaster, "To what land shall I turn, oh God? To whom shall I go with my praying?" '

" 'On that night his soul tasteth as much of suffering as the whole of the living world can taste.'

" 'On the third night where doth his soul abide?'

"The Lord God made answer and said, 'It rusheth and sitteth near the skull, singing the Kima Gatha, oh

[2] This is fresh butter made in the spring.
[3] The Gatha of lamentation.

holy Zoroaster, "To what land shall I turn, oh God? To whom shall I go with my praying?" '

" 'On that night his soul tasteth as much of suffering as the whole of the living world can taste.

" 'At the end of the third night, oh holy Zoroaster, when the dawn appeareth, it seemeth to the soul of him of the faith as if it were brought amongst snow and stench and as if a wind were blowing from the region of the north, a foul-scented wind, the foulest-scented of all the winds in the world. And it seemeth to the soul of the wicked man as if he were inhaling that wind with the nostrils, and he thinketh, "Whence doth that wind blow, the foulest-scented wind that I ever inhaled with my nostrils?"

" 'The first step that the soul of the wicked man maketh, layeth him in the Evil-Thought Hell; the second step that the soul of the wicked man maketh, layeth him in the Evil-Word Hell; the third step that the soul of the wicked man maketh, layeth him in the Evil-Deed Hell; the fourth step that the soul of the wicked man maketh, layeth him in Eternal Darkness.

" 'Then one of the wicked who departed before him, addresseth him, saying, "How didst thou perish, oh wicked man? How didst thou come, oh fiend, from the abodes full of cattle and full of the wishes and enjoyments of love, from the material world into the world of spirit? From the world of corruption into the world of incorruption? How long did thy suffering last?"

" 'And Ahriman, the father of lies, maketh answer for him, saying, "Ask him not what thou asketh him who hath just trod the dreary way, full of fear and distress, where the body and the soul part from one another. Let him eat of the food brought unto him, of poison and poisonous stench. This is the food, after he hath perished, for the youth of evil thoughts, evil words, evil deeds, evil religion; after she hath perished, this is the food for the devilish woman, rich in evil thoughts, evil words and evil deeds, evil religion, ill-principled and disobedient to her husband"'" (Yast XXII, c. II, 1-36).

The exceptional aptness of this account has long been appreciated by students of the religions of the world; it is scarcely matched, if at all, by any passage of a similar sort in other scriptures.

It is also noteworthy as marking the abandonment of what appears to have been the earlier idea that only the righteous achieve immortality at all, and the adoption of the belief that all souls are, by nature, necessarily immortal.

The three nights, during which life is treated rather as suspended than extinct, the soul remaining beside the body according to the account just given, correspond with the period of time that the body should be preserved, as is generally agreed in all countries, in order to assure that resuscitation will not take place. Among the Parsis these are known as the three nights of trial; during them the nearest relative is held responsible for maintaining a prayerful watch with appropriate ceremonies. Of this the Dadistan-i-Dinik (c. LV, 1, 2) says:

"What are the qualifications and relationship of the person who hath the duty of sustaining the soul that is in its three nights' trial, and who is that person? The answer is, according to tradition, that the husband must officiate to sustain through the three nights' trial the soul of a privileged wife, a father for his child and a master for his thrall."

The performance of these pious offices was most strictly enjoined by the Parsi authorities. The duty of such performance the Dadistan-i-Dinik (c. LXXXI. 1-4) discusses, as follows:

"What is the purpose of this ceremony for the surviving soul and why is it essential to require it? And, when it is required, in what way should the order go forth? . . . The answer is, that compliance with the ceremonies for them that have just passed away, during the three days they spend in giving account (of the deeds done in the body) is incumbent upon thinking men, just as to succor those newly-born is incumbent upon thinking men. He is, in sooth, a thinking man by whom the three days' ceremonies are observed for the soul of his father, his privileged wife, his minor child, his faithful thrall, when such hath passed away; and it is indispensable that the three days' ceremony be ordered."

The same book gives the following account, explaining by an apt simile what takes place at death:

"When they shall snatch forth the life from the body of man, how doth it depart? The answer is, according to tradition, that it is in semblance such as when the redness is drawn up out of the fire; for, when the inflammable material is burnt by the fire, and has reached the stage of ceasing to glow, and it doth not obtain new inflammable material, or when extinguishing matter cometh upon it; its redness and heat then depart from it; so the life, too, on the departure of the breath, remaining not in the body, but in like manner departeth" (Dadistan-i-Dinik, c. XXIII, 1, 2).

In another place the same book thus explains both the desertion of the body by the righteous soul, and the dispersion of the body:

"And of that, too, which is righteous and filled with great joy that ariseth from being really certain of the best existence, then the spiritual life which was in the body, on account of its great righteousness which was continually accumulated by it while in the body, fit for exaltation, is fully-developed; and the wonderfully-constructed body is cast off as a garment, so that its dispersion into its elements is occasioned thereby" (Dadistan-i-Dinik, c. XVI, 6).

The Aögemaïde Nask (84) thus identifies that which escapes extinction when life abandons the body:

"That which doth not mingle with the dust are the Ashemvohus (i.e. the praises of holiness) that the man hath recited in this world and the alms that he hath given to the holy and the righteous."

That is to say, the Good Mind is in it that persists; but, if so, how do those of the Evil Mind survive? This appears to be a recrudescence of the older notion that the good only are immortal, set forth in an allusive fashion.

Elsewhere the Nasks (Tahmura's Fragments, c. XXIV, 43-44) promise for the righteous soul admission to Paradise and its joys, saying:

"And every righteous man is borne up to Paradise; and joy is given unto the soul of the righteous man that hath departed."

The Nasks in another place furnish this explicit and detailed account of the welcome of the righteous soul into the realms of the blest, there to abide throughout all time:

"Up riseth Vohu-Manah (the Good Mind) from his golden throne.

"He will take the blessed one by the hand;

"And make him rejoice as much as doth the man

who rejoiceth most, when on the pinnacle of nobility and glory.

"And the souls of the righteous will bring to the soul of the blessed one those precious aliments that are made at the time of Maïdyozarm. . . .

"As the sheep, on which the wolf is pouncing, tremble at the odor of the wolf, so the Drujs tremble at the perfume of the blessed one" (Aögemaïde Nask, 12-15, 19).

CHAPTER XXX

THE SIFTING BRIDGE FOR SOULS

"Whoso, either man or woman, doeth what thou, oh God (Ahura Mazda), knowest as best in life, as fated for what is the Right, give him the Dominion through the Good Mind; with those whom I impel to adore thee, will I cross the Sifting Bridge."

These words the Gathas (Yasna XLVI, 10) ascribe to Zoroaster, in relation to his followers, the elect of mankind; for these, also, a promise that they shall safely cross this bridge, is found in the Nasks (Tahmura's Fragments, c. VI, 2) as follows:

"For all of them shall a path be opened across the Kinvad Bridge."

In the Vendidad the story of how the souls of the dead approach the Sifting Bridge and how the righteous pass over in safety is set forth in this passage (Fargard XIX, c. V, 27-30):

" 'Oh Maker of the material world, thou Holy One (Ahura Mazda), where are the rewards given? Where doth the rewarding take place? Where is the rewarding fulfilled? Where do men come to take the reward that, during their lives in the material world, they have won for their souls?'

"God made answer and said, 'When a man is dead, when his time is over, then the wicked, evil-doing Daëvas cut off his eyesight. On the third night, when the dawn appeareth and brighteneth up, when Mithra, the god with beautiful weapons, reacheth the all-happy mountains and the sun is rising, then the demon, named Vizaresha,[1] oh Spitama Zoroaster, carrieth off in bonds the souls of the wicked Daëva-worshippers who live in sin. The soul entereth the way made by Time and open both to the wicked and to the righteous. At the head of the Kinvad Bridge, the holy bridge made by God, they ask for their spirits and souls the reward for the worldly goods which they gave away here below.

" 'Then cometh the beautiful, well-shapen, strong and well-formed woman, with the dogs at her sides, one who can distinguish, who hath many children, happy, and with lofty comprehension.

" 'She maketh the soul of the righteous one to go up above the Hara-berazaïti mountain; above the Kinvad Bridge she placeth it in the presence of the heavenly hosts, themselves.

" 'Up riseth then Vohu-Manah from his golden seat. Vohu-Manah exclaimeth "How hast thou come to us, thou holy one, from that decaying world into this undecaying one?"

" 'Gladly pass the souls of the righteous to the golden seat of God (Ahura Mazda), to the golden seat of the Amesha Spentas, to Heaven, the abode of God, the abode of the Amesha Spentas, the abode of all the other holy beings.' "

The Dadistan-i-Dinik (c. XX, 1-4) gives a circumstantial account of this experience and also of that of the wicked man, in the following passage:

" 'To what places go the righteous and the wicked?'

"The reply is this, that it is said that the souls of those passed away and dead are three nights on earth; and the first night satisfaction cometh to them from

---

[1] Who sits at the gate of Hell.

their good thoughts and vexation from their evil thoughts, the second night cometh pleasure from their good words and discomfort and punishment from their evil words, and the third night cometh exaltation from their good deeds and punishment from their evil deeds. And that the third night, at the dawn, they go to the place of account at Alburz;[2] the account being rendered, they proceed to the bridge, and he who is righteous, passeth over the bridge on the ascent and, if belonging to the ever-stationary, he goeth thither where their place is; if along with an excess of good works, his habits are correct, he goeth even unto Heaven; and, if, along with an excess of good works and correct habits, he hath chanted the sacred hymns, he goeth even unto the supreme Heaven. He who is of the wicked, falleth from the lower end of the bridge, or from the middle of the bridge; he falleth head-foremost to hell, and is precipitated unto that grade which is suitable for his wickedness."

In the next chapter of that book is found this account:

" 'Moreover, the bridge becometh a broad bridge for the righteous, as much as the height of nine spears and the length of those whom they carry is each separately three reeds; and it becometh a narrow bridge for the wicked, even unto a resemblance to the edge of a razor. And he who is of the righteous passeth over the bridge, and a worldly similitude of the pleasantness of his path upon it is when thou shalt eagerly and unweariedly walk in the golden-colored spring and with the gallant body and sweet-scented blossom in the pleasant skin of that maiden-spirit, the price of goodness. He who is of the wicked, as he placeth his foot

---

[2] A chain of mountains at the Kinvad Bridge.

upon the bridge, on account of affliction and its sharpness, falleth from the middle of the bridge, and rolleth over head-foremost; and the unpleasantness of his path to hell is in similitude such as the worldly one in the midst of that stinking and dying existence there where numbers of the sharp-pointed darts are planted, inverted and points upwards; and they come unwillingly running, for they are not permitted to stay behind, or to make delay. So much greater than the worldly similitude, is that pleasantness and unpleasantness unto the souls, as that which is fit for the spirit is greater than that which is fit for material existence'" (Dadistan-i-Dinik, c. XXI, 5-9).

The selections of Zad-sparam (c. I, 13) identify the punishment of the wicked at the Sifting Bridge with mere retribution growing out of one's own misdeeds:

"The first is that, of all things, that is proper which is declared as the will of God (Ahura Mazda); so that, whereas that is proper which is declared the will of God, where anything existeth which is not within the will of God, it is created injurious from the beginning, a sin of a positive nature. The second is this, that whoever shall do that which is the will of God, his reward and recompense are his own; and whoever shall not do that which is the will of God, the punishment at the bridge, owing thereto, is his own."

This is an echo of that which the Gathas say (Yasna XLVI, 11) as follows:

"By their dominion the Karpans and Kavis accustomed mankind to evil actions, so as to destroy life. Their own souls and their own selves shall torment them when they come where the Sifting Bridge is; to all time they are dwellers in the house of the lie."

CHAPTER XXXI

HEAVEN, HELL, PURGATORY AND THE WAY OUT

"HEAVEN is for saintly souls; and none of them that are wicked can enter Heaven and its shining, wide, sacred streets (and approach) near unto God (Ahura Mazda)."

Thus the Ardibehist Yast (c. I, 4) sets Heaven apart for the saints, with access barred to the sinful.

The Shayast-La-Shayast (c. XI, 3) says of it:

"Every one ought to be unhesitatingly of one mind about this, that righteousness is the one thing, and Heaven the one place, which is good."

That it is a state and, indeed, a state of mind, however, and not a place, the Gathas thus imply:

"And when these two spirits came together in the beginning, then they set up Life and Not-Life, and at last the worst shall be for them that follow the lie but the best for them that pursue the Right" (Yasna XXX, 4).

As much is further implied in this passage of the same Yasna (10) although it is there spoken of as an abode:

"Then truly upon the lie will come the blow of destruction; while they that give them the good name shall partake in the promised prize in the fair abode of the Good Mind, of God (Ahura Mazda) and of the Right."

The "Ashem Vohu," an invocation prescribed by the

241

Zend Avesta (Fargard XIX, c. IV, 22) and in common use by the Parsis, runs thus:

"Holiness is the best of all good; it is also happiness. Happy the man who is holy with perfect holiness."

Which is really meant to say that such a man is in Heaven or, to put it in another way, has Heaven in him.

The latter idea is adopted by the Bahman Yast (c. XI, 56) in this passage which also indicates that Heaven is not postponed to the future life but is also possessed here and now:

"And, moreover, I tell thee this, oh Zoroaster, the Spitaman, that whoever, in that time, appealeth for the body, is not able to save the soul; for he is, as it were, fat and his soul is hungry and lean in hell; whoever appealeth for the soul, his body is hungry and lean through the misery of the world, and destitute, and his soul is fat in Heaven."

There is a strong reminder of "what profiteth it a man that he gain the whole world and lose his own soul?" in this saying from the Nasks (Sundry Fragments, c. III):

"He hath gained nothing that hath not gained the soul. He gaineth nothing that gaineth not the soul."

Heaven is, however, the state, or the abode, constantly of God (Ahura Mazda) and the Amesha Spentas; from it strains of holy music issue, with which the songs of the saints may be in harmony. For it is said in the Gathas (Yasna L, 4):

"Thus will I worship thee, oh God (Ahura Mazda), praising ever with the Right the Good Mind and Dominion, that they, desired of pious men, may stand as judges on the path of the obedient toward the house of song."

That which constitutes such harmony and that which
will entitle one to Heaven for all eternity, is thus
summed up in the Aögemaïde Nask (III):

"All the good thoughts, good words, and good deeds
done or to be done, here or elsewhere, we seize upon
and we transmit them, that we may be in the number
of the righteous."

This is also put in more definite words in another
Nask (Westergard's Fragments, Vispa Humata, c.
III, 2):

"All good thoughts, all good words, all good deeds
will reach Paradise.

"All evil thoughts, all evil words, all evil deeds will
reach hell.

"And all good thoughts, all good words, all good
deeds are the badge of the righteous for Paradise."

The Aögemaïde Nask (82, 83) records that Zoroaster
was admonished by the Almighty, thus:

"The wicked acquire cattle, the wicked acquire
horses, the wicked acquire sheep and corn; but the
wicked tyrant doth not acquire a store of good deeds.
Seek ye for a store of good deeds, oh Zoroaster and
men and women! For a store of good deeds is full of
salvation, oh Zoroaster!"

The Nirangistan Nask (Fargard II, c. V, 84) thus
contrasts these requisites with the conduct of him who
seeks for selfish satisfactions of his lusts:

"Woe to the struggler who struggles for the satisfaction of his own soul, oh Spitama Zoroaster!

"Woe to the deceiver who deceiveth for the satisfaction of his own soul, oh Spitama Zoroaster!

"Woe to the giver who giveth for the satisfaction of
his own soul, oh Spitama Zoroaster!

"For the gift that delivereth all the world of men,

consisteth in good thoughts, good words, and good deeds."

The Aögemaïde Nask (20) gives this warning to him who procrastinates as if life were assured and death far removed:

"For whosoever hath been born and whosoever shall be born, must act in such a way that, when the moment cometh to leave this world, he may have Paradise as his portion and Heaven as his reward."

And, when he passes out of this world, he is judged according to the state in which he already dwells, as the Gathas (Yasna XXXI, 12) say in this:

"Then lifts up his voice the true speaker or the false, he that knows or he that knows not, in accord with his own heart and thought. Passing forever, one to another, Piety pleads with the spirit which is wavering."

This the Aögemaïde Nask (51, 52) expresses in the following eloquent and beautiful fashion:

"There cometh a day, oh Spitama Zoroaster, or a night, when the master quitteth his cattle, or the cattle quit their master, or the soul quitteth that body, full of lusts; but his virtue, which is of all that is, the greatest, the best, the finest, never parteth from a man."

The Vendidad (Fargard XIX, c. V, 47) says that, whenever the Ashem-Vohu is spoken, "Holiness is the best of all good," then:

"They rush away yelling, the wicked, evil-doing-demons, into the depths of the dark, raging abyss of hell."

The Bundahis (c. III, 27) describes hell as an actual place and gives its location in quite the orthodox way, thus:

"Hell is at the center of the earth."

The Vistasp Yast (c. VI, 43) intimates that it is a veritable place below the surface of the earth, in this passage:

"He who hath little liking for the law, him place I down below to suffer."

The Vendidad (Fargard VIII, c. III, 21) thus identifies it with the polar region:

"Perish away to the regions of the north!"

In another place (Fargard I, 3, 4) the same book declares:

"Thereupon came Ahriman who is all death and he counter-created the serpent in the river, the winter, a work of the demons. . . . Winter falleth there, the worst of all plagues."

But the Dadistan-i-Dinik (c. XXXII, 10, 11) identifies it with a state existing in this life, inevitably connected with one's wrongdoing as effect of that cause, and continuing in the next life until the sin is utterly expiated by the purgatorial fires; the passage runs thus:

"Incarceration in hell is not at an end before the resurrection, and until the time of the renovation of the universe, he remaineth in hell. Also, out of his sin cometh the punishment connected with it, and that punishment cometh upon him, from the demon and spirit of his own sin, in that manner and proportion with which he hath harassed and vexed others, and hath reverenced, praised, and served that which is evil."

This principle that each sin brings with it its own punishment and that the evil spirit that prompted it, officiates at the ordeal, is peculiarly Zoroastrian.

The same book gives at another place this circumstantial account, both of how the demons of a man's lusts take vengeance upon him in this world and in the next, after their nature, and how he is at last to be delivered from their torments:

"The punishment for the soul of a sinner cometh from that spirit with which the sin, which was committed by it, is connected; fostered by the iniquity practiced, that punishment cometh upon the souls of the sinful and wicked, first on earth, afterwards in hell, and lastly at the organization of the future existence. When the punishment of the three nights is undergone, the soul of the righteous attaineth to Heaven and the best existence, and the soul of the wicked to hell and the worst existence. When these have undergone their punishment, at the renovation of the universe they attain, by complete purification from every sin, unto the everlasting progress, happy progress, and perfect progress of the best and undisturbed existence" (Dadistan-i-Dinik, c. XIV, 6-8).

That "there is none holy, not one" has, of course, occurred to the author of this scripture, and accordingly in another place (c. XIII, 1, 2) the Dadistan-i-Dinik deals with the "balance" between one's good deeds and his evil deeds and describes the shortened purgatorial penance appointed unto poor, frail mortals who do not measure up and yet are not wholly evil; it runs:

" 'In the fourth night, do they score off the sin by the good works, and doth he go by the residue? Or do they inflict punishment on him for the sin which hath happened to him, and give reward and recompense for the good works which he hath done?'

"The reply is this, that at the dawn of the third night the account is prepared, it is said, and about the sin which he hath atoned for and the good work which is its equivalent, there is no need for account, since the account is about the good works which may·be appropriated by him as his own, or about the sin which may remain in him as its origin (i.e. the surplus). . . .

"Of those living, at the just, impartial balance, the man of proper habits whose good works are more, though sin hath happened to him, undergoeth a temporary punishment and becometh eternally cleansed by the good works; and he of improper habits, of much sin and little good works, attaineth temporary enjoyment by those good works, but through the sin which they perceive in him, he suffereth punishment until the resurrection."

The impropriety of finding a man worthy of this is shown by this warning in the Shayast-La-Shayast (c. XII, 28, 29):

"The rule is this, that thou shouldst not consider anyone whatever without hope of Heaven, and men should not set their minds steadfastly on hell; thereby much sinning for which there may be lust, becometh undesirable, for in my religion there is nothing which is a sin for which there is no atoning. . . . And as to him, even, who is a very sinful person, through the desire of good works which is entertained by him, there yet may come to him in all its fullness the joy of a soul newly made worthy."

The same book (c. X, 22) quotes the Nihadum Nask (not now extant):

"That the duty and good works which a son performeth are as much the father's as though they had been done by his own hand."

Thus they point out a way out of purgatory for a wicked father through religious ceremonies provided at the son's cost.

The Dadistan-i-Dinik, however, limits this rule to sacrifices in some way authorized by the deceased, though in such case they may be provided by any person who is interested in the peace of the soul of the departed or at the expense of the estate of the deceased, if so provided in his will.

This is so similar to a practice that grew up under Christian and largely Catholic auspices that the following rules have special interest:

"The seventh question is that you ask thus, 'When a man is passing away, and after the occurrence of his passing away, how doth the good work then avail him and assist him, which others may do for him who hath gone out from the world, on the third night in the dawn, at which he goeth out to the balance? And doth it count as though it were done by his own hand, or otherwise?'

"The reply is this: 'When others do a good work for him who hath passed away, after the passing away, if he who hath passed away, did not order that good work in his lifetime, and did not bequeath it, nor was its originator, and it was not even his idea, then it is not accepted and doth not avail him at the balance. . . .

" 'If he who hath passed away, did not order that good work, and did not even bequeath it, but was consenting to it by design, that which shall be done in his lifetime then availeth in the three nights for the improvement of his condition but that which shall be done after his passing away, is not in the account of the three nights or in the balance, but availeth at the time the good work is proceeded with, for the peace of his soul.

" 'And if he who hath passed away, ordered that good work in his lifetime, or bequeathed it, or was the originator and cause of the soul's being engaged in it, then although it is proceeded with after passing away, it then availeth him for the welfare of his soul, since the originator of the service and he that ordered and owneth the good works are certain.

" 'Any good work whatever, which is proceedeth with, is clearly a like good work, as regards those who are responsible for it, as with him who is the doer of it; also, in the account of his soul, the good work is as much his as the man's who did it; but the soul of him by whom the good work is done by his own hand, is finer and stronger than that of him by whom it is ordered' " (Dadistan-i-Dinik, c. VIII, 1, 2, 4-6).

The same book (c. IX, 3, 5) further qualifies this form of vicarious atonement:

"And among the kinds of good work, that is more effectual which one practiseth himself and with his own toil; then that which one setteth going out of whatever is his own, by his own order, regarding which he afterwards bequeathes and ordereth it out of his own property and it thus cometh to be done; and, lastly, that which others may do for him.

"When not consenting to the good work, and it is not his by design, even though others may do it for him, it doth not then become his at all."

CHAPTER XXXII

RESURRECTION AND THE LAST JUDGMENT

"The dead shall rise, life shall return to the bodies and they shall breathe again."

Thus says one of the Nasks (Westergard's Fragments, c. IV, 3) concerning the resurrection of the dead, which was taught by the later Zoroastrian scriptures, notwithstanding their pristine doctrine that the soul survives, which appears to make it unnecessary to follow with a further account.

There is not very much about this in the most ancient of the Zoroastrian scriptures and the little there is might be glosses added at later date, or be susceptible of other explanation, except that Saöshyant is mentioned.

It is a most singular view for those who practice destruction of the body by beasts and birds, to hold; and it may be inferred that it came from the Egyptians after the Persians by their conquests came into contact with the already very ancient civilization, especially as there is little evidence of it in the Gathas.

Resurrection was prophesied to take place at the end of the world; in consequence of which the Dadistan-i-Dinik (c. XXXV, 1, 2) asks and answers the following question:

" 'Doth this world become quite without men, so that there is no bodily existence in it, whatever, and then shall they produce the resurrection, or how is it?'

"The reply is this, that this world, continuously from its immaturity even unto its pure renovation, hath never been, and also will not be, without men."

The same book in another place (c. XVI, 7) puts this question upon the lips, if such they may be called, of the spirit newly departed from the body:

"And the consciousness of a man, as it sitteth three nights outside the body, in the vicinity of the body, hath to remember and expect that which is truly fear and trouble unto the demons, and reward, peace, and glad tidings unto the spirits of the good; and, on account of the dispersion and injuring of the body, it uttereth a cry spiritually thus, 'Why do the beasts and birds gnaw this organized body when still at last the body and life unite together at the raising of the dead?' "

This disturbing question, how the particles that compose given bodies can be reassembled when at different times they must have been portions of many bodies, came up in the following from the Bundahis (c. XXX, 4-7):

"After Saöshyant cometh, they produce the raising of dead, as it saith, that Zoroaster inquired of God (Ahura Mazda) saying, 'Whence doth a body form again, which the wind hath carried and the water conveyed and how doth the resurrection occur?' God made answer and said, 'When through me the sky arose from the substance of the ruby, without columns, on the spiritual support of far-compassed light; when through me the earth arose, which bore the material life, and there is no maintainer of the worldly creation but this; when by me the sun and moon and stars are conducted in the firmament of luminous bodies; when by me corn was created so that, scattered about in the

252 THE ETHICAL RELIGION OF ZOROASTER

earth, it grew again and returned with increase; when by me color of various kinds was created in plants; when by me fire was created in plants and other things without combustion; when by me a son was created and fashioned in the womb of a mother, and the structure severally of the skin, nails, blood, feet, eyes, ears, and other things was produced; when by me legs were created for the water, so that it floweth away, and the cloud was created which carrieth the water of the world and raineth where and when it listeth; when by me the air was created which conveyeth in one's eyesight, through the strength of the wind, the lower-most upwards according to its will, and one is not able to grasp it with the hand outstretched; each one of them, when created by me, was herein more difficult than causing the resurrection, for it is an assistance to me in the resurrection that they exist; but when they were formed, it was not forming what becometh, out of what was, the future out of the past. Observe that when that which was not, was then produced, why is it not possible to reproduce that which was? For at that time one will demand the bone from the spirit of earth, the blood from the water, the hair from the plants, and the life from the fire, since they were delivered to them in the original creation.

"First, the bones of Gayomard are raised, then those of Mashya and Mashyoi, then those of the rest of mankind; in the fifty-seven years of Saöshyant they prepare all the dead, and all men stand up; whoever is righteous and whoever is wicked, every human creature, they raise from the spot where its life departeth."

The same book, however, relates that God assured the Devil at the outset that the resurrection was decreed and that then his own impotence would be demonstrated, thus:

"He (Ahura Mazda) also exhibited to the Evil Spirit his own triumph in the end, and the impotence of the Evil Spirit, the annihilation of the demons, and the resurrection and undisturbed future existence of the creatures forever and ever" (Bundahis, c. I, 21).

One of the Nasks (II, Zend Fragments, 5) says concerning what follows after the resurrection, according to the Zoroastrian scriptures:

"The whole physical world shall become free from old age and death, from corruption and decay, forever and ever."

There is, however, according to these scriptures, much human preparation necessary before this can come about, especially since those who have not passed through death, will then never need to do so. The Bundahis (c. XXX, 1) speaks of this as follows:

"On the nature of the resurrection and the future existence it says in revelation, that, whereas Mashya and Mashyoi, who grew up from the earth, first subsisted upon water, then plants, then milk, and then meat and, when their time of death hath come, first desisted from eating meat, then milk, then bread, until as death draweth near, they always subsisted upon water, so, likewise, in the millennium of Husedar-mah, the power of the appetite will thus diminish until men will remain three days and nights in overnutrition through one taste of consecrated food. Then they will desist from meat food and eat vegetables and milk; afterwards, they will abstain from milk and abstain from vegetables and they will subsist on water; and for ten years before Saöshyant comes, they will remain without food and yet not die."

The Dadistan-i-Dinik makes the same report concerning the preparation of mankind for that last day, in this passage (c. XXXV, 3):

"And near to the time of the renovation the souls yet in the flesh desist from eating and live without food; and the offspring who are born from them are those of an immortal, for they possess lasting and blood-free bodies. Such shall they be, who will yet exist in the flesh in the world when the dead shall rise and live again."

This circumstantial account of what takes place immediately after the resurrection of the dead is found in the Bundahis (c. XXX, 8-15):

"Afterwards, when all material things assume again their bodies and forms, then they assign them all to one class. Of the light accompanying the sun, one-half will be for Gayomard, and one-half will give enlightenment among the rest of men, so that the incarnate soul will know, 'This is my father,' 'This is my mother,' 'This is my brother,' 'This is my wife,' and 'These are some of my nearest relatives.'

"Then comes the assembly of the Sadvastaran, where all mankind will stand at this time; in that assembly everyone seeeth his own good deeds and his own evil deeds; and thus, in that assembly, a wicked man becometh as conspicuous as a white sheep among those which are black. In that assembly whatever righteous man was friend of a wicked one in the world, and the wicked man complaineth of him who is righteous, 'Why did he not make me acquainted, when in the world, with the good deeds which he practiced, himself?' And if he who is righteous did not inform him, then it is necessary for that man to suffer shame accordingly in that assembly.

"Afterwards, they set the righteous man apart from the wicked; and then the righteous is for Heaven and they cast the wicked back to hell. Three days and nights they inflict physical punishment in hell, and then he in the flesh is shown those three days' happiness in Heaven.

"It is said that, on the day when the righteous man is parted from the wicked, the tears of every one, thereupon, run down unto his legs. For, when they separate husband from wife, brother from brother, friend from friend, they suffer, every one for his own deeds, and weep, the righteous man for the wicked, and the wicked man about himself; for there may be a father who is righteous and a son wicked, and there may be one brother who is righteous and one wicked."

In the same chapter of the Bundahis (c. XXX, 18-20) this account of the purification by fire is given:

"As Gokihar [1] falleth in the celestial sphere from a moonbeam upon the earth, the distress of the earth becometh like unto that of a sheep when a wolf falleth upon it. Afterwards, the fire and the glow melt the metal of Khshathra in the hills and mountains, and it remaineth on this earth like a river. Then all men pass through that melted metal and become pure. When one is righteous, then it seemeth to him just as though he walketh continually in warm milk; but, when wicked, then it seemeth to him as though, in the world, he was treading in molten metal."

The same book (c. XXX, 31) tells of the destruction of the devil in this fire, thus:

"Gokihar burneth the serpent in the melted metal, and the stench and pollution which were in hell are burned in that metal, and it becometh quite pure. God

[1] A meteor.

(Ahura Mazda) setteth the vault into which the Evil Spirit fled, in that metal; he bringeth the land of hell back for the enlargement of the world; the renovation ariseth in the universe by his will, and the world is immortal forever and ever."

The Dadistan-i-Dinik furnishes this, which is really an explanation of the foregoing and especially of the efficacy of fire for purification and of the complete elimination of Ahriman, the Druj and all the demons:

"And at the time of the renovation, when the devil perisheth, the souls of the wicked pass into melted metal for three days; and all demons and evil thoughts, which exist because of their sin, suffer their final throes and are hurried away by the cutting and breaking away of the accumulation of sin from the wicked souls. And by that supreme ablution in the melted metal they are thoroughly purified from guilt and infamy and, through the perseverance and mercy of the supreme immortals, they are pardoned and become most saintly and pure.

"And after that purification there are no demons, no punishment, and no hell for the wicked; and their disposal also is just, they become righteous, painless, deathless, free from fear and from malice, and with them cometh the spirit of the good works which were done and caused by them in the world, and procureth them pleasure and joy in the degree and proportion of those good works. But the recompense of a soul of the righteous is a better and greater thing" (c. XXXII, 12-16).

The story of what actually takes place, according to the later Zoroastrian conceptions of the matter, is told in the Bundahis (c. XXX, 21, 24-25) in these words:

"Afterwards with the greatest affection, all men come together. Father and son and brother and friend ask one another, "Where hath thy soul been these many years, and what was the judgment upon it? Hast thou been righteous or wicked? . . .

"God (Ahura Mazda) completeth his work at that time, and the creatures become so that it is not necessary to do anything further about them; and it is not necessary that those by whom the dead are prepared, do anything further about them.

"Saöshyant, with his assistants, performs a Yaziz ceremony in preparing the dead, and they slaughter the ox Hadhayos in that Yazisn; from the fat of that ox and the white Hom [2] they prepare Hush, [3] and give it to all men, and all men become immortal forever and ever.

"This, too, it saith, that, whoever were the size of a man, they restore them with an age of forty years; they who have been little when not dead, they restore them with an age of fifteen years; and they give every one his wife, and show him his children with the wife; so they act as now in the world, but there is no begetting of children."

The new life is upon this earth, but it is a new earth, purified and transformed—in what manner the plainsmen, among whom the later Zoroastrian religion came into existence, themselves hating the mountains as the fastnesses of the dread marauders, conceived, is indicated by the following:

"This, too, it says, that this earth becometh an iceless, slopeless plain; even the mountain whose summit is the support of the Kinvad Bridge, they press down, and it will not exist" (Bundahis, c. XXX, 33).

The Dadistan-i-Dinik (c. XXXVII, 120-124) cele-

[2] The fabled flower from under the sea.
[3] Nectar for consumption by immortals.

brates the freedom from pain of all men after the destruction of the devil, in this realistic fashion:

"After the renovation of the universe there is no demon because there is no deceit, and no Druj because there is no falsity; there is no Evil Spirit because there is no destruction; there is no hell, because there is no wickedness; there is no strife, because there is no anger; there is no hatred, because there is no ill-temper; there is no pain, because there is no disease. There is no king, because there is no fear; there is no want, because there is no greediness; there is no shame, because there is no deformity; there is no falsehood, because there is no desire of falsehood; there is no heterodoxy because there are no false statements. . . .

"And on his disappearance (i.e. of Ahriman) every evil disappeareth; on the disappearance of evil every good is perfected; and, in the time of complete goodness, it is not possible to occasion any pain or distress whatever, by any means, to any creature. Those who are now sufferers, when there is a blow of a fist on the body, or the point of a nail is driven into a limb, are pained on account of the combination of a different nature, for the purposes of the fiend, in the body. But at that time of no complication, when a limb is struck upon a limb, or even such a thing as a knife, or sword, or club, or stone, or arrow reaches the body, there is no pain or discomfort whatever, corresponding to that present pain."

How this means, for every human soul, limitless and perpetual progress, the Bundahis (c. XXX, 27) indicates in this:

"Afterwards, Saöshyant and his assistants, by order of the Lord God (Ahura Mazda), the Creator, give every man the reward and recompense suitable to his deeds, that is, even the righteous existence where it is said that they convey him to Paradise and the Heaven of God taketh up the body as itself hath need. With that assistance he continually advanceth forever and ever."

At the close of all things terrestrial, the later Zoroastrian scriptures represent light as dispelling all darkness and Ahriman and his brood, together with all delusion, wholly disappearing.

This the Ardibehist Yast (c. II, 7, 8, 17) thus celebrates:

"Sickness fled away (before it); death fled away; the Daëva fled away; the Daëvas' counterwork fled away; the unholy Ashemaögha⁵ fled away; the oppressor of men fled away;

"The brood of the snake fled away; the brood of the wolf fled away; the brood of the two-legged fled away; Pride fled away; Scorn fled away; Hot Fever fled away; Slander fled away; Discord fled away; the Evil Eye fled away. . . .

"The Druj will perish away; the Druj will perish; the Druj will rush; the Druj will vanish. Thou perishest away to the regions of the North, never more to give unto death the living world of the holy spirit."

This redemption of God's creatures is, according to the Zamyad Yast (c. IV, 21-23) to be accomplished by the human servants of the living God, operating as guided by that wisdom which is the essence of the divine, thus:

"We sacrifice unto the awful, kingly Glory, made by God (Ahura Mazda) that belongeth to the angels in Heaven and to them in the material world, and to the

⁵ Infidel.

blessed ones, born or not yet born, who are to perform the restoration of the world.

"It is they who shall restore the world, which will (thenceforth) never grow old and never die, never decay and never perish, ever survive and ever increase, and be master of their wish, when the dead will rise, when life and immortality will come, and the world will be restored at its wish:

"When all creation will become immortal, the blest creation of the Good Spirit!"

CHAPTER XXXIII

THE SPIRITUAL UNIVERSE, NOW AND EVER

"As to the godly man who hath been purified, the wicked, evil-doing demons tremble at the perfume of his soul after death, as doth a sheep upon which a wolf is pouncing."

This saying of the Vendidad (Fargard XIX, c. V, 33) which quoted in one of the Nasks, closed an earlier chapter upon the departing soul, rightly opens this chapter upon the spiritual universe, which the Parsis, following the Zoroastrians, conceive of as composing the entire, sentient universe. It treats of spiritual lives other than lives which formerly were human and with which human lives may flourish both in bodies and after death.

The Aögemaïde Nask, from which the passage containing the quotation is taken echoes in another place (77) the sentiment that the soul has departed to "a bourne from which no traveler returns" in these words:

"The way may be traversed that is barred by a river springing out of the depths; but one way cannot be traversed, the way of the pitiless Vayu," i.e. of death.

Notwithstanding which, the later Dadistan-i-Dinik (c. IV, 1-3) thus eulogizes study of the spiritual existence as a thing entirely feasible and as peculiarly the province of the good man:

"The third question that thou askest, is: To what end doth the greatness of a righteous man exist?

"The answer is that it is to the end that what is

desired by his Creator, be performed by the worshipper of God (Ahura Mazda). . . . That intelligence, by which he comprehendeth that which the celestial beings desire, is not vouchsafed, but if the true, the pure religion which is knowledge of spiritual beings the science of sciences, the teacher of the learning of celestial beings and the source of all knowledge."

The first Sirozah (19) made invocation "to the awful, overpowering spirits of the sanctified," meaning the souls of the righteous that have departed this life and, lest it be supposed that these are to be invoked although they could not hear or answer, the Yast (XXII, c. II, 39, 40) records this question and its answer:

" 'Oh thou Creator (Ahura Mazda), how do the souls of the dead, the spirits of the sanctified, manifest themselves?' The Lord God answered and said, 'They manifest themselves by goodness of spirit and excellence of mind.' "

The Shayast-La-Shayast (c. X, 11) gives this rule, to be followed in praying forgiveness for an injury done to one who is dead, viz. that one should say:

"Whatever I have trespassed against him, oh Lord (Ahura Mazda), take thou into account, together with his trespasses against me, and let these trespasses conceal one another; but if he hath trespassed against me beyond this, so much take as a righteous gift from me unto him!"

This, it is declared, is more efficacious than the mere begging for pardon, which assumes that one knows which way the balance goes.

The Bundahis (c. XV, 4), another later book, thus discusses the genesis of the body, as the thing which is moved:

"It is asked, 'Which is created first, the soul or the body?' and God (Ahura Mazda) hath answered that the soul was created first and the body afterward for the soul that was already created. It is placed within the body that it may produce motion and the body is created only for motion."

The same book (c. XVII, 9) promises a spiritual body to the soul after death, "a counterpart of the body of man when it formeth in the mother's womb and when a soul from the world of spirit settleth within it which controlleth the body during life; when the body perisheth, its substance mingleth with the earth and the soul goeth again to (the world of) spirit."

The Farvardin Yast (c. I, 1, 2, 4-5, 9-10) attributes these words concerning the spirits of the faithful, who are ever about us, even if unseen, to God himself:

"God (Ahura Mazda) spake unto Spitama Zoroaster, saying: 'Do thou proclaim, oh holy Zoroaster, the vigor and strength, the glory, the help and the joy that are in the spirits of the faithful, the awful and overpowering spirits; do thou tell how they come to help me, how they bring assistance unto me, the awful spirits of the faithful.

" 'Through their brightness and glory, oh Zoroaster, I maintain that sky, there above, shining and seen afar, and encompassing this earth about. . . .

" 'Through their brightness and glory, oh Zoroaster, I maintain Ardvi Sura Anahita, the wide-expanding, the health-giving, who hateth the demons and obeyeth the laws of God; who is worthy of sacrifices in the material world, worthy of prayer in the material world; the life-increasing and holy, the flocks-increasing and holy, the fold-increasing and holy, the wealth-increasing and holy, the country-increasing and holy; who

maketh the seed of all males pure, who maketh the
wombs of all females pure for bringing forth, who
maketh all females bring forth in safety, who putteth
milk in the breasts of all females in the right measure
and the right quality. . . .

" 'Through their brightness and glory, oh Zoroaster,
I maintain the wide earth made by God, the large and
broad earth, that beareth so much that is fine, that
beareth all the material world, the living and the dead
and the high mountains; (the earth) rich in pastures
and waters, upon which run the many streams and
rivers; upon which the many kinds of plants grow up
from the ground, to nourish animals and men, to
nourish the Aryan nations, to nourish the five kinds
of animals, and to succor the faithful.

" 'Through their brightness and glory, oh Zoroaster,
I maintain in the womb the child that hath been conceived, so that it doth not perish from the assaults of
Vidhotu, and I develop in it the bones, the hair, . . .
the entrails, the feet, and the sexual organs.

" 'Had not the awful spirits of the faithful given help
unto me, those animals and men of mine, of which
there are such excellent kinds, would not subsist:

" 'Through their brightness and glory, the waters run
and flow out from the never-failing springs; through
their brightness and glory, the plants grow up from
the earth beside the never-failing springs; through
their brightness and glory, the winds blow, driving
down the clouds toward the never-failing springs.

" 'Through their brightness and glory, females conceive offspring; through their brightness and glory,
these bring forth in safety; through their brightness
and glory, these become blest with children.

" 'Through their brightness and glory, a man is born

who is a chief in assemblies and meetings, who listeneth well to the (holy) words, whom Wisdom holdeth dear, and who returneth a victor from discussions with Gaotema, the heretic.

" 'Through their brightness and glory, the sun goeth his way; through their brightness and glory, the moon goeth her way; through their brightness and glory, the stars go their way.

" 'In fearful battles they are the wisest for help, the spirits of the faithful.

" 'The most powerful amongst the spirits of the faithful, oh Spitama, are those of men of the primitive law or those of the Saöshyants not yet born, who are to restore the world. Of the others, the souls of the living faithful are more powerful, oh Zoroaster, than those of the dead, oh Spitama; and the man who in life shall treat the spirits of the faithful well, will become ruler of the country with full authority, and a chief amongst the strong.

" 'Thus do I proclaim unto thee, oh holy Zoroaster, the vigor and strength, the glory, the help and the joy, that are in the spirits of the faithful, the awful and overpowering spirits, and how they come to help me, how they bring assistance unto me, the awful spirits of the faithful' " (Farvardin Yast, c. I, 1, 2, 3, 5, 9-19).

Elsewhere in the same Yast after commanding the adoration by the faithful of the spirit of the Almighty and the spirits of his celestial choir, worship is admonished for the souls of the faithful, thus:

"We worship the spirits of all the holy men and holy women, whose souls are worthy of sacrifice, whose spirits are worthy of invocation.

"We worship the spirits of all the holy men and holy women, our sacrificing to whom appeareth good in the eyes of God (Ahura Mazda). Of all of these we have heard that Zoroaster is the first and best, as a follower of God and as a performer of the law.

"We worship the mind, conscience, perception, souls, and spirits of men of the primitive law, of the first who listened to the teaching, holy men and holy women, who struggled for holiness; we worship the spirit, conscience, perception, mind and soul of our next-of-kin, holy men and holy women, who struggled for holiness.

"We worship the men of the primitive law who will be in these houses, boroughs, towns, and countries;

"We worship the men of the primitive law who have been in these houses, boroughs, towns, and countries;

"We worship the men of the primitive law who are in these houses, boroughs, towns, and countries.

"We worship the men of the primitive law in all houses, boroughs, towns, and countries, who obtained these houses, who obtained these boroughs, who obtained these towns, who obtained these countries, who obtained holiness, who obtained the Manthra, who obtained the (blessedness of the) soul, who obtained all the perfections of goodness.

"We worship Zoroaster, the lord and master of all the material world, the man of the primitive law, the wisest of all creatures, the best-governing of all creatures, the brightest of all creatures, the most worthy of sacrifice amongst all creatures, the most worthy of prayer amongst all creatures, the most worthy of propitiation amongst all creatures, the most worthy of glorification amongst all creatures, whom we call well-desired and worthy of sacrifice and prayer, as much as any creature can be, in the perfection of his holiness" (Farvardin Yast, c. XXX, 148-152).

The same Yast continues (c. XXX, 154-157) thus

explicitly to dwell upon the duty of worshiping the souls of good men, as constituting, together with God, and his spirits of the faithful, the spiritual forces of the universe, working together for good:

"We worship the souls of the holy men and women, born at any time, whose consciences struggle, or will struggle, or have struggled, for the good.

"We worship the mind, conscience, perception, souls, and spirits of the holy men and holy women who struggle, will struggle, or have struggled, who teach the law, and who have struggled for holiness.

"The spirits of the faithful, awful and overpowering, awful and victorious; the spirits of the men of the primitive law; the spirits of the next-of-kin; may these spirits come satisfied into this house; may they walk satisfied through this house!

"May they, being satisfied, bless this house with the presence of the kind Ashi Vanguhi! May they leave this house satisfied! May they carry back from here hymns and worship to the Creator, the Lord God (Ahura Mazda), and to the Amesha Spentas! May they not leave this house of us, the worshippers of God, complaining!"

The reason for this worship is, unquestionably, given at the opening of this declaration of worship, before even the worship of God and his angels was pronounced; it is contained in this saying, "We worship all the good, strong, *beneficent* spirits of the faithful," i.e. the souls of such mortals as manifest in life and after death through all time the Good Mind and the thoughts, words and deeds that flow from it—such souls as the Gathas speak of when they say (Yasna XXX, 10):

"While they that get for them the good name shall

partake in the promised prize in the fair abode of the Good Mind of the Lord (Ahura Mazda) and of the Right."

The Bundahis relates (c. II, 10, 11) that, before the spirits of men set forth upon their wanderings in human bodies, they were consulted by the Most High concerning the course that should be laid out for them, thus:

"He deliberated with the consciousness, the spirits of men; and the Omniscient Wisdom (Ahura Mazda) coming forth among men, spake thus, 'Which seemeth to you the more advantageous, when I shall present you to the world? That you shall contend in a bodily form with the Druj and the fiend be slain, and in the end I have you prepared again perfect and immortal and in the end give you back to the world and you will be immortal, incorruptible and changeless; or that it be always necessary to provide you protection from the destroyer?'

"Thereupon, the spirits of men became of the same opinion with the Omniscient Wisdom about going into the world."

The Farvardin Yast, however, the great reservoir for enthusiastic tributes to the human soul, within the body or after death, speaks thus (c. XXII, 65-70) of the continuing interest of beneficent human beings in the welfare of their native land:

"And, when the waters come up from the sea, Vouru-Kasha, oh Spitama Zoroaster, along with the glory made by God (Ahura Mazda) then forth come the awful spirits of the faithful, many and many hundreds, many and many thousands, many and many tens of thousands, seeking water for their own kindred, for their own borough, for their own town, for their own country, and saying thus: 'May our own country have a good store and full joy!'

"They fight in the battles that are fought in their own place and land, each according to the place and house where he dwelt (of yore); they look like a gallant warrior who, girded up and watchful, fights for the store he hath treasured up; and those of them who win, bring waters to their own kindred, to their own borough, to their own town, to their own country, saying thus, 'May my country grow and increase!'

"And, when the powerful sovereign of a country hath been surprised by his foes and enemies, he invoketh them, the awful spirits of the faithful; and they come to his help, if they have not been offended by him, if they have been rejoiced by him, if they have not been harmed nor offended, the awful spirits of the faithful. They come flying unto him; it seems as if they were strong-winged birds of the air."

The same chapter (75, 76) pays this eloquent tribute to the spirits of the faithful, whether souls which once were in man or souls that perpetually look after all:

"We worship the spirits;

"We worship them, the liberal;

"We worship them, the valiant; we worship them, the most valiant;

"We worship them, the beneficent; we worship them, the most beneficent.

"We worship them, the powerful; we worship them, the most powerful.

"We worship them, the light; we worship them, the most light;

"We worship them, the effective; we worship them, the most effective.

"They are the most effective amongst the creatures

of the two spirits, they, the good, strong, beneficent spirits of the faithful, who stood, holding fast, when the two Spirits created the world, the Good Spirit and the Evil One."

Earlier in the same Yast (30-33) the souls of the faithful are identified and portrayed in words which leave little to the imagination, thus:

"We worship the good, strong, beneficent spirits of the faithful; whose friendship is good, and who know how to benefit; whose friendship lasts long; who like to remain in the abode where they are not harmed by its dwellers; who are good, beautiful afar, healthgiving, of high renown, conquering in battle, and who never injure first.

"We worship the good, strong, beneficent spirits of the faithful; whose will is dreadful unto those who vex them, powerfully working and most beneficent; who in battle break down the dread arms of their foes and enemies.

"We worship the good, strong, beneficent spirits of the faithful; liberal, valiant, and full of strength, not to be seized by thought, welfare-giving, kind, and health-giving, following with Ashi's remedies, as far as the earth extends, as the rivers stretch, as to where the sun riseth.

"We worship the good, strong, beneficent spirits of the faithful, who gallantly and bravely fight, causing havoc, wounding, breaking to pieces the malice of the malicious, be they demons or men, and smiting powerfully in battle, at their wish and will."

These qualities are again celebrated in another place (c. XXII, 64) of the same Yast in fewer words, but not less laudatory and appreciative, thus:

"We worship the good, strong, beneficent spirits of

THE SPIRITUAL UNIVERSE 271

the faithful, who are greater, who are stronger, who are swifter, who are more powerful, who are more victorious, who are more healing, who are more efficient than can be expressed by words."

The Dadistan-i-Dinik (c. LXVII, 1, 2) thus names a beautiful sign, which has not failed to call forth the marveling admiration of all peoples, by which it asserts the spirits of the departed reveal their presence, in this passage:

"What is this rainbow which girds the sky?

"The answer is, that it is the mingling of the sun's rays with mist and cloud that is seen; of this it is, at all times and seasons, a characteristic representation, so that it has become for spiritual beings their signal in the heavens unto beings of the earth."